Nationalism in American Thought 1930-1945

The Rand McNally Series on the History of American Thought and Culture

Nationalism in American Thought 1930-1945

Charles C. Alexander

University of Georgia
Athens, Georgia

Rand McNally & Company · Chicago

The Rand McNally Series on The History of American Thought and Culture

David D. Van Tassel, editor

European Origins of American Ideas. eds., David D. Van Tassel and Robert W. McAhren

American Thought in Transition: The Impact of Evolutionary Naturalism, 1865–1900. Paul F. Boller, Jr.

Nationalism in American Thought, 1930–1945. Charles C. Alexander

Forthcoming:

The Great Awakening and the Revolution. Cedric Cowing

The Progressive Mind, 1890–1917. David Noble

The Symbolic Revolt, 1917–1930. Roderick Nash

Printed in U.S.A. by Rand McNally & Company
Library of Congress Catalog Card Number 69-17202

For JoAnn and Rachel

Editor's Preface

The Rand McNally Series on the History of American Thought and Culture aims to fill the need for synthesis through a series of short, readable volumes covering broad, chronological periods. No such synthesis now exists in spite of the fact that the history of American thought and culture, although a relatively new area for scholarly inquiry, has had an enormous and rapid growth. The written histories are legion, and every college and university has a course or two in social, intellectual or cultural history. An increasing number have a plethora of courses embraced by American studies or American Civilization programs. Despite this flourishing condition, there are no new general surveys which cover the whole history, and only a few such works even by pioneers in the field. The cause lies in the fact that a particularly strong variety of viral specialization afflicted intellectual history before it ever established any boundaries as a field. Consequently, it developed neither orthodox approach, traditional organization nor core of accepted subject matter "to be covered." The "generalists" opened up the field, but now only specialists are cultivating isolated segments of it. Thus, most of the recent work even of a survey nature has been either topical, as defined by social institutions, or conceptual, limited by period, subject or sources. These approaches have proved very effective means for scholars to organize and extract meaning from such a vast range of human endeavor. But the general student is in need of a synthesis, a means of tying together developments in religion, education, philosophy or science, and relating significant portions of the growing literature in the field. *The History of American Thought* is designed to help bridge the gap between topical surveys and monographic studies by giving some conceptual framework to significant periods and thus drawing together the burgeoning knowledge of this vast area of the American past. Each volume embraces a chronological period that is characterized by a dominant theme, coherent patterns of ideas, or major intellectual movement. The authors are expert in their fields, but they do not represent any one "school" of intellectual history. Each author has chosen his own approach or emphasis, but the general aim is to present ideas in depth and point out the significant relationships between the developments in all areas of the intellectual and cultural expression of the period.

In the decade and a half between 1930 and 1945, Americans twice were forced to re-examine their assumptions about their country in order to face the crises of depression and war. As Charles Alexander demonstrates with insight, wit and apt quotation, the Great Depression of the thirties, although challenging many traditional American assumptions, nevertheless elicited responses that combined to give a new character and energy to a resurgent American nationalism. This was a nationalism far deeper and more self-confident than either the jingoism or the cultural self-doubt of the 1920's. Never since the experience of the thirties has there been any serious question of the federal government's responsibility for the health of the national economy. Scholars, artists and writers, today as never before, collect, study and draw upon a rich heritage of American culture without explanations or apologies. The 1920's questioned the existence of an American literature, but since the thirties the question has been irrelevant. Although still taught in English departments, American literature now occupies a significant place in the college curriculum.

Besides precipitating new expressions of American nationalism, the exigencies of the Depression accelerated the processes of nationalization through the centralization of economic and political power in federal bureaus and agencies. Governmental pressures and economic necessity forced the consolidation of transportation, communications and mass media, resulting in a country-wide standardization that has had effect on everything from manufacturing codes and farming practices to soap operas. Homogenization of such regional distinctions as language, dress and custom proceeded rapidly, a result not only of technological advances but also of federal application of national policies and programs to local areas.

Nationalism, however, was challenged at its very foundations by crises in Europe and Asia, by United States' entry into the Second World War, and by the final unleashing of the atomic bomb. In the 1930's, as the vision of a League of Nations dimmed, almost everyone accepted the nation-state as the largest viable political, economic and cultural unit. Even international Communism recognized the power of nationalism when it adopted the Popular Front strategy. The United States, more than most countries, turned inward, seeking to solve all problems on its own terms and alone. The War and its conclusion raised questions that have yet to be answered, but by 1945 it was clear that certain limits of nationalism had been reached.

History does not end neatly with all problems solved and loose ends tucked in, yet this book explains more about the history of the ideas and culture of the 1930's and early 1940's than any other single volume. In so doing it fulfills the major purpose of this series, which is to help meet the general student's need for a synthesis, by tying together in meaningful segments a burgeoning knowledge of this vast area of the American experience. Mr. Alexander skillfully utilizes the concepts of nationalism and nationalization to sum up and relate the essence of a huge body of scholarly literature about the 1930's, and at the same time he manages to describe developments in nearly every major phase of American cultural life in the period.

DAVID D. VAN TASSEL

Preface

The student who ventures into the period 1930–1945 of United States history soon becomes aware that he must climb a mountain of solid historical scholarship. Already a host of writers, enjoying access to an unprecedented quantity of manuscript and archival material, has meticulously examined and evaluated the political, economic, diplomatic, and social developments of the period. The meaning of the early Depression years, of the New Deal, of American involvement in the Second World War, and of the war itself has provoked heated and continuing controversy among the postwar generation of historians. As yet, however, scholars have given relatively little attention to the intellectual and cultural history of this crowded decade and a half. The aim of this book is to provide a meaningful overview of developments in American ideas and art from the collapse of the stock market to the Japanese surrender. I have tried to strike a compromise between the need for focus and direction in an extraordinarily complex era, on one hand, and the need for broad textual treatment, useful to both students and specialists, on the other.

Of the several organizing principles that might have helped order the period, I have chosen the theme of American nationalism, which, in these years of profound change and perpetual crisis, found many diverse, sometimes contradictory, expressions. Thus in chapter one the theme of nationalism relates primarily to Depression-inspired demands for national economic planning, the relationship between regionalism and planning, and reactions against the partial centralization of planning power in the national government under the New Deal. In the next two chapters the theme is applied to the "rediscovery of America" in literature, the visual arts, and music, where the characteristic responses in the thirties were a heightened social awareness, a renewed interest in national values and traditions, and a yearning for a uniquely American statement. Chapter four deals with popular culture—films, radio, and journalism—which in the thirties, more than ever before, worked to standardize, centralize, and therefore nationalize the thoughts and tastes of Americans. The principal relevance of the theme of nationalism to chapter five, "Science and Scholarship in an Age of Depression," has to do with various ways in which people in the natural sciences and the humanistic disciplines sought to make their activities meaningful and useful for a stricken nation. A similar concern for meaning and purpose in Depression America pervaded educational and religious thought (treated in chapter six), although educational theorists and theologians disagreed vigorously among themselves in their efforts to diagnose the ills of American society. In chapter seven the nationalism theme is equated with America's entry into the Second World War and the problems of defining the "American Cause" in a decade of crisis and convulsion in Europe and Asia. Finally, I have tried to analyze the responses of Americans to the experience of war and the prospect of peace, and to assess the impact of the worldwide conflict on the nation's intellectual and cultural life.

I wish to thank the following publishing houses for permission to quote selections from works published by them: Charles Scribner's Sons, from Thomas Wolfe, *Of Time and the River*; Philosophical Library, from John Dewey, *Problems of Men;* Little, Brown and Company, from Walter Lippmann, *The Good Society* and Alfred Kazin, *Starting Out in the Thirties*; McGraw-Hill Book Company, from Aaron Copland, *Our New Music*; Yale University Press, from Robert M. Hutchins, *The Higher Learning in America* and Carl Becker, *New Liberties for Old*; Houghton Mifflin Company, from Archibald MacLeish, *America Was Promises, The Irresponsibles,* and *A Time to Speak*; Viking Press, from Irwin Edman, *Philosopher's*

Holiday; Harper and Row, Publishers, Incorporated, from Thomas Wolfe, *You Can't Go Home Again*; Abelard Schuman, Limited, from Selig Adler, *The Isolationist Impulse*; Harcourt, Brace & World, Incorporated, from Carl Sandburg, *The People, Yes*, and Lewis Mumford, *Men Must Act* and *Faith for Living;* The John Day Company, Inc., Publishers, from John Chamberlain, *Farewell to Reform,* and George S. Counts, *Dare the School Build a New Social Order?* I also wish to thank Edmund Wilson for permission to quote from his *The American Jitters* and *The American Earthquake.*

In the preparation of this book I have also become indebted to a number of individuals, particularly to: David D. Van Tassel, editor of this series and longtime friend and mentor, for help in formulating the book's scope and content; Stephen B. Oates of the University of Massachusetts and Willard B. Gatewood, Robert W. Griffith, and other colleagues at the University of Georgia, for ideas, comments, and criticism; Fred Sakon and Frank Saunders, for research assistance; Hazel Lumpkin and Kathleen Kohan, for diligent typing; and my wife JoAnn, for understanding, patience, and forbearance.

CHARLES C. ALEXANDER

Athens, Georgia
March 1968

Contents

Editor's Preface • vii

Preface • x

Chapter

I. DEPRESSION YEARS: NEW ERA, NEW NATIONALISMS • *1*

II. AMERICA REDISCOVERED: LITERATURE IN THE THIRTIES • *25*

III. TOWARD A NATIONAL CULTURE: VISUAL ARTS AND MUSIC • *60*

IV. VARIETIES OF CULTURAL EXPERIENCE: FILMS, RADIO, JOURNALISM • *85*

V. SCIENCE AND SCHOLARSHIP IN AN AGE OF DEPRESSION • *108*

VI. STORM AND STRESS IN EDUCATION AND RELIGION • *139*

VII. DEFINING THE AMERICAN CAUSE • *164*

VIII. FOR A BETTER WORLD? • *190*

Bibliography • *231*

Index • *257*

Chapter I

Depression Years: New Era, New Nationalisms

One of the most striking things about the published record of the early 1930s is an acute historical awareness on the part of contemporary observers. Perhaps at no time in American history have men and women been as cognizant of having reached a turning point in their lives and in the evolution of their country, of having closed one era and begun another, as they were in the years immediately following the shattering stock market crash in the fall of 1929. "The Post-war Decade had come to its close," wrote Frederick Lewis Allen in *Only Yesterday,* a brilliant, remarkably detached survey of the twenties published two years after the crash. "An era had ended. . . . the United States of 1931 was a different place from the United States of the Post-war Decade; there was no denying that. An old order was giving place to new."

The old era, the twenties, had appeared to be the "new era," a time when America was supposed to have reached a permanent plateau of material abundance and mass happiness. Now, as the nation sank even deeper into the quicksand of the Great Depression, F. Scott Fitzgerald looked back nostalgically on the twenties and sighed, "after two years the Jazz Age seems as far away as the days before the War." The old way of looking at things, the old way of conducting the affairs of business and government, already seemed archaic. "Future historians may well regard the nineteenth century in America as having ended in the year 1929," remarked two economists. The stark economic questions of the Depression could not be evaded; if not fully answered, they must at least be confronted. John Chamberlain announced, "where the '20s were tired of Great Causes, the '30s will be forced to go crusading. . . . The common man is feeling gored once more." "Now once more the belt is tight," said Fitzgerald, "and we summon the proper expression of horror as we look back at our wasted youth."

Indicative of the new attitude was the return from Europe of most of the writers and artists who had gone into self-imposed exile in the twenties. Their return presaged a robust reawakening of nationalism in the arts in America. H.L. Mencken, whose gleeful excoriations of the hucksterish, doltish American "booboisie" in the pages of his *American Mercury* had made him the high priest of the discontented literati in the twenties, proved that he knew when to make the proper exit. In 1930 Mencken published his last book-length cannonade, an attack on religion in the United States; three years later, with the New Deal roaring through its first 100 days, he prepared to retire from the editorship of the *American Mercury* and return to his native Baltimore. There he would continue his learned studies of the American language and write his autobiography.

The return of the expatriates was symptomatic and the demise of Mencken symbolic of a new social seriousness and national consciousness among intellectuals, of a feeling that something might be made of America after all. But to many millions of Americans the Depression brought only lessened confidence, lowered morale, and finally despair. The literary and social critic Edmund Wilson described the apparent national dolor early in 1931: ". . . it seems to me that at the present time the optimism of the Americans is flagging, that the morale of our society is weak. The faith and energy for a fresh start seem not forthcoming; a dreadful apathy, unsureness and discouragement seem to have fallen upon our life. . . . What we have lost is, it may be, not merely our way in the economic labyrinth but our conviction of the value of what we are doing." Ralph Barton Perry, the Harvard philosopher, affirmed his faith in the democratic system but admitted, "while a few years ago the defense of democracy would have been hackneyed and banal, one who undertakes it now is suspected of seeking notoriety." Gilbert Seldes ended his grim chronicle of the "years of the locust," 1929–1932, with the mordant observation that since the national birth rate had been declining sharply for several years, at least fewer citizens would be alive to witness the conceivable downfall of American civilization.

Why had this economic and social catastrophe happened? The thirties were the years of peak interest in ideas presented decades earlier—chiefly by the sociologist William Graham Sumner and the historian Frederick Jackson Turner—about the significance of the American frontier, the steadily advancing line of westward settlement whose disappearance Turner had called attention to in a famous scholarly paper in 1893. Sumner, positing the essential link between democracy and economic opportunity as epitomized in abundant cheap land, had prophesied the destruction of democracy when "land hunger" could no longer be satisfied. Turner, emphasizing American attitudes and habits cultivated by the frontier (notably nationalism, democracy and individualism), had also suggested the economic basis of democracy and the passing of the older America.

The Great Depression of the 1930s, the worst in United States history, seemed to confirm such forebodings. A remarkable number of contemporary commentators, if they did not argue that the passing of the frontier and the closing of the West had helped bring on the crisis of 1929 as a delayed reaction, at least agreed that there was no longer a built-in antidote or "safety valve," in the form of westward opportunity, for periodic economic stagnation and discontent in American society. Although younger historians were already at work to demonstrate that many of Turner's contentions and implications were more metaphor and myth than history, the logical assumption in the early thirties was that the era of economic expansion, individualism, rapid population growth, and general freedom based on an advancing frontier had ended. The economic system of the United States, highly integrated, concentrated, and interdependent, had matured, leveled off, and reached its growth limits. Thus the problem of the thirties was not how to reach new orders of economic activity but how to achieve "recovery," which meant regaining the seeming paradise of 1929. The concept of a closed frontier and matured economy was not only one of the significant social myths of the thirties and an appealing explanation for the Depression, but also a powerful argument for government action. Franklin D. Roosevelt stated the rationale concisely in his famous Commonwealth Club speech during the presidential campaign of 1932:

> A glance at the situation today only too clearly indicates that equality of opportunity as we have known it no longer exists. Our industrial plant is built; the problem just now is whether under existing conditions it is not overbuilt. Our last frontier has long since been reached, and there is practically no more free land. More than half of our people do not live on the farms or on the lands and cannot derive a living by cultivating their own property. There is no safety valve in the form of a Western prairie to which those thrown out of work by the Eastern economic machines can go for a new start.

America no longer needed to open up new areas rich in natural resources or to increase the production of goods. What was needed, according to Roosevelt, was "the soberer, less dramatic business of administering resources and plants already in hand . . . of adapting existing economic organizations to the service of the people. The day of enlightened administration has come."

In the midst of the greatest domestic crisis Americans had faced since their Civil War, Roosevelt's campaign confidence and ebullience did not entirely compensate for the vagueness of his prescriptions. Since 1930 there had been increasing speculation on the possibility of a complete collapse of American economic and social institutions, followed by real revolution—perhaps fascist, more likely Marxist. The conservative journalist George E. Sokolsky thought Americans too faithful to their institutions, too naive about continuing opportunity, to heed the Communist party's call for a "Soviet America." "As long as every American believes that he has as many chances as John D. Rockefeller to become a millionaire, to join a country club, and to get into the upper social brackets," wrote Sokolsky, "he will not become a revolutionist. Hungry, he will pull in his belt. . . . He is what the Russians call a Kerenskyist—a man who takes it on the chin, smiling."

Others were not so sure. To Edmund Wilson the country had the "jitters." Karl Marx's predictions about the development of industrial capitalist societies "have gone just as he said they would, and are apparently producing the results he foretold." The economic polarization of the classes had already occurred in the United States; all that remained was psychological polarization, the creation of true class consciousness within the bourgeoisie and the proletariat. George Soule of the *New Republic,* writing in late summer 1932—after the

"Bonus Army" of unemployed veterans had been driven from Washington by tanks, tear gas, and bayonets—saw no immediate prospect for revolution. While the people "vaguely expect profound changes," said Soule, "searching for actual flesh-and-blood revolutionary proletarians is a thankless task. Most of those who really suffer from the Depression are, according to the best-informed reports, simply stricken dumb by it." Soule nevertheless thought violent upheaval would likely follow a middle-of-the-road government which instituted unsatisfactory "reforms from above." Although Soule did not say as much, the implication of his argument was that Roosevelt and his proclaimed but undelineated New Deal might furnish such a prelude to revolution. In any case, halfway measures would not avail. John Chamberlain, bidding farewell to moderate reform the same year, felt that "a contemplation of 'reform' in America . . . is productive of no further hopes in its tenets. The situation, looked upon with intelligence and considered as a long-range proposition, can lead to but one of two personal conclusions: it can make one either a cynic or a revolutionist."

As virtually every writer trying to assess the responses of Americans to the Depression pointed out, coherent radical sentiment could seldom be found in the bread lines of the cities or on the decaying farms. True radicalism was almost exclusively an intellectual phenomenon in the thirties. It was mainly among journalists, writers, artists, and teachers—from mostly middle-class backgrounds—that proposals for effecting drastic changes in the economic and social order flourished. The philosopher Irwin Edman recalled how Marxist ideology became a la mode in New York literary society: "It is not easy to say just when it was that the vocabulary of the dinner parties and the little groups began to change. . . . But suddenly it seemed . . . the talk had turned from sex to socialism . . . : at a certain point in the history of conversation among the articulates of New York, Marxism became the characteristic theme of conversation and almost a correct standard of deportment."

Plans for Democratic Planning

Yet corollary to the cocktail chatter and more serious talk about class warfare and the imminence of revolution was the notion that the historic American dream of material abundance and democracy of opportunity could be realized only in economic collectivism. Except for the small number of confirmed, orthodox Communists and their closest sympathizers, American radicalism in the Depression years can be viewed largely as a manifestation of American nationalism, not as a capitulation to foreign-bred ideologies. Viewed from this angle, the widespread and unconcealed admiration among intellectuals in this country for the Soviet Union takes on a somewhat different aspect. For much of the American intelligentsia, the way out of the Depression nightmare and toward fulfillment of the dream lay in observing, learning from, and partially emulating the great collectivist experiment going on in Russia.

As Frank A. Warren has shown in his study of American liberals and Communism in the thirties, the primary attractiveness of the Soviet Union was its comprehensive economic planning. The Five-Year Plan instituted by the Stalin regime in 1928 was producing incredibly rapid industrial and agricultural progress during the same years in which American capitalism appeared to be going to pieces. The key to the Russian "miracle," in the minds of the American leftists,[1] obviously was planning. The aging muckraker Lincoln Steffens, whose autobiography of 1931 was, like Chamberlain's book, one long testimony to the economic basis of politics and the consequent futility of political reform, put it succinctly: "That is the advantage of a plan. You can go wrong, you can tack, as you must, but if you know you are wrong, you can steer back on your course." Soviet Russia had shown that the energies of a whole people could be mobilized in one grand effort at national uplift. The resultant image of the U.S.S.R. was an intensely romantic one for many people on the American political left. To Steffens, Russia was "the land of conscious, willful hope." And Edmund Wilson, summing up what he had seen in travels over the Soviet state, wrote, "The strongest impression one gets in Russia . . . is one of extraordinary heroism. . . . you feel in the Soviet Union that you are at the moral top of the world where the light never really goes out."

Yet several points should be made clear regarding this "red romance"—to use Malcolm Cowley's phrase—experienced by a significant portion of the American intelligentsia in the thirties. In the first place, the characteristic view of non-Marxist leftists was pragmatic. They saw the Soviet Union as a 'great laboratory' in which an unprecedented experiment in collectivization was taking place. While Americans could profit in many ways from the Russian example, historical and present circumstances were so different in the two countries that the United States could not use the Soviet scheme as an exact model. Thus the Russian experiment was just that—an experiment—and not a Marxist blueprint. Planning was essentially a technique to be employed as conditions, not dogma, required; acceptance of the technique was more important than whether true socialism actually came about. George Soule and Alfred Bingham, editor of the weekly *Common Sense,* both called for a "democratic collectivism," with government ownership of major industries a desideratum; but for each, planning was the critical consideration, not socialism per se. For Stuart Chase, widely read popularizer of economic theories, outright government ownership of segments of the economy might be undertaken as a last resort. In any case, what was important was not who owned the means of production, but techniques of organization and distribution of economic resources. As the United States instituted planning and more overall government intervention in the economy, Chase predicted, the Soviet Union would authorize more private business activity; there would follow a period of "keen, fair competition," with the best features of both experiments ultimately fused in a new system which would replace capitalism as capitalism had replaced feudalism.

Not only did most advocates of planning eschew Marxist dogma in their approach to collectivization, but they insisted that systematic economic reform take place within the established framework of representative democracy. Presumably the desired reorientation of governmental and economic affairs could be brought about with popular support. This was implied in such calls to action as Chase's *A New Deal* (published the month after Roosevelt used the phrase in his 1932 acceptance speech), Soule's *A Planned Society,* and the popular writings of the historian Charles A. Beard. Almost all of the planning enthusiasts either had reservations about the Soviet system because of the dictatorial and repressive nature of the Stalin regime or, like Beard and John Dewey, forthrightly criticized the absence of political dissent in the U.S.S.R. Yet the whole point of planning, they contended, was to recapture the kind of economic democracy that had supposedly vanished with the western frontier. Real democracy must be a democratic collectivism founded on individual security from catastrophic swings of the economic pendulum. As Dewey said, "Economic determinism is now a fact, not a theory."

In the third place, the collectivists realized that the issue was not planning versus no planning; Soule, among others, reminded his readers that the formulation of plans and the regulation of economic activity to maximize private profit had been practiced by Americans since their colonial period. In fact, said the advocates of planning, the Depression had come about because the power to make monumentally important decisions for the entire economy had become overconcentrated in private business. Thus, in a sense, too much intraplanning, especially deliberate cutbacks in industrial production to effect scarcity (what Thorstein Veblen had called "capitalistic sabotage"), helped bring on the crisis. What was needed was overall coordination and rationalization of already highly rationalized economic interests in society. Soule and Chase both pointed to the War Industries Board of 1917–1918 as the outstanding example of how government could manage business and subordinate profit to the national cause in wartime, and as proof of what could be accomplished in peacetime. The choice was between privately induced confusion and public control, between what Dewey called "blind, chaotic and unplanned determinism, issuing from business conducted for pecuniary profit, and the determination of a socially planned and ordered development. It is the difference and the choice between one that is public and one that is capitalistic."

Finally, basic to national economic planning proposals was the idea that organized interests and the general public should voluntarily accept measures recommended by some sort of planning board. Expressing the old nationalist progressive faith in bodies of "qualified experts representing the nation as a whole," the collectivists proposed a variety of schemes: Chase advocated a Peace Industries Board analogous to the War Industries Board; Beard, a National Economic Council having representation from corporations, labor unions, agriculture, and consumers; and R. G. Tugwell, a mixture of socialism and economic syndicates. In their continuing attachment to voluntarism, most planners implicitly, if not overtly, broke with Stalin's Five-Year Plan. Stalin himself made a distinction between the Russian concept of planning and American "prognosis, guess-plans which bind nobody, and on the basis of which it is impossible to direct a country's economy." Real socialist planning, said Stalin, had to have "*instructions* which are *compulsory* for all managements. . . ." American advocates of planning, on the other hand, wanted direction, not dictation; recommendation, not regimentation.

Of the many manifestations of the national planning movement, the most publicized and most bizarre was Technocracy. The "Technocracy craze," as the popular press almost invariably termed it, belongs in the long American tradition of faith in engineering and managerial wizardry, which includes the scientific management theories of Frederick W. Taylor, the writings of Veblen, and even the ideas of Herbert Hoover, the "Great Engineer." The more particular origins of Technocracy are to be found in the early 1920s when a group of engineers and publicists, tenuously connected with the New School for Social Research in New York, formed the Technical Alliance, which was an organization devoted to the logical fulfillment of Veblen's ideas—especially those expressed in *The Engineers and the Price System* (1921). Scourging capitalistic society and bourgeois democracy for their greediness and inefficiency, Veblen described the potential benefits of government by an elitist "directorate" of engineers. Through comprehensive economic planning and direction, they would abolish the profit motive, maximize production, and eliminate waste. The Technical Alliance lasted only about a year. Its leaders included Chase, who used some of the Alliance's data for a study of economic waste published in the twenties, and a wraithlike civil engineer named Howard Scott.

What Veblen (who died in 1929) and other critics had said about the basic defects of American industrial capitalism seemed spectacularly borne out in the Great Depression. As the country drifted in the months between Hoover's defeat and Roosevelt's inauguration, Scott reemerged at the head of a movement called Technocracy to trumpet a new day of enlightened technology administration—of production for use, not profit. Operating initially out of the Department of Industrial Engineering at Columbia University, the "Technocrats," as Scott and his followers called themselves, blazed into public prominence with their plans for revolutionizing the economic system. What had to be done, they insisted, was abandon selfish, directionless capitalism and replace it with a system of centrally allocated resources and efficiently administered production. Under such a system, "energy units," not money, would become the standard of value. Presumably such a transformation would take place after the American people had willingly vested authority in Scott and his corps of professional and amateur engineers, although the Technocrats were always cryptic about how the actual assumption of power should come about. Moving his headquarters into downtown New York, Scott proclaimed that Technocracy had been conducting a ten-year survey of the nation's energy resources and would soon produce a multitude of charts and graphs to prove how proper use of technology could bring material abundance to everyone.

Newspapers, popular magazines, trade journals, and even some learned societies debated and publicized Technocracy's claims and anxiously awaited its disclosures. The weeks passed and still the heralded "energy studies" were not forthcoming. Then, in January 1933, Scott gave a rambling, nearly incoherent banquet speech broadcast over a nationwide radio hookup, embarrassing the Technocrats and amusing the newspapers. When serious press consideration turned to ridicule, and when some of the Technocrats repudiated Scott and formed a separate organization, the great Technocracy excitement became a national joke. A few weeks later, public attention shifted to the banking crisis and the beginning of the Roosevelt administration. The Technocracy phenomenon was important primarily as a symptom of the Depression disease and as an expression of the American faith in tinkering rather than as a plausible curative. As the New Deal's empirical recovery program got underway, Technocracy went the way of other panaceas—into the intellectual dustbin.

Yet the problems highlighted by the Technocrats persisted in Depression America. In a widely noted study of American corporate development in 1932, Adolph A. Berle and Gardiner C. Means of Columbia University showed that actual management and control of corporations had passed from stockholders to a relatively small number of executives holding only a small amount of stock. Berle and Means also disclosed that about 200 corporations controlled some 38 per cent of all non-banking activity in the United States. Between 1934 and 1936 the Brookings Institution of Philadelphia published a series of highly analytical and statistical volumes written by a group of professional economists who came to some rather striking conclusions about the operations of the American economy in the twenties. The problem in the previous decade had certainly not been overexpansion, the Brookings economists declared. In the years 1925–1929, supposedly the period of peak prosperity, no more than 85 per cent of productive plant capacity had been utilized; every important industry had had a substantial labor oversupply. "Our economic society lacked almost 20 per cent of living up to its means," they wrote. One-tenth of one per cent of the families at the top of the income scale had received almost as much as the poorest 42 per cent of the families. In short, "vast potential demands . . . exist in the unfulfilled wants of the masses of the people, both rural and urban." It was presently impossible "to produce more than the American people as a whole would like to consume."

The Roosevelt administration and its New Deal seemed to be making little headway toward achieving this potential of national abundance. Roosevelt, according to Daniel R. Fusfeld, came to the presidency with coherent views on such matters as labor, big business, welfare legislation, conservation of natural resources, and public power; but he lacked any real understanding of basic economic processes—investment, production, distribution, international trade. The New Deal did resort to a modicum of national planning, embodied mainly in the National Recovery Administration for industry and commerce and in the Agricultural Adjustment Administration. Yet in both cases the approach was planned scarcity: deliberate cuts in production, diminution of competition, and stabilization of prices at levels that worked to the disadvantage of the masses of consumers. Abandoning the Hoover quest for international remedies through monetary agreements, the Roosevelt administration focused on the Depression at home and joined the trend toward economic nationalism throughout the western world. A premise of the New Deal, according to one analyst, was that "we can carry out an adequate national industrial plan, regardless of what the rest of the world does, or fails to do. . . ."

Still, in its avoidance of abstraction—"its indifference to ideology" and "the tyranny of dogma," to use Arthur Schlesinger, Jr.'s words—the New Deal operated without the kind of overview and system the national planning enthusiasts demanded. George Sokolsky even saw Roosevelt's pragmatic, step-by-step approach as a repudiation of planning. The absence of central planning he thought consistent with American ideals: "Most Americans regard the intellectual planner as a strange creature. . . . There is something Russian or Italian about him, something that will not fit Toledo, Ohio, or Cairo, Illinois."

Piecemeal experimentation, with preponderant influence wielded by big business and big agriculture, was not enough for collectivists like the economist Tugwell, one of Roosevelt's original "Brain Trust" and increasingly one of his severest critics inside the government, or Soule and others who formed the National Economic and Social Planning Association in 1934 to propagandize for what Soule called "a planned society." Roosevelt's alleged pragmatism was thin stuff indeed to Dewey, the greatest of philosophical pragmatists. In a series of lectures in 1935 Dewey rebuked New Deal patchwork and called for purposeful, comprehensive planning. "Experimental method is not just messing around nor doing a little of this and a little of that in the hope that things will improve," said Dewey. "Just as in the physical sciences, it implies a coherent body of ideas, a theory, that gives direction to effort." As he had been doing for forty years, Dewey affirmed his faith in the enlightened power of human intelligence, utilizing the scientific method, to cope with economic and social problems. Only inclusive planning based on "a new conception and logic of freed intelligence as a social force" furnished a way out of the continuing crisis of American democracy.

And the crisis of democracy brought by the Great Depression had not abated. The melange of ideas and programs making up the New Deal proved enormously popular with the electorate, which returned Roosevelt by an unprecentedly lopsided margin in 1936. But while economic conditions had improved and capitalism seemed safer, the performance of the economy by virtually every measurement still fell substantially short of 1929 levels. Statistics on industrial output, corporate profits, agricultural prices, personal income, and unemployment made clear that a depression was still very much at hand. After the judicial execution of both the NRA and the AAA, its two grand schemes for industry and agriculture, the Roosevelt administration seemed to be thrashing around, to have lost the minimum direction it had in 1933. Discontented Americans continued to be numerous, as attested by the large nationwide followings of Father Charles Coughlin, the silverite, anti-Semitic admirer of Benito Mussolini, and Senator Huey Long, boss of Louisiana and champion of confiscatory income taxes to "share our wealth." Although American leftists of the thirties cried "fascist" nearly as freely and as carelessly as rightists of the 1950s would cry "Communist," it did appear that authoritarian elements, similar to those that had seized power in Italy and Germany and brought on civil war in Spain, were gaining strength in the United States.

Lawrence Dennis, the leading intellectual fascist in America, continued to publish widely, sometimes for quite respectable periodicals. In 1935, for example, he argued in the *Annals* of the American Academy of Political and Social Science that the only way to save America from Communism in the midst of collapsing capitalism was through "middle-class fascist revolution." Such a revolution would establish fascist councils which would abolish the archaic system of separated powers and checks and balances, then concentrate political power and centralize economic control in the state. Thus the people would get what they desired more than anything else—"public order and the elements of subsistence."

In fundamentally different ways, what democratic collectivists wanted (but never got from the New Deal), what Dennis wanted, and even what the American Communist party wanted, was national planning for maximum material welfare. The only New Deal agency that approached the democratic collectivists' ideal of an overall planning body was the National Planning Board, which began under the Public Works Administration in 1933. Given independent status the next year, it issued its first report, a curious document in which the Board seemed to be at pains to demonstrate its lack of central planning authority. "Planning," said the Board, "does not involve the preparation of a comprehensive blueprint of human activity to be clamped down like a steel frame on the soft flesh of the community by the United States government or by any government." Over the New Deal years the Board's name was changed periodically to comport with its somewhat broadened research and advisory functions. As the National Planning Board, the National Resources Board, the National Resources Committee, and finally the National Resources Planning Board, the agency before its dissolution in 1944 issued some seventy major reports—on topics ranging from public works, the organization of scientific research, and regional planning, to urban and rural population trends, consumer potential, and civil rights and liberties.

By whatever name, the Board was never more than a comparatively obscure information-gathering and advisory group whose reports were probably read more frequently and more closely by physical and social scientists than by Roosevelt and his immediate advisers. Reeling from the impact of the "Roosevelt recession"—really an intensified depression—in 1937–1938, the Roosevelt administration turned to a generally ineffective campaign of antitrust prosecutions and to larger budget deficits and massive government spending to pump life back into the flagging economy. Part of the attractiveness of heavy spending to promote recovery, as advocated by Marriner Eccles of the Federal Reserve Board and by the British economist John Maynard Keynes, was that such action could have maximum effect with a minimum of government controls. In short, while

Keynesianism (the generic term for various spending theories) entailed planning in the sense that long-term trends should be considered and budgetary policy manipulated accordingly, the partial acceptance of spending as the key to recovery meant the New Deal moved still further from the collectivist ideal of national economic planning. Roosevelt and his manifold relief and welfare programs may have won the hearts of the planning advocates, but he never won their minds.

Regionalism and Nationalism

One part of the New Deal, however, did look like the apotheosis of planning. The Tennessee Valley Authority, created in the first months of the New Deal, became to many planners a case study in what could be done through rational public predetermination—although it was actually a regional rather than national project and was concerned more with resource conservation and public power than with economic organization. The TVA was a product of various lines of thought: public reaction to revelations of legal and illegal abuses by private electrical power interests in the twenties; Roosevelt's longtime interest in soil conservation and the setting up of public 'yardsticks' for measuring the justice of private power rates; and growing national concern over the condition of the South, which Roosevelt described in the late thirties as "the nation's number one economic problem." One of the most backward parts of the most economically retarded region in the country, the Tennessee River basin could become a laboratory for testing the concept of regional development. As it became increasingly apparent that Roosevelt had little stomach for comprehensive designs, the TVA's example in regional planning became a compelling one for many national planning enthusiasts. Perhaps, after all, the realization of the American dream lay not in central direction and coordination but in a regional approach to national problems.

"Regionalism" became something of an intellectual fashion and almost an ideology for its governmental and academic proponents. Stuart Chase both recognized and abetted its attractiveness in his *Rich Land, Poor Land* (1936), a lively account of the way in which Americans, through their traditionally wasteful and haphazard uses of land and water, had destroyed soil fertility and contributed to periodically devastating drouths. Chase ended with a dramatic plea for federal and state action to set up a series of regional conservation, electrification, and resource-use projects modeled on the TVA.

In addition to soil conservation, promoted by several New Deal measures besides the TVA, regionalism drew on more idealistic motives. The regional approach, emphasizing the conservation and efficient use of both natural and human resources—of people as well as land and water—seemed particularly promising for the South. Regionalism could be a way of integrating the South more fully into the national way of life, of overcoming what W. J. Cash called "a profound conviction that the South is another land, sharply differentiated from the rest of the nation, and exhibiting within itself a remarkable homogeneity." Regionalism could perhaps close the "extraordinary chasm between [southern] potentialities as measured by resources and actualities as measured by facts," as the North Carolina sociologist Howard W. Odum said in his pioneering work in regional sociology, itself a symptom of the new enthusiasm. Paralleling the integrative attitude was another less obvious but equally strong manifestation of nationalism—one which defined the quality of American life in terms of its diversity. For people sharing this pluralistic outlook—paradoxically, they often included advocates of national integration—regionalism was a way to preserve the diversities of South, North, and West, while at the same time reducing the exacerbating economic disparities between the sections.

Both the South and the trans-Mississippi West, which Bernard De Voto termed "a plundered province," were predominately rural and agricultural in the thirties. In both, though more so in the South, the agrarian tradition, based on the supposed superiority of rural farm life, remained strong. New Deal agricultural policy was quite confused, as was shown by the contradiction between the AAA (which benefited the more substantial farmers and drove many thousands of tenants off the land) and programs for resettling and loaning money to tenants (which aimed to keep them on the land). Yet the New Deal did operate on the assumption that national prosperity was tied to agricultural prosperity; and on many occasions Roosevelt, who considered himself a 'scientific' gentleman farmer, spoke of the need to balance rural and urban populations. There is also little doubt that he had a personal attachment to farming and deep convictions about the inherent moral primacy of rural living. Regionalism and agrarianism easily joined in one formula for rural economic progress and rural cultural preservation.

An essential component of the collection of attitudes known as agrarianism was the Jeffersonian ideal of a nation of rural freeholders constituting the backbone of democracy. Regionalists saw a chance partially to realize this ideal through enlisting the people of a region in planning and making decisions which affected the development of their area. Here was a way to get government back to the people, to the "grass roots." In the magical phrase of the TVA's David Lilienthal, this would be "democracy on the march." During years in which Washington more than ever became the center of American life, the locus of power for numerous new government functions, Lilienthal and others, while supporting the New Deal, insisted that government must strive for decentralization, for local responsibility. Otherwise a Washington bureaucracy, "so distant from the everyday life of ordinary people," would "wither and deaden the average citizen's sense of participation and partnership in government affairs." Regionalism was a healthy centrifugal force preserving the involvement of people with government. "For in this citizen participation," declared Lilienthal, "lies the vitality of a democracy."

Beyond the TVA, the ideas of the regional planning enthusiasts went mostly unfulfilled in the thirties. Hopes for additional regional development projects, inspired partly by Chase's popularizations and by the National Resources Committee's *Regional Planning Reports,* found concrete formulation in Roosevelt's 1937 proposal for "seven little TVAs" to be set up primarily in the West. An increasingly recalcitrant Congress refused Roosevelt on that and subsequent occasions, and the TVA remained a unique regional effort in economic and social rehabilitation. Yet it soon became evident that even for the TVA there was a substantial gap between promise and reality. The regional planning concept steadily gave way to administrative concentration on electric power, flood control and navigation, and inexpensive fertilizer production; after 1938 the agency even officially stopped using the term "planning." By the late thirties it was also clear that, despite paeans about fostering grassroots democracy, the citizens of the Tennessee Valley had little share in making TVA's decisions.

If the TVA was to reclaim an entire debilitated region, the Works Progress Administration was to rehabilitate the spirits of the multitude thrown out of work by the Depression. Besides employing millions of workers on a host of construction and conservation projects, the WPA undertook to "salvage culture" through four programs—for writers, theater people, painters and sculptors, and musicians—which would give appropriate work to thousands of men and women who had become expendable luxuries in a depression-ridden society. "By 1935," claimed Charles and Mary Beard, "the number of unemployed musicians, painters, sculptors, architects, writers, playwrights, actors, and dancers had grown to such an extent that the country faced the possibility of an utter collapse in the art movement." Expanding on the precedent of the Public Works of Art Project organized late in 1933 in the Treasury Department, Roosevelt made wholesale federal employment of artists part of the overall work relief plan established under Harry Hopkins in 1935. Soon the Federal Writers', Theatre, Art, and Music Projects were carrying on a brilliantly variegated program, an unexampled American venture in public sponsorship of the arts.

Yet to Roosevelt and Hopkins, the WPA's cultural activities, while admirable enough, still comprised only a small portion of what was first and last a gigantic work relief scheme—to be reduced, then abandoned, as economic conditions improved. Apparently neither showed much interest when people like Hallie Flanagan, director of the Theatre Project, approached them with proposals for permanent federal subsidy of the arts. Certainly Roosevelt, under attack by congressional critics in both parties for the WPA's boondoggling and political machinations, remained silent in 1938 when the Coffee bill to provide for a Bureau of Fine Arts in the federal government came before the House of Representatives. This and all other efforts to sustain the WPA's cultural program proved futile, and by 1942 the national government's brief foray into broad-based cultural sponsorship had been virtually abandoned. The WPA's cultural projects, like so much of the New Deal, became just another experiment, a one-shot undertaking whose principal legacy was more promise than lasting achievement.[2]

In Defense of Tradition

While the proponents of national economic planning, regional planning, a permanent federal cultural program, and other new departures were ultimately disappointed by the New Deal, some elements in American society believed passionately that the New Dealers had gone much too far. Spokesmen for such groups as the American Liberty League, the National Association of Manufacturers, or the

United States Chambers of Commerce attacked Roosevelt's policies with arguments calculated to play on certain symbolic attachments presumably shared by Americans. As seldom before in American history, powerful national symbols—especially Thomas Jefferson and his ideals, the national Supreme Court, and the Constitution—moved Americans in the thirties. In part, of course, such symbols served organized economic and political self-interest; many of the wealthy Liberty League industrialists and financiers, for example, called themselves "Jeffersonian Democrats." Thurman Arnold, the Montana-born Yale law professor, acidly described this "folklore" of government and business expressed in such abstractions as "rugged individualism," the unchanging Constitution, objective justice, the personal property rights of corporations, and the free marketplace. Arnold urged all Americans, especially lawyers and legal theorists, to recognize the realities of modern industrial capitalism in the United States.

Yet, as Roosevelt discovered when he set out to revamp the Supreme Court in 1937, the people continued to cling to what the historian Carl Becker called their "useful myths." Lawrence Dennis was partly right when he asserted that "Ninety per cent of the American people have no grasp whatever of the ideological content of the system. . . . If they are moved by words or symbols, like 'Constitution,' 'liberty,' 'democracy,' 'representative government,' and so forth, it is purely a result of early emotional conditioning and the association of a given feeling with a given word, without the occurrence of any understanding process." But Dennis and other radicals of both left and right underestimated the durability of these components of the American dream. In the midst of the confusion and uncertainty created by the Depression, Americans as a whole sustained their national faiths.

Much of the popular conception of American life derived from the agrarian tradition, which, as has been noted, figured largely in Roosevelt's thinking and in various aspects of the New Deal, especially conservation and regional planning. Yet one group of agrarians saw the New Deal as part of a dangerous historical tendency in the United States toward concentration and conformity within a framework of urbanization, industrialization, and mass democracy. In the 1920s a literary coterie of young southern-born writers had formed at Vanderbilt University. These "Fugitives," as the members of the Nashville group called themselves, propounded an agrarianism that upheld the South as the last bastion of rural culture and looked back longingly at

antebellum slave society, "once the fine flower of men's lives." They identified a rural gentry, such as had supposedly reigned in the Old South, with the cultivation of the arts, the social graces, and the civilized life in general. In 1930 twelve of these Southerners published their manifesto, a collection of essays entitled *I'll Take My Stand: The South and the Agrarian Tradition.* John Crowe Ransom, poet and literary critic, stated their basic theme: While the South must inevitably accept "progressive" industrialism and thus have its leisurely rural culture altered, it must also "manage to maintain a good deal of [its] traditional philosophy. . . . It would be childish and dangerous for the South to be stampeded and betrayed out of its own character by the noise, force, and glittering narrowness of the industrialism and progress spreading everywhere. . . ."

The Agrarian writers carried on their collective resistance to urban industrial civilization in the pages of the *American Review* (1933–1937) and other periodicals. They insisted on maintaining the South's regional identity, although for them regionalism was primarily a cultural matter. They saw the TVA and the regional planning movement as only additional manifestations of the drive to fit the South into the national pattern of dehumanizing 'progress.' As literary people—poets, critics, novelists—they thought essentially in esthetic and philosophical rather than political terms. In the mid-thirties, however, the Agrarians became loosely associated with American exponents of a program called "Distributism," which had developed in England in the late twenties, particularly in the writings of Hillaire Belloc and G. K. Chesterton. Appealing principally to the urban lower middle class, the Distributists advocated a partial restoration of rural-based society through the widest possible distribution of land-holding. The most vociferous American Distributist was Herbert Agar of the Louisville *Courier-Journal.* Involvment with Agar and his group gave the Southern Agrarians somewhat more of a political stance.

In 1936 the Agrarians—notably Ransom, Allen Tate, Robert Penn Warren, Donald Davidson, and Andrew N. Lytle—collaborated with Agar, David Cushman Coyle, and others in a symposium whose title asked *Who Owns America?* Besides the familiar hymns to the agrarian life and the value of a rural-based regional literature, the book offered "an economic declaration of independence." All the writers agreed that "monopoly capitalism" and centralized industrialism were throttling intellectual and economic self-sufficiency; real property, which few Americans owned anymore, was the foundation of

democracy. In Lytle's words, "the small farm secures the state." Agar advocated distributing lands held in absentee ownership, decentralizing (but not destroying) industry, and regionalizing government power. Davidson, who came the closest of any Agrarian to a regional political statement, sketched what he would elaborate on two years later in *The Attack on Leviathan*—southern autonomy within a kind of confederation, with the South in its minority status secured by constitutional devices similar to John C. Calhoun's "concurrent voice."

The Southern Agrarians dealt mostly in myths and nostalgia when they described the Old South, and their ideas, largely racist and elitist, could be easily (if falsely) branded as fascist. They also failed to reach a popular audience in the thirties. As one critic observed at the end of the decade, classes in southern history at Harvard were familiar with the Agrarians, but the average Southerner had never heard of them. Their principal contribution come not in political discourse but in furnishing much of the basis in this country for a new kind of literary analysis called the "New Criticism." Nevertheless, the Agrarians, in rejecting the prospect of a congested, hurried nation of city-dwellers—of a standardized, centralized culture—raised questions which Americans, in their emphasis on quantitative material improvement, have yet to answer.

Whereas the Agrarians and Distributists spoke from a regional-agricultural standpoint in attacking the trend toward collectivism, other critics generalized from the recent European experience. And just as leftists, both Marxists and non-Marxists, actually believed an internal fascist threat existed in the United States and were willing, in 1935, to join the Popular Front against fascism, so spokesmen on the right became convinced that the New Deal was in line with the rise of the all-powerful state and the suppression of liberty in Hitler's Germany and Mussolini's Italy.

Perhaps the outstanding conservative intellectual critic of the New Deal was the journalist Walter Lippmann. While still in his twenties during the Wilson era, Lippmann had become a leading ideologist of the progressive movement. In the 1920s, after leaving the weekly *New Republic* to become editor of the *New York World,* he expressed growing pessimism about the whimsical, irrational nature of mass democracy but continued to have a devoted readership among social reformers. When the *World* folded in the early Depression years, Lippmann began a nationally syndicated column for the more conservative New York *Herald-Tribune.* Now reaching many more

readers than ever before, he analyzed and approved the moderate, largely business-oriented measures of the early New Deal. As late as 1934, when he delivered the Godkin lectures at Harvard, he argued for a "free collectivism," which he termed "the method of freedom in the Twentieth Century as laissez faire was its method in the Nineteenth," and the only system compatible with representative government. Collective responsibility, the essential response of the New Deal, must be perpetuated to provide protection for personal property, including the right to a job, and freedom of economic action within a climate of social concern. Thus could a maximum number be brought to a prosperous, secure "middle condition" conducive to freedom.

Within two years, however, Lippmann had abjured all forms of collectivism. Frightened by the spread of totalitarian thought and practice over the western world, he found his way to the conclusion that there was a fundamental relationship between government-directed economic collectivism and the growth of the totalitarian state. Since, as Lippmann saw it, the New Deal was obviously collectivist in its approach, Roosevelt was carrying the United States down the same road to statism other erstwhile democracies had traveled. Undoubtedly Roosevelt's increasingly belligerent anti-business rhetoric, his espousal of an advanced social welfare program in 1935–1936, and his verbal thrusts at the Supreme Court helped send Lippmann into open opposition to the New Deal.

In 1937, the year Roosevelt made his oblique assault on the Supreme Court bastion, Lippmann brought together his charges in *The Good Society*. In unusually polemical language, Lippmann renounced the whole conception of social control through centralized government planning. "All known examples of planned economy are military in origin and purpose," he declared. ". . . there is only one purpose to which a whole society can be directed by a deliberate plan. That purpose is war, and there is no other." There could be no compromise between freedom and planning, no partial direction, no "democratic collectivism." "Collectivists have no stopping place short of the totalitarian state." But while liberty and planning could not coexist, a modern industrial economy must be dynamic and responsive to the needs of the whole society. The only solution lay in a return to the historic principles of western liberalism: democracy and "human inviolability" grounded in the sanctity of private property, the restraint of government, and the common law. Government's primary responsibility was to maintain the free market and the division of labor, first principles of liberal capitalism. Thus Lippmann favored laws to curb the growth of monopolies and to insure truth-in-trading. But the initiative in safeguarding the free market should come not from a congeries of government regulatory agencies, but from individuals bringing suits to redress their grievances. The focus should be on improving law, creating a more respectable and favorable legal framework for business operations. Finally, Lippmann advocated using the resources of government credit—deficit spending—to stimulate a lethargic economy. He acknowledged his debt to Keynes, "who has done so much to demonstrate to the free peoples that the modern economy can be regulated without dictatorship."

There were several ironies in Lippmann's critique of the New Deal and in the general conservative reaction against Roosevelt's fancied socialist or fascist intentions. While Lippmann won some following among conservative businessmen because he denounced New Deal planning, collectivists censured Roosevelt for not doing precisely what Lippmann opposed. In fact, by the time *The Good Society* appeared, the New Deal had virtually abandoned even its earlier piecemeal planning. Secondly, while Lippmann would have nothing to do with planning, he did endorse the spending theories of Keynes; on the other hand, the Roosevelt administration, while partially implementing Keynes's ideas in 1938, never fully accepted his or any other formula as an operational recovery program. Finally, even if Roosevelt had abandoned his futile quest for a balanced budget and embraced Keynesianism, businessmen would have denounced deliberate deficit spending as the ultimate fiscal heresy. Yet Lippmann, whose arguments they otherwise found congenial, seconded Keynes. For that matter, so eventually did the planning enthusiast Stuart Chase, who in *Idle Money, Idle Men* (1940) explained Keynesianism to general readers and again filled his useful role as an intelligent popularizer.

Such contrasts, contradictions, and confusions were plentiful in the Depression decade. Despite Roosevelt's dogmatic shunning of dogma, his "bold, persistent experimentation," the passage of much long-needed reform legislation, and the creation of issues and rhetoric that would dominate American politics for a generation, the United States in 1940 still found itself wallowing in an economic quagmire. The simple, oft-noted fact was that the New Deal had not got the country out of the Depression. Only full-scale war in Europe, bringing new demands and new opportunities for industry and agriculture, put America on the road to recovery.

"How can society improve its economic organization so as to make full use of the possibilities held out by the march of science, invention and engineering skill, without victimizing many of its workers, and without incurring such general disasters as the depression of 1930–1932?" That was the question posed by President Hoover's Committee on Recent Social Trends in its report of 1933. Eight years later the question, described by Carl Becker as "the dilemma of modern democracy," was still there, and the status of the American dream was still dubious. Students of American society reported widespread pessimism as to whether the dream could ever become a reality. Not long after Pearl Harbor, Margaret Mead wrote that "The most striking change since 1929 is the alteration of the average man's expectation from his life, from an attitude of robust, overconfident optimism, in the face of which individual failure and individual unemployment were felt to be punishments for lack of effort, to an attitude of equally disproportionate pessimism, in which every individual's chances to succeed are felt to be narrow, constricted, and unrewarding."

Whether the conversion of popular attitudes was as complete as Mead maintained is debatable. Certainly the phenomenal sales of Dale Carnegie's guide to instant success, *How to Win Friends and Influence People* (1937), indicated that for millions of Americans the myth of rags-to-riches endured. That it did so suggests a continuing attachment to an older America, to a time when economic and social opportunity and mobility were taken for granted.

The Depression and America's later involvement in a second world war called forth bewilderingly diverse expressions of American nationalism. A sense of nationalism underlay both attacks on and defenses of individualistic capitalism. Nationalism found expression in both national and regional planning movements, and in both the glorification of national tradition and the rejection of tradition. The many other 'isms' encompassed by nationalism included internationalism and isolationism, socialism and conservatism, not to mention radicalism, liberalism, and even fascism.

Inescapably in this new era, a time of great crises and great causes, the entire spectrum of intellectual life in America was touched by a new concern with the welfare of the nation and of all Americans.

Some of the most spectacular manifestations of the new national and social consciousness affected literature, for which the rediscovery of America provided the central theme.

Notes

1. Advocates of collective action to achieve social betterment ranged from moderate reformers to confirmed Marxists in the thirties. Their labels included "progressive," "liberal," "radical," "Socialist," and "Communist," and were often used indiscriminately and interchangeably. Even the Communist party after 1935 described itself as part of the "progressive" element. Because of the great confusion of terminology that characterized political debate, I have used the term "leftist" to refer to the whole range of American collectivist thought during the thirties.
2. In subsequent chapters the work of the WPA cultural projects will be mentioned within commentaries on the various art forms in the thirties.

Chapter II

America Rediscovered: Literature in the Thirties

In 1915 a young literary critic named Van Wyck Brooks, in a little book with the ironic title *America's Coming-of-Age,* described the sad state of letters in a nation whose Puritan heritage of esthetic prudery and "catchpenny opportunism" had systematically frustrated literary genius. Brooks lamented that "no ideas in America are really strong or bold. There has not in fact been one thinker strong enough to create a resisting background in the vague element of American life." Three years later he asked: "How then can our literature be anything but impotent? It is inevitably so, since it springs from a national mind that has been sealed against that experience from which literature derives all its values." Yet, even as Brooks wrote, the greatest literary harvest in American history was ripening. Within ten years the harvest, hurried by the war and its disheartening aftermath, was at hand in the work of novelists like Dreiser, Sherwood Anderson, Fitzgerald, and Hemingway; of poets like Robinson, Sandburg, Frost, and Jeffers; and of the playwright O'Neill. Despite continuing indictments in the twenties of the stifling crassness, complacency, and "feminization" of society in the United States, the fact was that by 1930, at least in its literary expression, America had magnificently "come of age." That year Sinclair Lewis became the first American to receive the Nobel Prize for literature, an event that recognized the literary stature of the nation as much as it acknowledged the achievements of an individual writer.

The 1930s would see the process of maturation carried a step further. The pattern of trans-Atlantic literary traffic, which in the twenties had carried hundreds of American writers into self-imposed exile in Europe, would be reversed during the next decade; increasingly European writers, fleeing totalitarian suppression or simply seeking creative ferment, would come to the United States. By 1941, with Europe emptied of much of its intellectual resources, the United States had achieved literary preeminence, especially in the novel. And New York City, the center of culture in America, had, at least for the time being, replaced Paris as the world's esthetic magnet.

In the first three decades of this century, the philosophy—more properly the disposition—known as "naturalism" came to dominate the American novel and short story, to a lesser extent drama, and poetry still less. Although there are many definitions and almost as many varieties of literary naturalism, it can be described broadly as an effort to achieve an 'objective' view of life, characterized by realistic technique in the depiction of human actions and usually guided by some deterministic doctrine, or sense of sequential causation working independent of human will. Before 1930 the principal philosophical and scientific influences on literary naturalism in the United States, sometimes operating explicitly, sometimes vaguely, had been Darwinism and Freudianism. Darwinism, expressed most notably in the early years of the twentieth century in the writings of Frank Norris, Jack London, and Theodore Dreiser, gave way in the twenties to enthusiastic reception, fragmentary understanding, and partial application of Freudian psychology by American writers. In the thirties a new kind of determinism, sometimes mingled with biological and psychoanalytical viewpoints, permeated the work of Americans. Not surprisingly in a decade of depression and privation, numerous writers took economic determinism as a point of departure.

Descriptive realism had always been an important element in the naturalistic approach to literature. Writers had insisted on looking squarely at life's realities—its brutality, ugliness, violence, sensuality, obscenity—and describing them in detail. Consequently, the triumph of naturalism as a literary disposition brought numerous legal clashes between advocates of freedom in descriptive technique and the forces of censorship. The battle raged throughout the twenties. In

December 1933—coincidentally, the same month in which the national prohibition amendment was repealed—a federal district judge significantly enlarged the scope of American literary freedom by finally lifting the ban on the importation and sale of James Joyce's *Ulysses.* But while victories over censorship continued to be won for the rest of the decade, numerous national, state, and local restrictions on literary expression persisted. The outlines of the controversy over "hard-core pornography" versus writing with "redeeming social purpose" seemed clear enough in the thirties, but a generation later the controversy remained unsettled.

The last shots in the critical and philosophical, as opposed to legal, controversy over literary naturalism were fired not long after the stock market crash. During the twenties a group of literary critics centering around Paul Elmer More and Irving Babbitt of Harvard University had become identified as a movement called the New Humanism. There was little 'new' about what More, Babbitt, and their followers had to say; essentially their position amounted to a renewal of the historic resistance to attempts, beginning a century and a half earlier in European romanticism, to break down the duality of man and nature, of the human spirit and animal behavior. The New Humanists attacked virtually all tendencies in twentieth century literature, but especially naturalism with its ostensible abnegation of spiritual values, its concentration on the coarse, irrational aspects of human existence, and its milieu of science, technology, and industrialism. They reaffirmed man as a moral being and insisted that true art must have a moral basis.

The debate between naturalists and New Humanists reached its peak in 1930, when Norman Foerster collected essays by Babbitt, More, T. S. Eliot, and others into a volume entitled *Humanism and America.* Foerster in his introduction defined Humanism as "a working philosophy seeking to make a resolute distinction between man and nature and between man and the divine." The volume was widely reviewed and provoked much critical analysis, including a book of rebuttals by such diverse figures as Edmund Wilson, Malcolm Cowley, Allen Tate, and Kenneth Burke. But the debate over the place of moral values in literature proved short lived. Within a year or so the whole furor seemed anachronistic, irrelevant. The Great Depression had raised basic questions regarding not so much the moral as the social and political significance of literary activity, and had riveted attention on the here and now of life in stricken America.

American Writers and the "Red Romance"

"The soil of American perception is a poor little barren artificial deposit . . . void of all that nourishes and prompts and inspires the artist," wailed a young painter in Matthew Josephson's 1930 book *Portrait of the Artist as American.* "We poor aspirants must live in perpetual exile!" Within a year, however, the Lost Generation, homeless and expatriated in the prosperous twenties, was coming home to find itself in a nation plagued by bank failures, hordes of unemployed, and crops rotting in the fields for want of decent market prices. As Malcolm Cowley, one of the returned exiles, put it, "They rediscovered America, in one book after another, and it was a different America from the country they had deserted in the 1920s." Paradoxically, the Depression, instead of shattering the few social values the war and post war disillusionment had left for American writers, gave most of them a whole new set of values.

The resurgence of social concern among artists in all fields, but especially in literature, was a phenomenon that escaped few observers. Some agreed with the aristocratic, acerbic Albert Jay Nock, who predicted that the "license of indiscriminate affirmation" in the thirties would be just as distasteful as the "license of indiscriminate negation" which had dominated the twenties. But most literary critics welcomed the renewal of the writer's conscious commitment to his society. It seemed that the age of 'constructive' writing had returned. "Literature, after a decade of pure individualism split off from any 'social consciousness,' is returning to its functions of 1902–1917," enthused John Chamberlain, "and with its return the whole general field of pamphleteering and propaganda will be reopened to discussion of these matters and possibly advanced beyond the state of 1902–17."

In one sense, of course, social consciousness had never disappeared from American writing. Here it is useful to note Granville Hicks's distinction between "social protest" literature, which aims at a specific wrong that can be righted, and "social criticism," which is concerned with institutions and patterns of life, goes broader and deeper in its analysis, and has an influence that is harder to measure. In denying the artist's place in American society and withdrawing to Europe or to querulous detachment at home, the Lost Generation literati of the twenties had obviously engaged in social criticism. But their criticism had been generalized—dealing with such abstractions as "the

Puritan tradition," "Philistinism," or "materialism"—and their objectives had been to achieve freedom for the individual in his personal life and freedom of artistic technique and content. Thus in the twenties literary radicalism was essentially apolitical and individualistic.

In the thirties radicalism in literature usually meant radicalism in politics as well. As Hicks said, "it takes a peculiar kind of sensitivity, not usually found among writers, for a man to remain indifferent when the world threatens to tumble about his head." Social protest literature, focusing on the plight of factory workers, migrant farm laborers, Negroes, and other downtrodden groups, experienced a remarkable renascence, while social criticism both narrowed to a primary concern with the economic basis of society and broadened to encompass the great social aggregate. 'Individualism,' the shibboleth of the twenties to both Herbert Hoover and the literary rebels, now became something of a dirty word. 'The people,' denounced as yahoos, yokels, and Ku Kluxers in the previous decade, took on heroic qualities in their poverty. And America, which had seemed so dull, commercialized, and hopeless when prosperous, looked vital and exciting, just awakening to its national promise in the depths of depression.

One obvious paradox in this rediscovery of America was that the novelists, poets, and playwrights who produced the flood of social protest literature beginning about 1932 envisioned the destruction or at least radical revision of the capitalist system, which before the Depression had been generally equated with Americanism. For the first time a large portion of the literary output in the United States revealed a direct infusion of Marxist ideology. In one way or another, perhaps a majority of American writers during the thirties were influenced by theories of economic determinism, class struggle, capitalist decadence, and proletarian revolution. Just as advocates of national economic planning pointed to the Soviet Union's Five-Year Plan and embraced collectivism as the means to recovery and restoration of opportunity, so hundreds of writers accepted Marxism as a philosophical guide and an esthetic maxim. If genuine political and social radicalism flourished mainly among intellectuals in the Depression years, then it is probably true that within the American intelligentsia radical sentiment was most widespread and most intense among writers.

Apart from the general appeal in the Soviet example of economic progress and the attractiveness of 'Marxist science' as an intellectual system, various explanations can be offered for the powerful pull that Marxism exerted on literary people in the thirties. In the first place, some of them had either been vaguely socialist in the twenties, reading and even contributing to the *New Masses,* the Communist party's literary organ, or had grown up in urban families, often of central and eastern European origin, with socialist proclivities. But the Socialist party of America, with its traditionally moderate, evolutionary approach to the abandonment of capitalism, seemed to have little to offer radicals in the Depression. The reaction of Alfred Kazin, a young writer just beginning in the thirties, was typical: ". . . the Socialists seemed to have only their own virtue. I was tired of virtue, and now wanted to see some action."

Secondly, just as many writers had made a moral and intellectual decision to repudiate the collective concerns of a greedy, provincial America in the 1920s, so after the crash they swung to the other extreme, to total commitment to the revolutionary transformation of their society. Although their conception of revolution was abstract and few of them ever tried to figure out what kind of society they really wanted, they insisted that nothing short of upheaval would suffice. Marxism showed such upheaval to be inevitable; the Communist party claimed to be the instrument for imminent revolution. Conceivably, writers, whose whole reason for being was to try to understand and portray the human condition, were touched more deeply as a group by the turmoil and suffering of the Depression than other types of intellectuals. At any rate, many gave themselves fervently to revolutionary politics and revolutionary esthetics. "Wherever I went now," recalled Kazin, "I felt the moral contagion of a single idea." 'The people' in their agony—this was the stuff of the new literary radicalism. As the novelist Jack Conroy proclaimed to the first Congress of American Writers in 1935, "a strike bulletin or an impassioned leaflet are of more moment than 300 prettily and falsely written pages about the private woes of a gigolo or the biological woes of a society dame as useful to society as the buck brush which infests Missouri cow pastures and takes all sustenance out of the soil."

A final factor drawing writers to Marxist radicalism involved the station and function of the writer in American society. Communist theory reserved a major role for the intellectual who understood that "ideas are weapons," who committed his scholarship or his art to molding revolutionary sentiment. Leon Trotsky, forced to flee Russia after his break with Stalin in the late twenties and thus vilified in official Communist publications, nonetheless remained the epitome of the revolutionary intellectual for a large number of American writers. After the revolution men of letters would continue to be indispensable in transforming society. Writers had a worthy place in the Soviet system, Josephson told the 1935 Writers' Congress. They addressed a "colossal public," which insured them of handsome royalties by buying their works from the state publishing house for only a few pennies a copy. "The security, the prosperity that I noted in Russian writers," Josephson said, "offered a striking contrast to the condition of writers in my own country, where . . . the majority starve in garrets still." Obviously the overthrow of capitalism would enhance the financial position of writers. "It seems that . . . before we can raise the status of workers in the field of literature, there must be a social revolution."

Nevertheless, as was true with the social and economic theorists who excitedly called for American emulation of Soviet central planning, the "red romance" for most American writers was, as Daniel Aaron has shown, a shaky affair at best. A relatively small number of writers actually joined the Communist party, and an even smaller number were willing to write according to Communist canons, to turn out material "worked up by proletarian slide rule," in John Chamberlain's phrase. If it took a particularly insensitive person not to be moved by the Depression experience, it took an equally insensitive writer to follow faithfully the rigid demands for structure and content decreed by the *New Masses* and other party literary arbiters. The formula for Marxist fiction dictated that a novel or short story be a work of action (involving a strike, wandering unemployment, or slum life); that it subordinate character development to action; that it feature attention to detail to give it a veneer of documentary realism; and that it have a hero or heroine who, starting from confusion and divided loyalties, comes to understand proletarian realities and is transformed into a militant revolutionist. As Murray Kempton observed wryly, "The standards of the proletarian novel were so demanding as to amount almost to a conspiracy against the writer. . . ."

Few writers could or would submit to such a schema, although numerous works which the *New Masses* criticized before 1935 contained one or more criteria for good Marxist fiction. That year Moscow instructed Communist parties in the countres of western Europe and the United States to begin cooperating with liberals, Socialists,

Trotskyists, and other leftists in order to form united or popular "fronts" against international and domestic fascism. Quickly Communist literary critics muted their esthetic preachments and began praising almost any piece of writing that attacked the common enemy, fascism. Radical writers who had insisted on maintaining the integrity and independence of their art now found it possible to participate with party members in a great variety of "front organizations," such as the League of American Writers or the American League against War and Fascism.[1] Communists welcomed such free spirits as Theodore Dreiser, the aging patriarch of American literary naturalism; or John Dos Passos; or Ernest Hemingway; or the celebrated young James T. Farrell. The thing was to combat the forces of militarism and reaction and preserve 'democracy,' both American and Soviet styles. But the immediate crisis was in Spain, where from 1936 to 1939 the republican government lost its fight for survival against the insurgent Franco fascists, armed and otherwise aided by Nazi Germany and fascist Italy. A few thousand Americans, including a few hundred writers and artists, fought in Spain for the republican cause.

All along, of course, the principal purpose of non-Communist radicals had been to further economic, social, and political democracy at home. When Edmund Wilson urged "progressives" to "take Communism away from the Communists" and "prove that the Marxian Communists are wrong and that there is still some virtue in American democracy," he spoke for the great majority of American radicals in the thirties. Cooperation with the party faithful seemed feasible enough in 1935 for many (although by no means all) leftist intellectuals, and the Front even worked fairly well for awhile despite mutual misgivings. The political and literary left generally applauded when Earl Browder, head of the American Communist party, declared that "Communism is the Americanism of the twentieth century."

Yet the undulations of official Communist policy ultimately proved intolerable for all except the most devoted party members. The incredible Stalinist judicial lynchings of the once-lionized "old Bolsheviks" between 1935 and 1938, together with the growing dominance in the Spanish republican government of Communists who proved to be as cynical and ruthless toward non-Communists as the fascists, alienated a considerable number of American leftists from the Front. But what really shattered liberal-radical-Communist comradeship and brought the whole Popular Front experiment to a thunderous termination was the Nazi-Soviet Pact of trade and non-aggression signed in Moscow on August 23, 1939. Overnight the American Communist party ceased calling for common action against fascism and joined other groups in demanding that the United States maintain strict neutrality in the event of war in Europe. The Russo-German treaty opened the door for the invasion of Poland, which came on September 1 and brought prompt declarations of war by Great Britain and France. Unfortunately the weekly edition of the *Nation* had already been printed by the time the pact was signed; when it appeared three days later it carried a statement, endorsed by some 400 people in various fields of scholarship and the arts, which extolled Soviet material and cultural progress and proclaimed that "the Soviet Union continues as always to be a bulwark against war and aggression, and works unceasingly for a peaceful international order."

The pact amounted to the ultimate duplicity, a rapprochment between the two presumed mortal enemies, Naziism and Communism. The agonized recantations (for the majority who repudiated the party and Stalinism) and rationalizations (for the minority who managed to keep the faith) would have been amusing had they not issued from such grim circumstances. Granville Hicks, a party member and zealous Marxist literary critic before the pact, publicly resigned from the party. Fifteen years later he summed up his two intellectual "blind spots": "(1) I refused to see that the Communist party of the United States was completely subservient to the Soviet Union; (2) I would not admit to myself that the Soviet Union was basically and incurably a totalitarian dictatorship."

While Hicks and others were resigning from the party, almost all non-affiliated radicals were throwing over the Popular Front, leaving only confirmed Communists in control of the front organizations. For most writers the red romance had ended. The period of exuberant radicalism, of strident camaraderie, of confident commitment to the job of remaking America into a land of democratic socialism and cultural enrichment, had passed. They had seen the right purpose—to eradicate the undeniable social and economic evils in American life—but they had misplaced their trust. As Norman H. Pearson said, "It was not the least of the triumphs of the values impelling them that so many writers had the humility to admit the error of their assessment." A chapter in American literary history had come to a close.

Radicalism and Reconciliation in the Novel

Quite obviously, not all writers in the thirties were political leftists, or even politically involved. A fair number of literary and other artists managed to remain aloof from the political storms and struggles of the decade; others, although showing increased social consciousness in their work, refused to become identified with specific political groups or movements. For the most part the writers who were least political in the thirties were those who had been influenced little if at all by literary naturalism before 1930, and hence had little interest in economic determinism after the crash. Important exceptions to this generalization were two novelists who could hardly be further apart in temperament, outlook, and (some would say) writing talent.

If H. L. Mencken was the high priest of the Lost Generation intellectuals in the twenties, F. Scott Fitzgerald was their exemplar, the brilliant embodiment of the Jazz Age's legendary disillusionment and dissipation. In 1934 Fitzgerald published *Tender Is the Night,* a deeply sensitive novel about expatriates, set in the twenties, with the theme of psychoneurosis—in other words, a work whose mood belonged to the previous decade. After that he went to Hollywood, where he spent most of the rest of the thirties squandering his talents and his energies writing film scripts. At his death he left the fragment of a last novel published as *The Last Tycoon* (1941).

While Fitzgerald haltingly carried on the tradition of psychologically based naturalism, Upton Sinclair continued to write social protest fiction in the tradition of the muckrakers, with whom he had mistakenly been identified during the progressive era. In the Depression, Sinclair, a confirmed Socialist of the Eugene Debs, not the Marxist, variety, kept producing his fictionalized tracts besides finding time to make a sensational but unsuccessful gubernatorial campaign in California on his own EPIC (End Poverty in California) ticket. To the literary Marxists, however, Sinclair's utopian socialism and unconcealed devotion to political democracy spelled bourgeois sentimentalism, while to most other critics his work was artistically inadequate.

Among novelists who had reached prominence before the twenties, who continued to write through that decade and into the thirties without being greatly affected by the changing literary and political moods, and whose work has, for lack of a better term, been called "traditional," are Ellen Glasgow, Willa Cather, and Edith Wharton.

Each worked from a humanist (not necessarily New Humanist) point of view, and each wrote in a manner that, while realistic enough regarding motivation and detail, had a kind of genteel, polished reticence. After 1930 Glasgow continued to write of her native Virginia and Virginians; Cather, of cultural interaction and the conflict between tradition and modernity; and Wharton, of the interplay of ambition, convention, and class in American society. Certainly Wharton had done her best writing before the crash, and perhaps Glasgow and Cather had as well. All three still had their faithful readers and even acquired some new admirers, but their restraint, subtlety, and genuine esthetic refinement ill-fitted the age of depression and war. About the only younger writer of the thirties who perpetuated the novel of manners and polite realism was John P. Marquand, who moved from popularity as a detective storyteller to stature as a novelist with *The Late George Apley* (1937).

Sinclair Lewis also expressed the humanistic tradition, and his work after 1930 clearly revealed an attachment to and reconciliation with America. After getting his Nobel Prize in 1930, the man who had delighted a large masochistic readership in the twenties with his needling treatments of American middle-class culture seemed to lack anything significant to say. What seemed most appropriate in the Depression milieu was not satire—the needle—but condemnation and forthright criticism—the bludgeon and the axe. Lewis found his way to the "problem novel," in which he dealt with such varied topics as social ambition, the domestic fascist threat to American democracy, and intra-family relations. *It Can't Happen Here* (1935) received widespread critical praise as a militant defense of democratic institutions. *The Prodigal Parents* (1937) portrayed with great sympathy a petit-bourgeois hero who, turned inside out, could easily have passed for the vulgar city booster Lewis had ridiculed with such relish in *Babbitt* (1922). In different ways Lewis's post-1930 novels revealed that, despite his reputation as the scourge of bourgeois America, he basically idealized his middle-class countrymen, whose solidity, generosity, and democratic outlook were for him synonymous with Americanism.

Perhaps Lewis's affirmation of traditional American values—thrift, honesty, the democratic wisdom of the people—was part of the larger quest for tradition, certainty, and stability by Americans unsure of their institutions. One manifestation of this questing attitude was the remarkable upsurge of historical fiction, which in the 1930s accounted for an unprecedentedly large proportion of the reading fare of middle- and upper-class America. Such historical romances as Hervey Allen's picaresque *Anthony Adverse* (1933), MacKinlay Kantor's *Long Remember* (1934), Kenneth Roberts's *Northwest Passage* (1937), and especially Margaret Mitchell's epic of the mythical South, *Gone with the Wind* (1936), were enormously popular. Many people, of course, simply wanted to escape into the past, to another, simpler, more romantic time; the combination of bulk, action, and subdued sexuality which characterized most of these novels offered an attractive means of escape. But many others wanted to reaffirm the validity of their ideals by discovering the continuity of those ideals in the national past. And it was the whole of the national experience that they embraced. *Gone with the Wind* speeded the process by which the Lost Cause of the Confederacy became almost as much an object of veneration in the North as in the South. Roberts made the best-seller lists with *Oliver Wiswell* (1940), a glorification of American Tory resistance in the Revolutionary War. Perhaps the popularity of period fiction was tied to declining economic opportunity and social mobility. Malcolm Cowley thought so. "A man rising in the world is not concerned with history; he is too busy making it," wrote Cowley. "But a citizen with a fixed place in the community wants to acquire a glorious past just as he acquires antique furniture. By that past he is reassured of his present importance; in it he finds strength to face the dangers that lie in front of him."

If the work of some people who had gained literary distinction before or during the twenties seemed incongruent with the temper of the thirties, John Dos Passos and Ernest Hemingway effectively bridged the emotional chasm between the two decades and between the old naturalism and the new. Although both were still in their early thirties when the Depression began, they had received much critical acclaim and acquired bands of loyal readers and emulators. The thirties would be a transitional period for these novelists; by 1941 each supposedly had moved to a different literary-philosophical position. Hemingway's attitudes did change considerably during the thirties, while for Dos Passos the transition was more apparent than real.

In the 1920s Hemingway had written two major novels, had given new greatness to the art of the short story, and had honed what Frederick Hoffman has called his "esthetic of simplicity," which involved not commonplace writing but an effort to achieve accuracy and purity in the correspondence of words to experience. Concentrating on individual conduct and individual relationships, he had developed for his characters and for himself a personal "code" based on man's primal needs—food, drink, sex, physical exertion. Insofar as individuals had a responsibility, it was to themselves—to eat and drink well, to make love well, and to die well, with discipline and dignity. This basic viewpoint Hemingway continued to express in the early thirties in his study of bull-fighting, *Death in the Afternoon* (1932), and in a collection of essays, stories, and travel accounts entitled *Green Hills of Africa* (1935).

In the late thirties, however, largely under the impact of the Spanish Civil War, which he covered brilliantly as a reporter, Hemingway broadened his social outlook. Although never a collectivist and never really interested in social protest, he did begin to write more about mankind's common ideals and interdependence and about causes worth dying for. A clue came at the end of *To Have and to Have Not* (1937), when the dying smuggler Harry Morgan gasps, "A man alone ain't got no bloody fucking chance." But with *For Whom the Bell Tolls,* Hemingway made a much more explicit statement of his growing social awareness. The title itself, taken from a poem by John Donne, expressed a sense of the collective responsibility men have for creating and destroying evil. Set in Spain and published in 1940, after the Spanish Loyalists had capitulated, the Nazi-Soviet Pact had been signed, and the Popular Front movement had collapsed, the novel nevertheless retained most of the idealism of the Front years. Throughout Hemingway affirmed his by-now famous personal code, with its emphasis on sensory enjoyment and the nobility of dying properly. Yet his hero, Robert Jordan, gives up his career as a college teacher in America to go to Spain, fight with Loyalist partisans, and die with a vague feeling of having defended the same principles of freedom and democracy for which his grandfather fought in the American Civil War. *For Whom the Bell Tolls* may not be Hemingway's finest novel, but it was one of the important social documents of the prewar period. If Hemingway did not rediscover America in this book, at least he rediscovered some of his country's historic values, linked them to the struggle of free men everywhere, and recaptured an idealism he had apparently lost in the First World War.

Dos Passos also had lost his idealism in the war, but he expressed his postwar disillusionment in a concern with the intricacy of modern mass society in America and with the seemingly aimless movements of its people. In *Manhattan Transfer* (1925) he had begun to use such techniques as stream of consciousness and rapid scene-switch-ing and to develop a narrative style which Alfred Kazin likened to a conveyor belt that carries the characters along to their disparate fates. That this novel was essentially preparatory, however, became clear with the appearance in 1930 of *The 42nd Parallel,* the first volume of the trilogy *U.S.A.,* which continued with *1919* (1932) and concluded with *The Big Money* (1936).

U.S.A. was perhaps the most ambitious undertaking and surely one of the greatest achievements in American literary history. Outraged by the social callousness of the 1920s, especially the executions of Sacco and Vanzetti in 1927, and made militant by the Depression, Dos Passos tried to tell the story of an entire generation of Americans growing up in a robust, tremendously fast-paced, and brutal capitalist society. He narrated the interconnected life histories of twelve men and women and a large number of secondary characters, interspersing passages of the "Camera Eye," an autobiographical, stream-of-consciousness commentary; "Newsreels," or headlines, popular sayings, and snatches of songs to give the atmosphere of the period; and sardonic historical profiles of people as varied as Woodrow Wilson, Eugene Debs, Henry Ford, and a lynched striker named Wesley Everest.

Although Dos Passos developed his characters inadequately and often appeared confused in his ideas, his three volumes added up to a stunning literary tour de force and a slashing criticism of the overpowering capitalist system. The *New Masses* and almost all other critics greeted each volume with enthusiasm. If *The Big Money* had come out before the Popular Front period, however, the *New Masses* would probably not have liked the book. For in fact *U.S.A.* can be read as revealing Dos Passos's evolution from Communist sympathizer to Communist critic. In *The 42nd Parallel* he romanticized the early century Industrial Workers of the World and its wandering, alienated "working stiffs," while *1919* was largely a pro-Marxist critique of the First World War. But the final volume, after praising radical heroism in the cause of Sacco and Vanzetti, ended by showing that factionalism and careerism can infect Communists as readily as capitalists; that, specifically, an ambitious party worker can throw over his loyal Marxist mistress to marry for advantage within the party, much as an aspiring young business executive might try to further his career.

Dos Passos was implying that urban, industrial society—"the system"—thwarts, distorts, and ultimately corrupts people's determination to maintain their integrity and their independence. In the conflict between the one and the mass, the individual's values are ground under by the social machine. His writings over the next ten years left little doubt regarding his ultra-individualistic, almost anarchistic views and his inability to accept any kind of collectivism. In *Adventures of a Young Man,* published toward the end of the Spanish Civil War—a year before the appearance of *For Whom the Bell Tolls*—Dos Passos's hero is an American Marxist who becomes disenchanted with the war. He is tortured, then sent to his death by the Spanish Communist secret police. The novel was roundly condemned by some of the same Marxist reviews who had earlier praised Dos Passos, who had also criticized Hemingway's 'nihilism' and apathy, and who now were lauding Hemingway for his pro-Loyalist reporting of the war. By the time of Pearl Harbor, Dos Passos had made his full reconciliation with American traditions and ideals, although those traditions and ideals, he suggested, may mave been lost along the way. In essays on American historical figures and in travel accounts he reaffirmed his confidence in the nation's root principles, however unsure he may have been about the direction contemporary society was heading. At the end of the Second World War he was well along on another trilogy called *District of Columbia,* of which the second volume (1943) indicated that he was heading backward, toward a rural-based Jeffersonian liberalism.[2]

A substantial number of young novelists and story-writers coming along in the thirties were plainly influenced by Dos Passos and Hemingway—by Dos Passos's vigorous, deterministic social criticism, by Hemingway's sparse, staccato writing style and his concern with physical experience, particularly sex and violence. The influence of Dos Passos and Hemingway was especially pronounced in the work of Nelson Algren, Robert Cantwell, John O'Hara, James M. Cain, Erskine Caldwell, Richard Wright, and James T. Farrell, who were collectively called the "hard-boiled school." Although clearly distinct from the party formula writers, these men were invariably political leftists and often avowed Marxists. Striving to picture objectively what Depression America was like and what capitalism did to people, they combined economic determinism with extreme descriptive realism to constitute a new kind of literary naturalism.

Yet despite their militant radicalism, their purposes usually appeared confused, even contradictory. Shock, sex, and violence, the staples of the new naturalism, seemed to be included as much to tease the libido as to arouse the social conscience. For example, in Caldwell's *Tobacco Road* (1932) and *God's Little Acre* (1933) what comes across is a farcical depiction of human depravity, not a record of the hopeless plight of Georgia sharecroppers. Wright's *Native Son* (1940) leaves one in doubt whether the author was describing the consequences of the white man's ubiquitous oppression of the black man, the brutalization of Negro slum-dwellers by a society that is both capitalist and racist, or perhaps the inherent degeneracy of one young Chicago Negro. Even Farrell, a Marxist with a talent particularly suited to the Depression era, with an insistence on cataloging every excruciating detail of life among the Irish of southside Chicago, and with a grim, mechanistic style reminiscent of Theodore Dreiser, was not unyielding in his determinism. In Farrell's most famous work, the trilogy *Studs Lonigan* (1932–1935), it is unclear whether Lonigan's deterioration and death at thirty result from the enervating influences of his grubby surroundings or from his own obvious personal deficiences. The metaphysical implications of Lonigan's rejection of Catholicism also seem strikingly out of place in what was hailed as a proletarian novel. In a tetralogy beginning with *A World I Never Made* (1936), Farrell, although continuing to operate within his dreary urban setting, showed a little more tenderness in his handling of characters, even intimating that his youthful hero would eventually escape the deterministic social trap. The shell of the hard-boiled writers was not unbreakable; this fact revealed, more than anything else, their sensitivity as literary artists.

Despite all the heady talk among literary radicals about creating a "revolutionary esthetic" and a "proletarian literature," the truth was that, as Louis Adamic sadly reported from his travels over the country, the mass of American workers, insofar as they read anything, consumed mostly cheap romance magazines, tabloids, and comic strips. "Ninety-nine and one-half per cent seem to me to be practically beyond the reach of radical printed propaganda or serious, honest writing of any sort," concluded Adamic. The 'reading public' in the thirties, as today, included only a minority of Americans, most of whom were literate yet not very perceptive people in relatively comfortable circumstances. The radical novel that probably reached the largest portion of this reading public, and thus had the most substantial social impact, was John Steinbeck's *The Grapes of Wrath,* published near the end of the Depression and the New Deal in 1939.

Steinbeck's variegated earlier work disclosed no great amount of radicalism and scarcely suggested that he would produce one of the foremost pieces of American social protest literature. In three novels before 1939—*To a God Unknown* (1933), *Tortilla Flat* (1935), and *Of Mice and Men* (1937)—and in a number of stories, he had displayed a kind of mystical naturalism which tied man to his primeval urges and to the land, specifically to Steinbeck's native California. *In Dubious Battle* (1939), although it sympathetically portrayed agricultural workers striking, also showed Steinbeck's disdain for the fanaticism of Communist ideologists and his compassion for the whole man, the individual apart from his socio-economic framework.

Then came *The Grapes of Wrath,* which towered over his other books in every respect. Steinbeck combined great narrative skill, an appealing story with elements of odyssean adventure, and a social 'message' to achieve much more than had the doctrinal Marxists with all their missionary zeal. If it is possible to separate the social content of a work of fiction from its formal esthetics, then *The Grapes of Wrath* is probably not great literature. Certainly there is no question of the intense conviction Steinbeck poured into the novel. But the mingling of back-country ribaldry, folk wisdom, worship of the undefined 'people,' agrarian mysticism, allegory, and numerous other moods and attitudes pointed up the author's rather considerable philosophical confusions. After more than 600 pages, the characters still lack completeness. Moreover, the novel's structure—which alternates chapters of heavily symbolic general commentary with the narrative of the Joad family's dispossession from their Oklahoma tenant farm, their painful journey across mountains and desert to California, and their endless tribulations there—becomes mechanical and monotonous. Yet the sheer force of many of Steinbeck's passages is overpowering. No geophysicist has ever said so much about the effects of a drouth, no geographer has even described so well the crossing of the southwestern desert, no sociologist or historian has ever conveyed such a sense of the social upheaval involved in the mechanized expulsion of hundreds of thousands of farm people. If less than satisfying esthetically and intellectually, *The Grapes of Wrath* was nevertheless a remarkable fusion of art and protest. Nothing else written in the thirties spoke to Americans with such fire and moral outrage.

While categorization and typology are indispensable tools of literary scholarship, such convenient labeling and boxing is usually hazardous business, and there always remain people whose work resists forced-fitting. Two such literary figures of the 1930s are William Faulkner and Thomas Wolfe. The outstanding characteristic of these writers, according to Kazin, was their "sensibility," their preoccupation not with the larger collective concerns of society, but with the individual's intensely personal experience and its psychological and metaphysical implications.

Some critics in the thirties tended to tab Faulkner a "regionalist" since he appeared to be interested in writing only of his native South. As his novels and stories accumulated, however, it became evident that, despite his frequent injections of broad, rowdy southern humor, he belonged not in a regional tradition but more nearly in the tradition of psychological horror—the tradition of Edgar Allen Poe, Ambrose Bierce, and some of Henry James's writings. More important than his literary antecedents, however, was his effort to compress the whole range of human experience into the past and present of the South, more exactly the imaginary county in northern Mississippi which was the setting for almost all his writings. The result was not historical fiction or contemporary social criticism. Rather, as Cowley has pointed out, it was the creation of a collection of myths woven into a legend of the South, expressed especially in *Absalom! Absalom!* (1936). In fashioning his county-full of characters around this legend, Faulkner showed an ability to shock and disgust that outdid the hard-boiled school of writers. Novel after novel and numerous short stories pictured the turmoil, violence, lust, perversion, insanity, and above all the degeneracy and decadence of his Southerners, who were, presumably, representative of humanity in general. Faulkner's superb management of mood and point of view created cumulative effects which were extraordinarily powerful. Yet his own point of view, and even the sense of particular passages, became obscured in prose that was often excessively rhetorical, sometimes incoherent. The recondite nature of much of Faulkner's work fascinated literary scholars who, in succeeding decades, would offer a variety of judgments on its meaning. At the close of the thirties it remained doubtful whether what one critic called his "outraged romantic idealism" left any room for optimism.

More relevant to the theme of the present book are the writings of Wolfe. If Faulkner created a legend of the South as an allegory of all mankind, Wolfe equated his own life experience with the experience of his country; and he hurled both passionately and unceasingly into the four novels he wrote before he died in 1938, still short of his thirty-eighth birthday. Wolfe tried to do nothing less than encompass all America, to tell everything about his country's character, to illumine every facet of a nation that was ugly, cruel, misdirected, rootless, yet incredibly rich and strong. "I will know this country when I am through as I know the palm of my hand," he wrote his mother as a student at Harvard, "and I will put it on paper and make it true and beautiful." In his effort to put it all down, to make some supreme comprehensive statement about American culture, Wolfe produced a seemingly uncontrollable flood of words. From boxloads of manuscript his editors cut, reorganized, and reassembled his novels. The published books still included much that was melodramatic, ponderous, affected, and discursive; yet they also contained some of the most lyrically descriptive prose written by an American.

Wolfe's four novels constituted a tortured and tortuous autobiography. The first two—*Look Homeward Angel* (1929) and *Of Time and the River* (1935)—were painfully intimate, only slightly fictionalized accounts of his growing up in "Altamont" (Asheville, North Carolina), his education at the state university and Harvard, and his young manhood in New York and abroad. Supposedly stung by charges that he could write only autobiographically, he started over with a new story and a new protagonist, but ended up writing essentially the same story of himself and his experiences begun in the 1920s. *The Web and the Rock,* which he had finished at his death, was published in 1939. A fourth manuscript, only roughly composed and put together by his editors, brought Wolfe's story almost up to date, including his stay in Nazi Germany. It appeared in 1940 as *You Can't Go Home Again.*

Wolfe failed in the impossible task of capturing all America. But he did come closer than anyone since Walt Whitman to cramming its geographical and social totality into the range of one man's vision and expression. Although he understood fully the effects of the Great Depression and described them better than most of the so-called proletarian authors, he had little sympathy for the political-literary radicalism espoused by so many of his fellow writers. The basic, intrinsic strength of the United States, not radical programs, would bring the country out of the present crisis. "I believe that we are lost here in America," Wolfe wrote at the end of *You Can't Go Home Again,*

> but I believe we shall be found. And this belief . . . is for me—and I think for all of us—not only our own hope, but America's everlasting, living dream. . . .

> I think the true discovery of America is before us. I think the true fulfillment of our spirit, of our people, of our mighty and immortal land, is yet to come. I think the true discovery of our own democracy is still before us. And I think that all these things are certain as the mornings, as inevitable as noon. . . . our America is Here, is Now, and beckons on before us, and . . . this glorious assurance is not only our living hope, but our dream to be accomplished.

In the writing of Wolfe, the ultra-romanticist, the two elements of man and nation merged into a metaphysical one. Kazin and others have contended that this tormented, tumultuous man yearned for "ambiguous, universal victory" and that his last novel suggested he had found a kind of philosophical equilibrium, had come home again to himself. If this is true, then here the analogy between Wolfe and his nation reaches its limit. Perhaps America yearned for the same kind of victory. But when Wolfe died, America was still trying to find itself, still trying to fulfill the dream.

As Wolfe struggled in huge novels to catch and hold America within his prism, so did the Writers' Project of the Works Progress Administration, albeit in collective, non-fictional, and less resplendent fashion. Under the directorship of a journalist named Henry Alsberg, the Writers' Project put to work thousands of writers—some virtually incompetent, some brilliantly competent—for a maximum of 25 to 30 hours a week and maximum weekly wages of $8–10. Some down-and-out literary people spurned WPA employment, agreeing with the defiant young James Agee when he proclaimed, "A good artist is a deadly enemy of society; and the most dangerous thing that can happen to an enemy, no matter how cynical, is to become a beneficiary." Yet most unemployed writers—as well as actors, dancers, painters, sculptors, and musicians in other WPA cultural activities—were delighted to be receiving a steady income, to be doing work that at least partly used their skills, and to have plenty of free time for their individual interests. Some of the best young artistic talent in America found expression in a wide variety of WPA undertakings.

Between 1935, when the WPA was established, and the fall of 1940 the Writers' Project maintained an average of 5,000 people on its payroll and sent to press more than 100 books and some 500 shorter items. Its publications included several photographic essays; an anthology of prose and verse called *American Stuff*, written by 50 project workers; studies of ethnic groups; and invaluable inventories of state and local archival materials in some 3,066 counties, 5,400 towns and cities, and 20,000 churches. The outstanding achievement of the Writers' Project, however, was the American Guide Series, a huge collection of anonymously written state, territorial, regional, and city guidebooks. In this vast compendium of historical, geographical, cultural, and economic information, the nation was introduced to itself in uniquely comprehensive fashion. What the guidebooks lacked generally in charm and occasionally in accuracy, they made up for in detailed honesty, in recording the false starts and failures of some communities as well as the successes and progress of others. Far from Chamber of Commerce brochures, they embodied a literal rediscovery of America, part of the national turning inward in search of assurance during the Depression years. The irony was that the Guide Series would never have happened without the Depression, and that the series was put together by destitute writers who, more than other Americans, felt anger and bitterness at what had happened to themselves and their country.

From their inception the Writers' and other WPA cultural projects had powerful critics in and out of Congress who denounced their wastefulness, branded them socialistic, and ridiculed the whole idea of the federal government paying people to write books, act in plays, perform concerts, or paint murals. Labor troubles, almost inevitably resulting from the combination of art and relief, also helped arm the critics. One day in 1938 Alfred Kazin, entering a New York Writers' Project office for a job interview, saw "men and women lying face down on the floor, screaming that they were on strike. . . . I had to make my way over bodies stacked as if after a battle; and as I sat in the supervisor's office, he clamly discussed a job while shouts and screams came from the long hall outside." Forced to raise a quarter of its funds from local sources beginning in 1939, the Writers' Project struggled on for a few more years before its termination during the Second World War.

Theater in the Thirties

While the Writers' Project, with modest enough ambitions, produced little that could be strictly termed literary art, the Federal Theatre Project, under the gifted leadership of Hallie Flanagan of Vassar College, saw itself functioning both as a tonic for the entire dramatic art in the United States and as an instrument for social change. Much was written in the early thirties about the "sickness" of the American theater, both esthetic and financial, which supposedly derived in large part from New York City's near-monopoly of theatrical talent, money, and audiences. John Mason Brown wrote that the United States had an "island theatre," a theater not of the nation but of the city of New York. While this situation did not greatly concern Brown, it did worry other observers. Some saw hope for the theater in the Depression and the impending financial collapse of Broadway, out of which could come regeneration through the decentralizing influence of off-Broadway and community theater groups over the nation. Broadway survived the worst years of the Depression, but the lingering economic malaise worsened the plight of theatrical companies even in such previously stable satellites as Boston, Philadelphia, Chicago, and San Francisco—and, if anything, accelerated the concentration of theater activity in New York. Thus to many commentators what had occurred was not only a financial disaster for impresarios, directors, actors, and theater people generally, but a cultural crisis which threatened to destroy what little exposure the American masses had to the dramatic art.

Whether the masses really wanted available theater was questionable, but in the fall of 1935 Hallie Flanagan and her associates zealously organized the Federal Theatre Project on the assumption that they did. The project's first objective, of course, was the same as the rest of the WPA—to give people work, presumably at what they were best qualified to do. But Federal Theatre had much broader aims than that. Here, it seemed, was the chance to create what America had never had—a truly national theater. Federal Theatre should strive for both physical decentralization to make quality dramatic productions accessible to almost all Americans, and esthetic decentralization to achieve full utilization of regional-local talent and full expression of the nation's richly diverse cultural heritage. Thus a combination of nationalist, regionalist, pluralist, and anti-urban attitudes furnished an internal rationale for perhaps the most urbane of the WPA's cultural ventures.

Federal Theatre never completely realized its aim and did not even survive the thirties. Yet its career, if short, was meteoric. Employing some 10,000 people, from janitors and stagehands to playwrights and directors, Federal Theatre had working companies in forty states; published a national theater magazine; conducted a research bureau for its companies and other local groups, churches, and some 20,000 schools; and played in every corner of the country to millions of Americans who had never seen a live stage production. For admissions of a few pennies for children and usually fifty cents for adults, people got to see a great variety of offerings—from puppet shows and children's plays, to performances of works by established American and European writers, to the controversial "Living Newspaper," an impressionistic dramatization of such current problems as flood control, rural poverty, slum-living, and the anti-New Deal Supreme Court.

Among the innovative, sometimes highly experimental things done by Federal Theatre groups were Orson Welles's production of *Macbeth* with an all-Negro cast and a Haitian setting; a dramatization of Sinclair Lewis's *It Can't Happen Here,* which opened simultaneously in eighteen cities and had Lewis himself appearing in the lead in New York; staging of Marlowe's *Doctor Faustus* without scenery; a "swing" version of *The Mikado;* and plays performed in Spanish, Yiddish, and other languages. Federal Theatre officials encouraged aspiring playwrights over the country to write works on regional themes for performance by local theater groups. Although it was generally and predictably the case that, despite the campaign for decentralization, the best productions were in New York, local groups did stage plays about Dunkard settlers in Reading, Pennsylvania; Hoosier life in Indianapolis; and mountaineers in Asheville, North Carolina. Of course some Federal Theatre efforts were banal, affected, propagandistic, and plain bad. For a few years in the late thirties, however, the always changing personnel of Federal Theatre, for the most part energetic and imaginative people, gave the United States the closest thing it has ever had to a national theater.

Federal Theatre provoked the most vituperative and most effective political opposition of any of the WPA's cultural projects, and it was the first to go. The opposition focused on the obvious 'leftism' of much of its work. Frequent proscriptive actions by WPA officials, such as the last-minute cancellation of Marc Blitzstein's left-wing opera *The Cradle Will Rock* in June 1937, did little to assuage congressional critics of federally sponsored culture.[3] Productions like the Living Newspaper's *Triple A Plowed Under* and *The Revolt of the Beavers* by the WPA Children's Theatre provided much-needed ammunition for those demanding an end to the Federal Theatre experiment. Federal Theatre died in 1939 when Congress refused its entire appropriation request.

The political radicalism of many of the previously jobless men and women who worked for Federal Theatre was understandable. Actually, the occasional leftist plays and reviews presented under WPA auspices accounted for only a small fraction of the spirit of social protest and criticism which affected drama as much as other forms of artistic expression in the thirties. "Drama is a weapon" became the slogan for a pronounced left-wing theater movement, centered in but by no means confined to New York.

The leading leftist dramatic companies, all off-Broadway, were the Theatre Union, the New Theatre League, the Theatre Guild, and Group Theatre. Theatre Union was the most militantly radical; all eight of its plays between 1933 and 1937 had class-struggle or antiwar themes, the most famous being John Howard Lawson's *Marching Song* (1937). The New Theatre League's outstanding production was Irwin Shaw's one-act pacifist play *Bury the Dead* (1936), which went on to a respectable run on Broadway. Perhaps the finest talent could be found in Group Theatre, directed by Harold Clurman and featuring such subsequently well-known figures as Franchot Tone, Luther Adler, Elia Kazan, Jules (later John) Garfield, and Sam Jaffe. Besides staging Shaw's anti-fascist allegory *The Gentle People* (1939), Group Theatre served as the vehicle for the most celebrated young playwright of the period, Clifford Odets. Odets wrote out of his own struggling background as a member of a lower middle-class Jewish family in New York; and his two most famous plays in the thirties were anti-capitalist—explicitly so in the powerful one-act polemic *Waiting for Lefty* (1935), suggestively in the much-lauded *Awake and Sing* (1935). In his less controversial *Golden Boy* (1937) and *Rocket to the Moon* (1939), however, he subordinated social doctrine to individual failures and conflicts in explaining the tragedy that eventually overwhelms his urban characters.

Today most of the leftist plays from the Depression years appear anachronistic, contrived, simplistic, even occasionally a bit silly; their sustaining value is primarily sociological and historical, not esthetic. This is even largely true of the plays of Odets, about whom Joseph Wood Krutch, drama critic for the *Nation,* said in 1938, "his gifts as a playwright are far more conspicuous . . . than his gifts as a political thinker." Yet, despite its glaring shortcomings and the fact that it was more a symptom of than a 'weapon' against social injustice, the left-wing theater movement of the thirties did, as Harold Clurman wrote in 1960, "produce a creative ferment that is still the best part of whatever we have in our present strangulated and impractical theatre."

As is the case with other aspects of American life in the thirties, it is easy to exaggerate the importance of political radicalism in the theater. Certainly the Communist party did not take over the American stage; as Morgan Y. Himelstein has shown in his study of leftist drama, "The Communists failed to control the new theatre movement because they were unable to control either the playwrights or the audience." Nevertheless, the work of several less radical playwrights expressed the same marked increase of social consciousness—manifested in an emphasis on contemporary problems and reinvestigation of the relevant American past—that influenced all literary forms after 1930. In different ways and degrees, collectivism, national rediscovery, and democratic affirmation characterized plays by such well-established dramatists as Robert E. Sherwood, Maxwell Anderson, Lillian Hellman, S. N. Behrman, and Thornton Wilder. Sherwood's *The Petrified Forest* (1935) could be read as a democratic pragmatist's critique of both amoral force and effeminate pacifism, while his *Idiot's Delight* (1936) satirized munitions makers and militarists and his *Abe Lincoln in Illinois* (1938) was a hymnic review of Lincoln's early career. Anderson attacked political cynicism and corruption in *Both Your Houses* (1933), and managed to do the same thing while glorifying George Washington and his ragtag revolutionary army in *Valley Forge* (1934). Sherwood's *There Shall Be No Night* (1940) tried to arouse Americans to the threat of fascism, as did Behrman's *Rain from Heaven* (1935) and Hellman's *The Watch on the Rhine* (1941). Hellman in *The Little Foxes* (1939) depicted the downfall of a newly rich southern family under late nineteenth century American capitalism, while Wilder's technically experimental and enduringly popular *Our Town* (1938) celebrated the resilient values of small-town America from a vantage point not far from that reached by Sinclair Lewis in the thirties.

Some of the best and most memorable dramatic works of the decade, however, furnished exceptions to the pervasive concern with collective crisis. William Saroyan gained almost overnight fame in 1934 with his short story, "The Daring Young Man on the Flying Trapeze," about a youth unable to find work and dying of starvation. But Saroyan proved that he was no protest writer in two exuberant, entertaining, perhaps too-genial plays of 1939–1940, *The Time of Your Life* and *My Heart's in the Highlands.* Anderson dealt with the conflict between universal good and universal evil in essentially personal terms in such plays as the verse-drama *Winterset* (1935), *High Tor* (1936), and *Key Largo* (1939). Hellman handled sensitively but forcefully the problem of attitudes toward sexual deviation in *The Children's Hour* (1934). Behrman and Philip Barry continued to write what was tritely but correctly termed "sophisticated comedy," although Barry became introspectively philosophical in his allegorical *Here Come the Clowns* (1938).

Finally, Eugene O'Neill, whose several brilliant works in the twenties had almost by themselves given the American stage world stature, continued to write on a variety of themes and in a variety of moods. In 1931 appeared *Mourning Becomes Electra,* probably O'Neill's greatest play before the posthumously produced *Long Day's Journey into Night* (1956). *Mourning Becomes Electra,* a work of almost pure psychological naturalism based closely on the Aeschylean tragedy of the house of Atreus, told of the ruin of a New England family through the inevitable conflict between man's primitive impulses and his social norms. Then, in 1933, O'Neill executed a startling about-face with *Ah, Wilderness,* a sentimental, homely play about a boy coming to maturity in a comfortable, mostly happy, middle-class environment. His last play of the decade was *Days without End* (1935), showing that love and forgiveness through religious experience could ameliorate the tragic conflicts within man. O'Neill's plays of the thirties and after, written basically outside the contemporary sociopolitical context, demonstrated that writing talent, not lavish productions, attractive performers, or immediately relevant social themes, furnished the key to a flourishing theater. What the critic Arthur Hobson Quinn said in 1933 would still be true a generation later: "There is just one road to success in the theater, and that is a good play, well acted and well directed, produced by a manager who has the courage to produce *only* good plays."

Varied Moods of Poetry

Of the different literary forms, poetry, involving the greatest degree of subjective experience, imagination, and introspection, was least affected by the Depression crisis at home and the rise of totalitarianism abroad. The enthronement of 'realism' in the thirties—whether in politics, in economic theory, in consideration of the social structure, or in the arts—worked against the esthetic of imagination. The political and economic circumstances of the day seemed to fit novels, stories, plays, and documentary non-fiction better than verse, and some poets turned away from the form altogether. Efforts to create a Marxist-inspired poetry of protest were not notably successful, although the deadly serious compositions of Muriel Ruykeyser, the wisecracking anti-capitalist ironies of Kenneth Fearing, and the often stirring verses of the Negro poets Langston Hughes and Horace Gregory, appeared regularly in Marxist and occasionally in non-Marxist publications.

Two of the greatest poets produced in the United States, T. S. Eliot and Ezra Pound, had long since followed the example of Henry James and become permanent expatriates—Eliot in England (where he eventually took citizenship), Pound on the Continent. Each continued to have a significant influence on poetry as well as on drama and literary criticism in this country, but neither was truly an American writer by 1930. No more than a handful of outstanding new poetic talents appeared in the thirties; for the most part the memorable verse of the decade came from men and women who had first gained notoriety during the American "poetic renaissance" of 1913–1918 or during the twenties. Most of these established figures were not deeply moved by the crises and crusades around them, or if they were their poetry scarcely showed it.

Edwin Arlington Robinson, one of the most metaphysical of American poets, died in 1935 after completing *King Jasper*. From the end of the continent on the California coast, Robinson Jeffers continued in his powerful, brooding verse to catalog man's sins and proclaim the immanence of evil. Robert Frost continued to set his deceptively simple poems in rural New England, although his work in the thirties, tending toward argument and satire and reflecting his essentially conservative reaction against the transformations of the Depression period, is perhaps his poorest. Ignoring the rules of syntax, punctuation, and capitalization, E. E. Cummings continued to write abstrusely of love and death. Wallace Stevens, a Hartford, Connecticut, insurance executive, began the decade with a small, devoted following and solidified it with two collections, *Ideas of Order* (1935) and *The Blue Guitar* (1937). Increasingly admired by literary critics, Stevens's poetry, focusing on the opposition of reality and imagination and the heightened esthetic awareness achieved in artistic distortion, remained specialized in viewpoint and quite limited in appeal.

Among poets of the thirties who expressed an aroused social consciousness and a collectivist point of view, yet showed little real interest in dogma, were Edna St. Vincent Millay, Stephen Vincent Benét, Carl Sandburg, and Archibald MacLeish. Millay, who began the decade writing of hedonism and esthetic delights in the vein of the twenties, made a dubious effort to analyze various contemporary attitudes and ideologies in *Conversation at Midnight* (1937), then denounced Francoist fascism in *Say That We Saw Spain Die* (1938) and called for collective democratic resistance to Nazi aggression in *There Are No Islands Any More* (1940). Benét, whose stridently nationalistic *John Brown's Body* (1928) had gone against the esthetic grain of the twenties, passionately condemned fascism and militarism in *Litany for Dictatorships* (1935) and *Nightmare at Noon* (1940). At his death in 1942 he was at work on an epic of American colonization, *Western Star*. Sandburg gave his long-standing interest in American folklore and folk themes and his deep commitment to humanity in the mass a new militancy in his pounding *The People, Yes* (1936). His faith in the collective wisdom of Americans and their ability to overcome their present adversities was crystallized in a rousing last stanza:

> In the darkness with a bundle of grief
> the people march.
> In the night, and overhead a shovel of stars for
> keeps, the people march:
> 'Where to? what next?'

No writer of the thirties combined the characteristics of political activism, devotion to the democratic faith, and doctrinal independence more effectively than MacLeish. A disheartened young intellectual, an admirer of Eliot, and briefly an exponent of estheticism in the twenties, MacLeish gave hints of his growing post-crash social awareness in his Pulitzer Prize-winning *Conquistador* (1932), a stylistically eclectic narrative of Cortez' invasion of Mexico told as the blurred recollection of a participant. In *Frescoes for Mr. Rockefeller's City*, published the next year, he ridiculed both capitalists and Communists while affirming the energy and strength of the American people. His collection of essays and poems called *Public Speech* (1936) argued that artists must throw themselves into the immediate task of trying to build a better society, while his verses written to accompany a collection of proletarian photographs, entitled *Land of the Free* and published in 1938, amounted to some of the best leftist poetry of the period. By the end of the next year, however, with the Popular Front gone and Europe at war, MacLeish was no longer interested in anti-capitalist criticism. Now he was telling his countrymen that "America was promises," that "promises are for the taking," that they must be ready to defend their freedoms. Henceforth he would give his energies to essays, speeches, and poems designed to steel Americans for the war he was convinced must be fought against totalitarian aggression.

The Bridge, Hart Crane's finest work, provided a promising poetic beginning for the 1930s. But two years later, unable to resolve his own personal turmoil, Crane took his life at the age of thirty-three. Crane's career and work offer several parallels to that of Thomas Wolfe. Both Wolfe the novelist and Crane the poet died young, presumably still at the height of their creative powers. Neither was noticeably aroused by the collective issues of the Depression, yet each had a deep emotional attachment to his country and a sense of personal restlessness and rootlessness, which he equated with the national character. And both Crane and Wolfe strained in Whitmanesque fashion to comprehend the entire American experience within a metaphor. Whereas Wolfe's metaphor was himself, his own life, Crane chose the Brooklyn Bridge as his unifying figure. Using historical and geographical themes, Crane in his epic *The Bridge* tried to describe the "myth of America" from its beginnings, to distill the essence of modern American urban, mechanized civilization, and to point up the spiritual, life-giving character of man's industrial artifacts. Crane was making a conscious effort to refute Eliot's morbid and pessimistic *The Waste Land* (1922). Yet, despite Crane's determination to declare a kind of idealistic materialism and the magnificence of many of his passages, his poem achieved neither the profundity of Eliot nor the grandeur of Whitman.

Critical Maturity

Nothing revealed better the richness, vitality, and variety of the literary life in the United States during the thirties than its literary criticism. In fact, it can be argued that in the field of criticism the literary "coming-of-age" for which Van Wyck Brooks had yearned in 1915 did not occur until after 1930, following three decades of spectacular qualitative growth in the novel, the short story, drama, and poetry. As America emerged from the thirties and moved toward another world war, one could look back on a decade of similar growth in the critical art, now a tonic for as well as a consequence of the nation's literary development.

The dichotomy between social consciousness and esthetic sensibility, which characterized so much American primary literature in the

Depression years, also marked a large part of the literary criticism of the period. Something of a harbinger of the militant leftist literary analysis to come out of the Depression appeared between 1927 and 1930 in the form of Vernon L. Parrington's three-volume *Main Currents in American Thought.* The unfinished, posthumously published last volume brought into the early twentieth century what was fundamentally an agrarian liberal history of America told through its literature. Parrington's lively volumes, written from a Jefferson-Jackson orientation and offering no quarter to business conservatives, represented a reaction to business domination in the twenties, not a radical response to economic distress. Yet their polemical, populist tone furnished an effective example of ideological literary criticism.

The spirit of radicalism among American writers spawned by the Great Depression produced a vigorous, influential Marxist movement in literary criticism. For critics like Michael Gold, literary editor for the *New Masses,* Joseph Freeman, Granville Hicks, or Bernard Smith, the worth of a piece of literature could be measured mainly by its social utility, its efficacy as an ideological tool. As one literary historian put it, "leftism was so much a part of the intellectual atmosphere that many critics, in and out of the Communist Party, admired or disapproved of writers almost exclusively on the grounds of their political sentiments." Hicks's *The Great Tradition* (1933) did little more than describe American literary history by substituting the Marxist dialectic for Parrington's Jeffersonian liberalism, with praise reserved for those writers who had attacked capitalist injustices and sternest censure given to the majority who had lacked sufficient social commitment. That same year, in a *New Masses* article, Hicks called for the "perfect Marxian novel," then laid down the rules for its composition. Most of the fiction turned out in accordance with the prescriptions of Hicks and other Marxist guides were heavy-handed efforts, unrelieved by either humor or personal insight; some of them were truly wretched. Their authors were lauded nonetheless for helping build the revolutionary purpose.

Such formula creation and formula criticism soon proved unpalatable for the preponderance of non-Marxist leftists and even for a number of critics who called themselves Marxists. Max Eastman, an admirer of Trotsky with an intense hatred of the Stalin regime, condemned doctrinal writing in two books and numerous articles and reviews. V. F. Calverton, whose *The Liberation of American Literature* (1932) had been the earliest attempt to apply Marxist criteria to this country's literary development, nevertheless enthusiastically published a great variety of esthetic and political views in his *Modern Monthly*. *Partisan Review*, denounced as Trotskyist by the party writers after breaking with the party in the late thirties, maintained high standards of artistic quality, not political suitability, in its offering of essays, stories, and criticism. But perhaps the most effective refutation of the Marxist literary argument was James T. Farrell's *A Note on Literary Criticism* (1936), all the more damaging because its author was an indubitable economic determinist, a self-described "amateur Marxist," and one of the favorite young radicals of the Communist critics. Eschewing all literary creeds—whether estheticism, Humanism, or Marxism—Farrell argued that Marx's approach to literature had been completely undoctrinaire, and that Marx had recognized writing had a basic duality as both an instrument for social change and a branch of the fine arts. Thus some kinds of literature could be important simply because of their "refreshment value." "Living literature," Farrell concluded, could not be "merely synonymous with formal ideology, generalized themes, and the explicitly stated ideas of its writers. Rather it is the shaping of life itself into literary form—a way of feeling and thinking and seeing life that the creative artist conveys to his audience. . . ."

Farrell's cannonade was symptomatic of the decline of Marxist ideology, and indeed of all political radicalism, in critical writing; the Nazi-Soviet Pact virtually eliminated leftist criticism as a dynamic force. The other 'school' of criticism coming to prominence in the thirties was a complex movement called "the New Criticism," which paralleled, then far outlived radicalism in intellectual respectability and became the dominant influence in the field after the Second World War. The principal sources of the movement were, first, the esthetic-linguistic-psychological criticism partially practiced decades earlier by Henry James and then carried further in the twenties by the English philosopher I. A. Richards, by Eliot, and by Pound; and, second, the conservative social philosophy of the dissident Southern Agrarians. Like the fading New Humanists, the Agrarians disdained both urban industrial society and literary naturalism with its rhetoric of determinism, especially economic determinism in the thirties. Unlike Babbitt, More, and their followers, however, the Agrarians had little interest in the morality of literature, insisting instead that writing could be analyzed quite apart from the author's values or social purpose.

Although the Southern Agrarians furnished much of the impetus for what came to be called the New Criticism, those writers classed as New Critics made up a considerably larger and more varied group than the original Agrarians. Yet, despite striking differences among such people as Kenneth Burke, John Crowe Ransom, Cleanth Brooks, Yvor Winters, Allen Tate, and R. P. Blackmur, the New Critics held in common the principle that literature existed in and of itself, not as a consequence of social and historical circumstances, and that the task of the critic was to examine and analyze the structure, texture, and symbolic meaning of a piece of literature as, first and last, a work of art. Not surprisingly, the New Criticism, stressing the inner logic and meaning of a work, favored poetry over other literary forms. In *The New Criticism* (1941), one of several efforts to give direction and definition to the movement, Ransom referred to "the most fundamental pattern of criticism: criticism of the structural properties of poetry." And the New Critics subscribed wholeheartedly to Eliot's dictum that modern poetry must be "difficult," capable of inspiring an inexhaustible number of analytical responses. "Wallace Stevens was content with thirteen ways of looking at a blackbird," noted Willard Thorp. " A New Critic could find thrice thirteen ways of looking at the poem Stevens wrote about his ornithological observations."

The New Criticism provided a needed antidote to the politically inspired, bantering, and frequently crude criticism rife in the thirties. Yet the New Criticism in its own way could be just as doctrinaire as leftist criticism, and certainly more arid and theoretical. One does not have to agree with Robert E. Spiller's contention—that for the New Criticism "literature becomes a substitute for rather than an involvement in life," and that its acceptance meant "the main dynamic phase of the twentieth-century literary movement was over"—to acknowledge that it helped speed academic specialization and the insulation of English departments from other equally insulated groups of scholars.

Not only 'independent' Marxists like Eastman, Calverton, Farrell, or the editors of *Partisan Review,* but perhaps a majority of professional critics, steered between the critical extremes which demanded an immediate social purpose for literature on one hand and a criticism detached from exterior considerations on the other. Respected literary arbiters like Malcolm Cowley of the *New Republic* or John Chamberlain of the *New York Times,* though politically left, usually maintained a balance in their esthetic judgments, while Ludwig

Lewisohn and a few others continued to write the kind of reasonably informed psychoanalytical criticism that had first come into prominence in the twenties. And Edmund Wilson, who became in the thirties America's most distinguished literary critic, scrupulously preserved his freedom from all the critical schools, even as he effectively used their techniques. After publishing a classic study of European Symbolist writers in 1931, Wilson became a thoroughgoing leftist, skeptical of Communism yet profoundly moved by the Depression disaster. Wilson also wanted to overcome the pervasive divorce of art from life in American society, and he speculated that Marxism might be a way to deal with both problems. Over the years, however, he became increasingly disgusted by Communist dogmatism, literary and otherwise, so much so that he refused to close ranks with the Communists during the Popular Front period. He explicitly disavowed Marxism in the late thirties, abandoned much of his interest in politics, and in *The Wound and the Bow* (1941) examined the relationship between psychological and physical abnormalities and artistic achievement. Despite Wilson's intellectual peregrinations, his approach to the study of literature remained historically oriented, with the artist seen as a product of his past and his times.

Van Wyck Brooks, by emphasizing historical origins and milieu, had done as much as anyone to elevate literary criticism in America from the level of personal taste to the level of art. The 1930s saw a sweeping transformation in the outlook of this man, who had once bemoaned his nation's cultural immaturity and written of "the ordeal of Mark Twain" and "the pilgrimage of Henry James." By 1932, when Brooks published his intellectual biography of Ralph Waldo Emerson, he had ceased to believe his own earlier preachments about the barrenness of American culture—"a youthful promise that is never redeemed," he had said in 1918—and had become convinced that, after all, this country had a rich literary heritage, part of the democratic, humanitarian canvas which was the native writer's "usable past." "After almost twenty-five years of quarreling with the national character," Alfred Kazin observed, "Brooks suddenly fell in love with it." There followed a series of volumes—the best known being *The Flowering of New England* (1936) and *New England: Indian Summer* (1940)—in which Brooks eloquently, nostalgically, almost protectively surveyed the intellectual life of nineteenth-century New England. The result was both less and more than historical criticism, an amber-hued rendering of a great tradition—not Hicks's tradition of anti-capitalist protest, but one of beauty and dignity. By 1941 Brooks was saying pointedly that contemporary American writing should be consciously grounded in this tradition, that it should repudiate Freudianism, Marxism, estheticism, and all other "decadent" foreign influences, and that it should seek to instill in Americans patriotic pride.

Brooks's reconciliation with the national past was only the most conspicuous example of the phenomenon of rediscovery which was so much the energizing element in American literature after 1930. The phrase "usable past," popularized by Brooks, became part of the literary jargon of the decade; in 1939 *Partisan Review* even polled a number of leading literary figures as to whether America had such a literary stimulant. Although their answers generally revealed distaste with the phrase and confusion about its meaning, the respondents willingly acknowledged that the nation's literary history was a vital influence on present-day writers.

As the United States neared Pearl Harbor, there remained little doubt that America had achieved much in literature since 1930, or that, simply by continuing to grow and by taking new directions, it had brought about a heightened national consciousness. But in the other arts, despite a decade or more of debate among creators and critics, doubts persisted as to what Americans had achieved by way of building a national culture.

Notes

1. The term "front organization," in its original meaning, indicated a group formed by people of various shades of leftism united in opposition to the forces of fascism, thus forming a "Popular Front." In the Cold War period the term acquired a more sinister connotation, "front" becoming synonymous with cover-up activity for Communist subversion.
2. Although Dos Passos apparently did not intend it as such when it was published, *Adventures of a Young Man* became the first volume of the *District of*

Columbia trilogy. The second volume, published in 1943, was a study of demagoguery called *Number One;* the final volume was the anti-New Deal *The Grand Design* (1949).

3. In one of the most famous incidents in New York theater history, John Houseman and Orson Welles, who had produced and directed *The Cradle Will Rock* for the WPA, moved cast and audience to the old Venice Theatre. There, with Blitzstein playing the score and the characters singing their parts from the audience, the opera was performed the same night of its cancellation.

Chapter III

Toward a National Culture: Visual Arts and Music

The Great Depression was the central, overwhelming fact of American life in the thirties. Wherever one went, whatever one did, he was confronted by evidences of the economic sickness. The Depression momentously affected American culture both in the newer, anthropological sense (meaning the aggregate social organization), and in the narrower, traditional sense (connoting a people's highest intellectual and esthetic activities). Although literature, the most direct means for trying to understand and interpret man's experience, offered the most explicit responses to the crises of the 1930s, the other arts—the visual arts of architecture, painting, and sculpture and the aural art of music—were discernibly, sometimes signally, altered. By 1930 maturity of both content and technique was taken for granted in American literature. The position of the non-literary arts in America, however, was roughly the same as that occupied by literature at the opening of the century—nascent, promising, aspiring, but as yet unfulfilled and undefined. Not surprisingly, the decade of the thirties, with its spirit of vigorous democratic nationalism, rediscovery, and reaffirmation, brought determined efforts to delineate what was or should be "American" in the visual and aural arts, to give them national direction and purpose, and to push them toward cultural maturity.

A People's Architecture?

No profession in the United States was hit harder by the Depression than architecture, simply because no industry was hit harder than construction. Between 1928 and 1932 the total value of building contracts let under the supervision of architects dropped from $3.6 billion to about $500 million. The number of architectural firms in the country fell from around 9,000 to 5,000; the average volume of business per firm shrank from $400,000 to $100,000. In thirty-seven states east of the Rocky Mountains, architects were doing less than 1⁄7 the volume of work in 1932 they had done in 1928, and total income from architectural practice in 1932 was less than 1⁄5 what it had been in 1928. "Behind these figures lie the poverty and the smashed hopes of a great part of the architectural profession," observed the *Nation*'s architectural critic. Thousands of architects, whose livelihood had depended on a continually expanding economy in the twenties, found themselves joining the swelling hordes of unemployed. Some never returned to the profession.

Yet the Depression meant more than financial reverses for architects, contractors, and construction workers. In the absence of massive support for public housing—and public projects were rare in the United States before the thirties—experimentation in design and use of materials depended largely on prosperity, on the ability and willingness of firms and individuals to pay architects to be imaginative. In other words, the various factors that enrich architectural 'taste,' that cause the architect to spend an extra amount of time and energy and the client to invest more money than he has to, were severely affected by the Depression. As a consequence, American architectural design in the thirties, especially in the early part of the decade, revealed a widespread willingness to "play it safe." Such conservatism was evident in most of the commercial architecture of the period, which tended to follow the complacent, eclectic style of the twenties. Firms continued to build towering skyscrapers that combined modern steel-shell construction with various exterior ornaments to connote Gothic grandeur and dignity. The culmination of the era of Gothic skyscrapers came in Manhattan in the first half of the thirties with the completion of the Empire State Building, whose 102 stories were crowned by a mooring-mast for dirigibles, and with the construction of the enormous commercial complex known as Rockefeller Center, which one observer called "the tangled growth of a group mentality."

Nevertheless, despite persistent business insecurity and consequent design conservatism, demands for cheaper and less adaptable building materials, and soaring labor costs arising from the increasing power of building trades unions, the thirties did bring substantial improvement in the quality of architecture in the United States. The period saw growing acceptance of new concepts and approaches which American and European architects had developed in previous decades. Increasingly in the thirties, American proponents of architectural "modernism," men who had argued over the years against complacency and grandiosity and in favor of simplicity and function, were joined by emigre architects from the totalitarian countries of Europe. The whole course of American architectural development was affected by these European designers, some of whose writings, such as LeCourbusier's *Vers une Architecture,* had been enthusiastically read by architects and architectural critics in the United States during the twenties. The European architects who did the most to help educate Americans in the principles of modern design were LeCourbusier himself, who made a celebrated lecture tour of the country in 1935, and the emigres Walter Gropius, Ludwig Mies van der Rohe, and Richard Neutra. Neutra settled in the United States during the twenties; Gropius and Mies came to this country after the famous German art center called the Bauhaus was closed by the Nazis. LeCourbusier, Gropius, and the others, despite significant differences among themselves, all held to an ultra-mechanistic and functional philosophy. They propounded a severely geometrical architecture—usually called the "International Style"—which was stripped of all ornament in an effort to develop universal forms to serve human needs under virtually any circumstances.

The acceptance of modernism did not come quickly nor without tenacious resistance by traditionalists and eclecticists. The Chicago exposition of 1933—whose theme, "A Century of Progress," seemed bitterly ironic in the depths of the Depression—was for all practical purposes the American layman's introduction to the new architecture. Even some devotees of modernism dismissed the buildings and architectural displays as "pallid and superficial" and "meaningless eccentricity"; the harshest criticism, however, came from conservatives, who used such epithets as "communistic," "barn-like," and "inhuman" to describe the Chicago designs. For the most part, real estate interests, mortgage firms, and public taste seconded these charges. Among professional architects the most vigorous critic of the new influences was Ralph Adams Cram, a votary of medieval architecture who made little effort to conceal his aversion to industrialism, urbanism, and mass democracy. To Cram, the International Style and the whole modern tendency in building design were symptomatic of the degradation and disintegration of society. ". . . it is the particular business of architecture (and ought to be of the other arts as well)," he wrote in 1938, "to counteract such an unwholesome tendency by proclaiming the integrity of the continuous idea—by refusing to make a human dwelling a 'machine for living,' a school like an automobile factory, and a church like a movie house."

As the thirties moved along, however, the advocates of unadorned structures, built to serve the material needs of their inhabitants above all else, created an ever-expanding circle of interest and admiration. The harsh economic facts of the Depression years seemed to compel a concentration on surface reality throughout American intellectual life. The effect of the vogue of realism on architecture was to emphasize the immediate problems of habitability and usability, not traditional esthetic considerations. The Museum of Modern Art, established in 1929 and moved into a striking new modernist structure ten years later, consistently displayed photographs and models of functionally conceived buildings, especially those of Gropius and his followers, and filled the role of middleman between the proponents of the new architecture and the public. Among architectural and social critics, Lewis Mumford, an editor of the *New Republic,* was undoubtedly the most important voice for modernism. For Mumford, function in architecture was only part of the larger desideratum of social planning to decentralize the urban, overconcentrated civilization of the twentieth century and presumably make life more liveable. In his two major works in the thirties, *Technics and Civilization* (1934) and *The Culture of Cities* (1938), he argued that mankind stood poised on a new phase in history, the "biotechnic." Now, through "a more organic utilization of the entire environment"—with the industrial arts subordinated to the biological and social arts, and with agriculture, medicine, and education given priority over engineering—modern society could be reclaimed.

Mumford's conception of what could be done to improve the urban American's existence was clearly utopian, with its insistence that decentralization was feasible under modern communications and transportation technology and its idealization of the small medieval city. But Mumford at least recognized that people came to cities because they offered certain advantages, and that population concentration produced cultural ferment. For the architect Frank Lloyd Wright, however, the city was the mortal enemy of individualism, a social cancer that ate away at man's roots in the land. The city's only redeeming quality, as far as Wright was concerned, was its economic diversification. Yet economic diversification could be achieved in small towns, too, if they were surrounded by fertile farm land and supported by small-scale, localized industry. Although frequently portrayed as an anti-capitalist radical, Wright actually expressed a kind of anarchistic, agrarian humanism which had little relevance to the basic infirmities of urban, industrial America. His much-heralded design for an ideal suburban community called Broadacre City, exhibited first in 1935, was aptly described by two architectural historians as "more a compilation of Wrightiana . . . than a great and serious solution of the urban problem."

Wright expounded his strident, vaguely anti-urban theories in several books during the thirties, most notably in his eloquent, epigrammatic *Autobiography* (1932). But his social criticism and social schemes were of much less value to American thought than his work as an architect was to American art. After 1930 Wright emerged from the partial eclipse in which he had found himself in the prosperous, conservative twenties to design a series of startlingly beautiful commercial and residential structures. Wright was convinced that the city held no creative opportunities for the architect, and he also rejected the cool, impersonal forms in steel and glass of the International Style. He worked instead on suburban and rural sites, where he could use a variety of materials, especially wood and stone. On such sites he could implement his philosophy that architecture should be organic, logically growing out of as well as integrated into its surroundings. Naturally he had to have clients with wealth and an outlook as ruggedly individualistic as his own; fortunately he found several in the thirties. His outstanding creations during the decade were "Falling Water," the cantilevered house at Bear Run, Pennsylvania, probably the most famous residential structure in America, and the huge Administration Building for the Johnson Wax Company at Racine, Wisconsin. By 1942 two of the projected fifteen buildings he was designing for Florida Southern University, at Lakeland, Florida, were complete.

Wright's designs were hailed in some quarters as providing the key to what the country had never had, a national architectural style, one that would fit the character and needs of modern America. Some writers saw regionalized styling, involving an extension and amplification of Wright's organic principles, as a viable alternative to both the unsentimental practicality of the modernist "space envelopes" and the oversentimentalized effects of eclecticism and "period" architecture. Ramsay Traquair argued that "every good architecture has been local—the product of local needs, local materials, and local climate. A few telephones and aeroplanes are not going to change human nature, and for us, as for our forefathers, our locality will remain the moulding feature of our lives and of our architecture." In the thirties regional taste and tradition continued to influence American building, as in the clapboard houses of New England or the hybrid "colonial" homes of the South. Yet, aside from the ongoing development of the low-roofed "California style" (which Neutra, in particular, helped make more flexible and functional in the thirties and forties), advocates of a genuinely American architectural style found little to admire in the various regional expressions.

Nor, for the most part, were advocates of a national architecture pleased by the results of the Roosevelt administration's program for public housing. The heterogeneous housing activites carried on by various New Deal agencies received much publicity and aroused great hopes for cultural nationalists and urban reformers. But the New Deal's housing ventures scarcely touched the problem of providing decent living quarters for the ill-housed one-third of the nation to which Roosevelt referred in 1937, and thus contributed little to the movement for urban planning. Federal housing also produced architectural efforts that were generally undistinguished. The New Deal could have built more than the three "Greenbelt" suburban working-class communities constructed under the Resettlement Administration, and it could have used its individual dwelling projects to promote prefabrication and standardization practices, which some architects and city planners saw as the key to attractive low-cost housing. Despite charges that it was extravagant and socialistic, the New Deal's Public Works Administration accomplished relatively little in public housing. The PWA completed only 51 multi-unit developments containing but 21,800 individual units. The planning of these projects could have been more imaginative, their architecture more innovative and esthetically pleasing. Frederick A. Gutheim, surveying seven years of the federal housing program, probably expressed the critical consensus when he wrote, "The architectural record of PWA is an account of pure eclecticism in action as well as in style, a pandering to every pressure, every taste, every dictate.

Architecturally it has stood for nothing." By Pearl Harbor the New Deal's foray into the nearly barren field of public housing was still hardly more than an experiment.[1]

One of the brightest spots architecturally in the thirties was public school design where, for the first time, modernism became an important influence. The "finger-plan" buildings erected in a number of communities over the country in the last half of the decade broke sharply with the multi-story eclecticism dominant in school design since the late nineteenth century. Seldom more than two stories high and spreading over the landscape, the new buildings were safer, better lighted, and better ventilated. They may not have fulfilled the ideals of those educational theorists who wanted to eliminate the child's sense of confinement, of rigid separation from the outdoors. Nonetheless, for many boys and girls the public school became a pleasing contrast with their dreary home surroundings.

While some of the school construction done by the PWA or the Works Progress Administration showed evidences of functional design, site-planning, maximum use of natural light, and other aspects of modernism, most schools built with federal money were bulky, poorly lighted, and monumental, thus conforming to the public's notions of what a school 'should' look like. The same attachment to 'institutional architecture' characterized the preponderance of college and university buildings and federal government structures completed in Washington. The critical out-cry against the massive new Commerce Building and National Art Gallery—both done in the style of the Greek Revival, with huge colonnades and piles of steps—was exceeded only by the storm of disapproval that greeted the Jefferson Memorial, designed by John Russell Pope and begun in 1938. Combining Greek and Italian classical forms, the Memorial symbolized and climaxed the national rediscovery of Jefferson and his ideals of democratic liberalism. Defenders pointed to the attractive site, the simple white beauty of the design, and the fact that the style had been favored by Jefferson in his plans for the University of Virginia. For the numerous and vocal critics, however, the Memorial was esthetically and philosophically intolerable, smacking of Toryism in politics and art and betraying Jefferson's progressive, egalitarian principles.

The whole argument, caught in a swirl of liberal-conservative, modernist-traditionalist, nationalist-internationalist rhetoric, had its ludicrous aspects. Yet it was symptomatic of the fiercely democratic spirit of the period and the related yearning for a national architecture, "an architecture of the people." The architect William Lescaze, disgusted with Pope's plans for the Jefferson Memorial, declared that Americans must have "architecture which makes them aware that it's good to be alive today in the twentieth century, it's grand to be alive today in a democracy—in America."

The search for a national architecture, featuring the mystical combination of esthetic modernism and democratic nationalism, never reached its perhaps unattainable goal. At the close of the thirties there were various indications that the minority of Americans who could afford to express their tastes still leaned toward the older styles. *Architectural Forum* reported in 1939 that the notable new houses of the year were still mostly of traditional design. The next year the Society of Architectural Historians was founded to analyze, preserve, and presumably foster pre-Revolutionary American styles. And as economic conditions improved, more and more tourists flocked to admire the seventeenth- and eighteenth-century restorations of Colonial Williamsburg, completed in the thirties with Rockefeller philanthropies to become another in the growing collection of national shrines. While modernists might grant the admirable patriotic intentions behind Colonial Williamsburg, they generally agreed that its architectural influence was reactionary. As John Marston Fitch lamented, "this project has done more to stultify and corrupt American taste than any single event in our history, the Columbian Exposition [of 1893] possibly excepted."

Nevertheless, the end of the decade of the Great Depression found modernism triumphant among professional architects and architectural critics. The prevailing intellectual disposition toward realism and function had helped promote acceptance of the new architecture. The approaching war would widen the American architectural conception, expose Americans to still more cosmopolitan esthetic influences, and in turn engraft American building designs throughout much of the world.

Painting and Sculpture: American Scenes and "American Scene"

Like architects, painters and sculptors in the thirties manifested a preference for realism at the same time that they tried to serve a social purpose and groped toward a national expression. In the twenties painting and sculpture had been dominated by a mood of experimentalism, by an urge to liberate art from pictorial realism through the highly subjective use of colors, lines, and shapes. But in the Depression period many American artists began concentrating on all aspects of the national life in an effort to close the chasm between the artist and popular tastes which had yawned ever wider since the public's startling introduction to "modern art" at the Armory Show of 1913. Artists in the decade of the Depression seemed intent on changing the condition Frederick P. Keppel and R. L. Duffus described in 1933: ". . . when all has been said and all allowances made, it must be admitted that for the overwhelming majority of the American people the fine arts of painting and sculpture in their non-commercial, non-industrial, forms, do not exist."

Painters and sculptors in Depression America, losing their commissions, unable to sell their work, being dropped from their teaching jobs, had plenty of reason to be embittered with a society whose attitudes toward art had traditionally exhibited what the art critic Suzanne LaFollette called "a chronic adolescence." Art and artists had been popularly regarded not as essential interpreters of life, but as luxuries to be enjoyed when times were good, then unceremoniously eliminated when business was bad. Yet, instead of attacking their country's cultural immaturity with blistering satire, a large number of artists, like so many writers of the period, rediscovered and embraced America. Holger Cahill understood this as early as 1931: "The artist . . . finds it possible to live and study and work in the United States and to bring his art closer to the life of a community that needs him and is learning to understand him. . . . Europe is the land of [his] desire no longer. . . . Today the expatriate period is over. The expatriate artist is out of fashion. He dates."

The emphasis on realism involved largely the same considerations for painters as for writers. Artists wanted to paint "things as they are," which often meant painting in a vein of protest against the injustices of a vicious system of industrial capitalism. But whether or not they consciously tried to achieve an art of social protest, numerous painters in the thirties wanted to achieve an "art of the people." As the painter Edward Hopper proclaimed, "a nation's art is greatest when it most reflects the character of its people. The domination of France in the plastic arts has been almost complete for the past thirty years or more in this country. If an apprenticeship to a master has been necessary, I think we have served it."

Presumably the new sense of nationalism and social purpose could be served most effectively by techniques that provided a greater degree of pictorial realism. As a consequence, abstractionism, which had flourished in the twenties, was temporarily eclipsed, while surrealism, preoccupied with spontaneity and the subconscious, attracted few followers during the Depression years.[2] Man in his societal state and the collective problems of society hardly seemed susceptible to abstract or surrealistic treatment. In the thirties, therefore, the dominant techniques in painting, and to a lesser extent in sculpture, were expressionism, which featured recognizable distortions of natural forms; romantic realism, which was representational yet still offered considerable freedom of form; and strict or "photographic" realism.

The practitioners of a more 'realistic' art calculated to get closer to the people received sturdy philosophical support from John Dewey. In *Art as Experience* (1934), Dewey applied his instrumental principles to esthetics, arguing that art should be not "the beauty parlor of civilization" but "an example of life realized." Art must be related to and reflective of place, time, and social context. Cultural maturity was not just having museums filled with the work of the "masters" and studying the art forms of earlier societies; it was the creation of an esthetic expression that belonged to the strivings and struggles of a people.

The phrase most often used to describe the kind of painting that became prevalent in the Depression years was "American scene." The term was misleading for various reasons. In the first place, the American landscape had been painted by thousands of artists over the generations; in the broadest sense Americans had always painted American scenes. Secondly, the term was used to connote a great variety of art showing increased concern with the whole of American existence, including much work that seemed preoccupied with the ordinary, the ironic, the drab, and the ugly. Thus the romantic realists comprising the Fourteenth Street School in New York City—most notably Reginald Marsh and the brothers Isaac, Moses, and Raphael Soyer—were ardent students of the American scene in their paintings of shopgirls staring longingly into store windows, of unemployment offices, of weary passengers on the elevated railway, of crowds on Coney Island. Charles Sheeler and Edward Hopper also brought a new vividness to the description of life in the United States. Sheeler turned from severely formal abstractionism to photography and realistic portrayal of a mechanized, urban America, while Hopper painted hotel lobbies, deserted smalltown streets, and nocturnal city scenes, achieving a startling mastery of both natural and artificial lighting effects. Sheeler and Hopper, as well as Charles Burchfield, seemed to paint primarily from a feeling of resignation, in contrast with both the enamoured proletarianism of the Fourteenth Street group and the spirit of protest and criticism of William Gropper, Jack Levine, Joseph Hirsch, or Ben Shahn. The American scene label unquestionably belonged on Gropper's savage caricatures in oil, Levine's and Hirsch's political and social satires, and Shahn's poignant, bitter pictures of working-class Americans.

Yet the label, with capital letters, also described a group of painters whose attitudes were actually distinct from, and even antagonistic to, most of the leftist and urban-oriented work of the thirties. As employed especially by Thomas Craven, art critic for the *New York American,* the term "American Scene" meant not the general disposition to treat Americans and American locales which pervaded painting in the 1930s, but a particular movement composed of particular painters. Although other critics had their own notions about which artists belonged to the American Scene movement, Craven invariably referred to the "Triumvirate" of Thomas Hart Benton of Missouri, grandson and namesake of the antebellum Missouri senator; John Steuart Curry of Kansas; and Grant Wood of Iowa.

Craven took it upon himself to become the spokesman for a militant cultural nationalism, which he saw expressed most forcefully in the work of Benton, Curry, and Wood, and less forcefully and less frequently in pictures by Burchfield, Marsh, and the muralist Boardman Robinson. Craven argued that American artists had too long been "groveling in the emasculated tradition of the French modernists." "Ashamed of his heritage and his environment," the American "parades the exaggerated niceties, the polite mannerisms of cultures which, being most remote from his own social roots, seem to be, by the very magic of distance, worthy of imitation." The artist, Craven contended, must be an organic part of his society, and his work should be representational, a realistic form expressing the spirit of that society. Yet while Craven maintained that he wanted a national art, an art belonging to all Americans, he and the painters he idealized really were self-conscious regionalists. They repudiated cubism, surrealism, and other European abstractionist influences and denounced the East, specifically New York City, for its effeminacy and decadence. They proclaimed that only in the heartland of America, the great Midwest, could the true soul of the country be plumbed.

Here was to be found the real American life. And as Benton said, "no American art can come to those who do not live an American life, who do not have an American psychology, and who cannot find in America justification for their lives."

Hence the American Scene regionalists set out to capture the national essence, which meant, to these painters of midwestern origins, depicting primarily the people, artifacts, and landscapes of their native region. Benton was the only one of the American Scene triumvirate who consistently reached outside the midwest for his subjects; his murals contained, in addition to midwestern yeomen and townspeople, many southern sharecroppers, urban subway-riders, and factory workers. The theme of most of Curry's paintings was the violent struggle between man and the natural elements in a rural setting. His most famous work, however, was the magnificently powerful figure of John Brown which formed part of the mural he completed for the Kansas state capitol in 1940. Wood could paint with tongue-in-cheek, as in *Daughters of Revolutio*n (1932), or in the severely, even grimly realistic manner of the German primitives, as in his celebrated *American Gothic* (1930); but most of his work in the thirties consisted of romantic realist midwestern landscapes and town and farm scenes.

While the position of Craven, the propagandist, and of Benton, Curry, and Wood, the painters, amounted to little less than esthetic chauvinism, they were not greatly impressed by political radicalism and their interests and tastes remained primarily rural and agrarian. Their repugnance for urbanism and industrialism—Benton called the city "a coffin for living and thinking"—and their attachment to their region, to the land, and to farming as a way of life provided obvious similarities to the Southern Agrarians. Although there was never any formal connection between the two groups, the midwestern artists almost certainly would have approved of Donald Davidson's dicta that "the goodness of life [is] measured by a scale of values having little to do with the material values of industrialism," and that "the chief subject of art, in the final sense, is nature."

Of course much of what critics said about the American Scene midwesterners was true: They were dogmatic, provincial, and reactionary, and in trying to shake free of European influences they ignored a simple fact of culture and psychology: An artist can never divest himself of his heritage, which in the case of Americans is largely European. Yet they represented only one vociferous contingent in the larger movement toward national expression in the arts. And even the most cosmopolitan and sophisticated commentators acknowledged that the cultural nationalists were right in saying true ripeness in the arts meant not just appreciative but also creative activity. As Virgil Barker wrote of American art in the mid-thirties, "Even if it be tenth-rate it will be better for us in the end than the better art of other nations. Only by making an art which in turn makes us can we attain spiritual maturity."

The anti-urban attitudes of the American Scene painters furnished additional evidence of the decade's curious revulsion against the city. Seemingly intensified by the crisis of industrial capitalism, anti-urbanism took such varied forms as the New Deal's faltering rural resettlement and suburban housing programs, the economic regionalism of the Tennessee Valley Authority, the cultural and political regionalism of the Southern Agrarians, the activities of the Federal Theatre Project, and the social and architectural theories of Lewis Mumford and Frank Lloyd Wright. One further indication of the widespread desire to counteract the centripetal force of the city was the Works Progress Administration's Federal Arts Project. Unlike the other WPA cultural programs, the Arts Project antedated the WPA. It began in 1933 as the Public Works of Art Project, a combination building-decoration function and limited artists' relief scheme under the Federal Emergency Relief Administration. Early in 1935 the Works of Art Project was transferred to the Fine Arts Section of the Treasury Department; then it was brought under the WPA when Harry Hopkins's agency got underway in mid-year.

Despite the capable and imaginative leadership of Holger Cahill, the distinguished art critic Roosevelt appointed to head the Federal Arts Project, the WPA's efforts to foster painting and sculpture while providing relief for jobless artists encountered the same problems and frustrations as the other federal cultural activities of the thirties. Charges of leftist propagandizing (not always unfounded), of waste and duplication, and of incompetence on the part of both administrators and employees dogged the Arts Project almost from its inception. Before it was terminated during the war, however, it had striven mightily to reverse the trend toward centralization of creativity in the cities and had actually accomplished a great deal to bring art to the people and the people to art.

The Arts Project had two principal themes—collective effort and localized expression. Collective effort meant that most of the work done in posters, murals, sculpture, and handcrafts would be anonymous. Hence while some of the finest younger artists in the country —Shahn, Gropper, Benton, Stuart Davis, and Jackson Pollock, to name a few—drew WPA wages at one time or another, they often failed to receive due recognition. To achieve localized expression, the Arts Project established a maximum of 103 art centers throughout the nation, mostly in small communities. Besides encouraging local artists and staging frequent exhibits of their work, the centers offered instruction in painting and sculpture, in crafts, and even interior decorating. They also contributed their local research findings and reproductions to the most ambitious enterprise initiated under the Arts Project—the Index of American Design.

The Index began under the direction of Constance Rourke, who probably did more than anyone else before her death in 1941 to call attention to the creative heritage in American folk art. Over the years Rourke argued that America had a rich native tradition not only in its formal letters and fine arts, but also in the ordinary, everyday esthetic expressions of the people. Accepting the new concept of culture developed by cultural anthropologists, Rourke maintained that culture was not the sum of national contributions in the arts and letters, but a "configuration," a whole. Thus what was important in the life of a people was not the epic achievement of a few, but the diversity, multi-colorings, and multi-layerings of society. Rourke brought these ideas to the Index project and received the enthusiastic endorsement of Cahill, who had himself written much on the value of folk art (pointing out, for example, the sculptural qualities in such folk carvings as duck decoys, toys, and cigar store indians). The Index of American Design set out to discover and illumine the nation's vernacular esthetic. The result was a compendium of some 20,000 plates—selected from many more precise drawings by Arts Project employees —which illustrated early American furniture, textiles, pottery, glassware, and other crafts. The Index, as one art critic said, "showed that thousands of nameless Yankees had wrought superbly in wood and iron, silver and wool. . . ." Despite the often excessive rhapsodizings of its admirers, the Index was one of the most brilliant manifestations of American democratic nationalism in the 1930s.

The enthusiasm for recognizing and fostering a native art reached its extreme in the vogue of primitivism. What could be a more fundamental expression of Americanism than the creations of untrained and sometimes unlettered 'little people' who simply painted avocationally, because they enjoyed it? Suddenly, it seemed, critics were praising and collectors were buying paintings by such "amateurs" as John Kane, a former coal miner from Pittsburgh; Horace Pippin, a Philadelphia Negro whose oil painting of the trial of John Brown conveyed considerable power; and Anna Mary Robertson "Grandma" Moses, an elderly woman from upstate New York, whose simple rural scenes would maintain their popularity—and increase their monetary value—over the next generation.

Most features of the Federal Arts Project helped give impetus to the primitivism phenomenon, especially the Index of American Design; but the Arts Project activity that literally brought art closest to the people was the mural program, inherited from the Treasury Department and broadened under the WPA. In hundreds of post offices and other public buildings over the country, worn old prints and posters came down from walls, and colorful murals appeared to fill the vacant spaces. Mural art was uniquely suited to the task of providing an art for the people. Covering vast interior and exterior walls, murals could be viewed free of charge by generations of citizens, regardless of wealth or status. Inspired by the stunning accomplishments of the contemporary muralists of Mexico, the WPA mural painters tried to capture the panorama of American life from pre-Columbian days to the doldrums of the Depression.

Many of the people who worked on the Arts Project murals tried to emulate not only the form of the Mexican muralists, but the radical political content of their art as well.[3] Often the WPA muralists displayed more social protest sentiment than talent, and their labors accomplished little more than to fill empty wall space. Criticism of the WPA's mural efforts was sharp and continuous, from both politicians and respectable art critics. Such criticism was partly justified; on the whole the federal mural program seems to have produced mediocre results. Yet some of the murals, painted by men of extraordinary talent like Benton, Robinson, and Henry Varnum Poor, represented perhaps the finest American mural art. Moreover, thanks to the government's murals and the rest of its Arts Project, more Americans were exposed to more art in the thirties than during any previous period of the nation's history. The WPA Arts Project heightened American tastes, improved the market for American artists, and helped enlarge the nation's artistic community.

Of course, not everything in the visual arts during the decade fitted the moods of leftist protest and democratic nationalism. Although many painters used expressionism as a critical weapon, Max Weber, often concerned with Jewish religious themes, and Marsden

Hartley, who usually painted New England landscapes, continued to demonstrate by their apolitical expressionism that technique and mood were not necessarily related. Moreover, the late thirties saw the resurgence of abstractionism. The two principal factors that brought abstractionism back into prominence were the immigration of several outstanding German abstractionists to the United States after the closing of the Bauhaus, and the growing reaction of some American artists against the chauvinism of the American Scene regionalists and the polemics of the leftist painters. John Marin, whose vigorous watercolors had made him perhaps the foremost American abstractionist in the twenties, now was joined by a growing number of highly talented "non-objectivists" like Willem de Kooning; Jackson Pollock, who would eventually compose with a dripping paint bucket; and Stuart Davis, who tried to achieve a "visual jazz," as in his *Hot Still-Scape for Six Colors* (1940). The Museum of Modern Art continued through the thirties to display large amounts of abstractionist work, while the Museum of Non-Objective Painting, established by the Guggenheim Foundation in New York, provided abstractionism with its own exclusive national gallery, beginning in 1937. The renewed interest in abstractionism meant the gap between the public and good art, closed somewhat during the Depression years, would grow wider than ever after the Second World War.

In more subdued fashion, American sculpture went through the same developmental process as painting—from increased realism in form and content during the early years of the Depression to growing abstractionism by the end of the decade. Genre sculpture, the depiction of ordinary people in ordinary and contemporary settings, was the sculptural equivalent to the American scene disposition in painting. Sculptors like Chaim Gross, Robert Cronbach, Hugo Robus, and Heinz Warneke realized the esthetic possibilities of everyday life in the United States, the "real America." One of the better pieces of the period was Robus's expressionist *Girl Washing Her Hair,* whose bold sweep was first seen at the New York World's Fair in 1939. For the PWA's Harlem housing project Warneke produced representations of Negro life that were appealing in their unheroic simplicity. Even so, the thirties was not a time of great American achievement in sculpture. Despite the upsurge of collective consciousness, the most striking new development in sculpture was Alexander Calder's dangling "mobiles," the ultimate in individualized abstractionism since the viewer could redesign the composition simply by touching it. The United States had always lacked a tradition of greatness in sculpture;

the work of the thirties represented only a modest advance toward the creation of such a tradition. "Fine talents are to be detected in all parts of the country," observed Shelton Cheney in 1938, "but the brutal truth is that there doesn't seem to be much place for sculpture in our contemporary environment." And Oliver Larkin came away from the World's Fair of 1939 with "the impression that the sculptor's place in American life was as marginal as it had been half a century before. . . ."

On the whole, however, the years of Depression at home and incipient war abroad were rich ones for the visual arts in America. One small indication of the flourishing state of the arts in the thirties was the fact that New York's Whitney Museum of American Art, established in 1930 to show solely native work, became one of the major galleries in the country. To be sure, the goal of a truly national expression seemed as illusive and as protean as ever. Yet whether the expression was defined as "American" or whether it was simply offered by Americans, it was there, vital and growing. "Civilization is shaky, therefore the United States is shaky, therefore American art is shaky," said Cheney. "But among the component parts or forces of American civilization, art is at last well up as an accomplishment." Cheney was not thinking specifically of music, but if he had been he would probably have reached the same optimistic conclusion.

Music: Americanism in Form and Content

The Great Depression was as much an economic disaster for musicians as for people in the other arts media. One writer estimated that by 1934 some sixty per cent of the musicians who had formerly held jobs were out of work. The case of the musicians playing in a WPA symphony orchestra in Florida, who explained that their performances were below par because their hands were stiff from working on road gangs, was not unusual. Throughout the country, musical groups had trouble staying together in the face of declining public patronage. San Francisco demonstrated its spartan devotion to high culture by imposing a half-cent tax increase to support its symphony, while the Metropolitan Opera in New York had to appeal to its millions of radio listeners for contributions to "save the Met."

Despite the economic privation of the period, there apparently was a quite considerable enlargement in the American audience for the more formal and complex forms of musical expression. The arrival from Europe of increasing numbers of musical artists, impelled toward the United States by political upheavals in their native countries, acquainted Americans with diverse musical forms and presumably broadened their range of appreciation. At the close of the thirties the "big three" of modern musical composition—Igor Stravinsky, Arnold Shoenberg, and Paul Hindemith—all resided in this country. The most famous of the musical emigres was the conductor Arturo Toscanini, whom the National Broadcasting Company brought to America late in the thirties to lead its symphony orchestra in weekly nationwide radio concerts.

The fame of Toscanini and the NBC Symphony pointed up the signal role of radio in the quantitative improvement of the musical situation in the United States. Although in the twenties a number of concert artists, conductors, composers, and critics had bemoaned the destruction of musical taste that would perforce follow the mass acquisition of radio, the new communications medium apparently did a great deal during the next decade to educate the public's taste. Undoubtedly the late thirties and early forties saw radio reach its apex as a disseminator of formal music. Two musical historians recalled that "it became as difficult to avoid hearing good music as it had been in past years to get the opportunity to hear it." By 1939 the combined radio audience of the Metropolitan Opera and the NBC Symphony on Saturday, and of the New York Philharmonic and the Detroit Symphony's "Sunday Evening Hour" the next day, was an estimated 10,230,000.

Evidently the increasing exposure to formal music through radio affected other areas of public taste. The RCA Victor Company reported a jump in its record sales of 600 per cent between 1933 and 1938, with most of the increase coming from sales of symphonic, opera, and chamber music recordings. By 1940 there were about 270 symphony orchestras in the United States, of which at least 16 were classed as "major" groups. Of the "lesser" ensembles, one-half had been formed since 1929. "It is . . . possible that a sound and deep appreciation among the masses of our people is growing in music," concluded Dickson Skinner in 1938. ". . . the signs are clear that the American people, in the mass, are at the threshold of a cultural maturity."

For some observers of music in America, however, maturity could not be measured solely by such general quantitative factors. "If top-notch performances and an active musical life were the only things needed for musical maturity," wrote the composer Aaron Copland, "we should by now be at the top of the list of auditory-minded nations. But . . . first-rate orchestras, brilliant conductors, imported opera singers, child prodigies, and the like cannot by themselves constitute an important musical culture." The essence of the problem of developing an indigenous musical expression was producing first-rate composers. Certainly there could be little argument with the conclusion of the composer and critic Howard Hanson: "If America produces great composers, we are a great country musically. If we do not produce great composers, we are a musical failure, regardless of whether we may or may not have a hundred orchestras, every one of which is better than the best orchestra abroad." Nor could one reasonably dispute the complaints of American composers about their troubles in trying to gain recognition. The outstanding symphony orchestras in the country were led by European-born conductors, most of whom showed little disposition toward music written by Americans. For the most part, the programs of the major orchestras featured the European "masters" of past centuries. Such a condition was justified as representing the good judgment of the conductor or, more likely, as giving the audiences what they wanted to hear. Neither explanation was acceptable to the musical nationalists. "As a matter of fact," growled Copland, "this continual preoccupation with the embalmed masterwork to the exclusion of any lesser music is one of the outstanding signs of our immaturity. . . . Being alive seems to relegate the composer automatically to the position of an 'also-ran.' "

The usual reply to the nationalists was that given by Henry Bellamann of the Catholic weekly *Commonweal* in 1934. Bellemann accused American composers of striving to do too much, of trying to turn "water colors into Michelangelo." After an American work had been performed once, it often was not repeated simply because audiences did not want to hear it again. Having the privilege of hearing a work conducted by Toscanini, for example, audiences wanted to be assured that the music matched Toscanini's talents. But that was the whole point, countered Hanson. Conductors, orchestras, chamber, choral, and operatic groups had a duty to perform the best compositions of Americans, to repeat them, regardless of audience reaction, and to keep performing them until the American public became educated to an appreciation of native talents. Only then would American music attain true stature; only then would American audiences, including many music critics, overcome their annoying habit of calling indigenous compositions "experimental."

The Federal Music Project of the WPA, like the Writers', Theatre, and Arts projects, was supposed to encourage and develop native talents, as well as disseminate culture and put people to work. Like the other WPA cultural activities, the Music Project could point to impressive quantitative achievements. WPA administrators estimated that more than one hundred million people attended Music Project concerts before the project ended in 1941. Besides forming full symphony orchestras, chamber groups, and bands, the WPA hired unemployed music teachers to hold classes for young people and adults throughout the country. Hundreds of WPA research workers went into cities, towns, and remote rural areas to record the ballads of cowboys and mountaineers, Negro slave songs, and obscure blues tunes. The Music Project, as well as the activities of people like John and Alan Lomax and Woody Guthrie, both reflected and furthered the growing national interest in folk art. Nikolai Sokoloff, who left the directorship of the Cleveland Symphony to head the project, invited American composers to submit their manuscripts to a national audition board, which would pass on their suitability for performance by WPA music groups. Unquestionably the federal musical authorities were more receptive to American compositions than were regular orchestras; between October 1935 and January 1937, according to Sokoloff, WPA orchestras performed forty symphonic works, many from manuscript, by native-born composers. Yet the overwhelming majority of the pieces offered under the auspices of the Music Project were European; such music undoubtedly evoked the greatest responses from audiences over the country. It appears that, however much the Federal Music Project may have helped to broaden American musical appreciation, it did relatively little to answer demands for a nationalized musical expression.

The controversy over a national music involved two separate considerations, a distinction which was commonly overlooked or obscured by nationalists. Most supporters of musical nationalism simply wanted to gain recognition for American-born composers, of whatever stylistic, generic, or thematic inclination. Hence Hanson and Copland saw no inconsistency in praising composers who made little conscious effort to be "American," but who rather worked essentially with European forms and influences, whether as modernists, traditionalists, or eclecticists. Composers of this type included Virgil Thomson, an outstanding music critic as well as a fine artist; Walter Piston, chairman of the music department at Harvard; Roger Sessions; and Samuel Barber, whose *Adagio for Strings* (1936) and *Essay for Orchestra* (1937) were chosen by Toscanini as the first American pieces to be played by the NBC Symphony.

A second and smaller group of musical nationalists, made up principally of young composers, wanted to achieve a music that was uniquely American in its content. Such a music should feature the use of native themes and the development of meters and rhythms suited to national scenes and attitudes. For Roy Harris, born, appropriately enough, in a log cabin in Oklahoma, genuine American musical expression must recognize that the American temperament and musical sense were fundamentally different from the European. Whereas European musicians were taught to think of rhythm in broad, symmetrical meters, Americans "are born with a feeling for its smallest specific units and their possible juxtaposition." Harris also indicted conductors, audiences, and music teachers for their apathy toward American compositions. He noted that when Toscanini toured Europe with the New York Philharmonic, he refused to offer a single work by an American, yet he always offered selections by composers native to the countries in which the orchestra was performing. Harris found such an attitude intolerable. "When foreign conductors and soloists refuse to perform our works," he declared, "they are denying American creative musicians the right to speak to American people. When they surround us with the idioms of eighteenth and nineteenth century European masters, and thus directly insist that these idioms must be our ultimate musical values, they are subtly and circumspectly curtailing our musical liberty and our pursuit of musical happiness."

Yet throughout the thirties American composers, both 'neutralists' and 'Americanists,' did manage to have their works performed by prominent orchestras. The Boston Symphony, under Serge Koussevitsky, introduced Harris's self-consciously nationalistic *First Symphony* in 1934 and *Third Symphony* in 1939. Other composers who chose American themes and tried to integrate folk songs, jazz, and other influences into their works were Douglas Moore, William Grant Still, Ernst Bacon, Ferde Grofé, and George Gershwin. Moore's major symphonic composition was *Overture on an American Theme* (1931);

Bacon's was a collection of suites called *Country Roads, Unpaved* (1936). Grofé's *Grand Canyon Suite* (1932) was an effective piece until it became the theme for a cigarette commercial; his other attempts to describe aspects of the national life included *Tabloid Suite* (1933) and *Hollywood Suite* (1935). Grant Still, a Negro, arranged and played night-club music while writing his *Afro-American Symphony,* finished in 1930. His *Symphony in G Minor* was performed by the New York Philharmonic in the late thirties. Gershwin had startled, intrigued, but not wholly won music critics in the twenties with his *Rhapsody in Blue,* an ambitious effort to capture the atmosphere of New York City, especially its Negro and Jewish rhythms.[4] After 1930 Gershwin continued to pursue parallel careers as a successful popular song-writer and as an increasingly acclaimed composer of formal music. In *Second Rhapsody* (1932) he again gave an orchestral impression of urban life, while in *Cuban Overture* (1935), finished two years before his death, he experimented with Latin idioms.

All of these composers received respectful attention from directors and courteous hearings from audiences. Yet the prevailing reaction was skeptical, the descriptive language often condescending. With regard to opera, for example, most critics ignored the fact that numerous European composers had taken their themes from national history and legend, and insisted on attaching the label "folk opera" to music drama written on American themes. Such was the fate of Moore's one-act *The Devil and Daniel Webster* (1939), based on a story by Stephen Vincent Benét, and Gershwin's immensely popular *Porgy and Bess,* featuring an all-Negro cast. Ironically, in view of its "folk opera" tag, *Porgy and Bess* emphasized not Negro folk tunes but the milieu and argot of contemporary urban Negro life. By contrast, Deems Taylor's opera *Peter Ibbetson* (1931), European in theme and tradition, was favorably received for what it was. Performed by the Metropolitan Opera Company, it ran for four seasons, longer than any other opera written by an American.

Although America may still have lacked maturity in formal music in the thirties, there was no denying that the United States was a musical nation. Virgil Thomson observed that "The United States is the one country in all the world that produces all kinds of music that there are. Only here do composers write in every possible style and does the public have access to every style." The enormous popularity of phonograph records and radio music, of musical comedy in New

York and elsewhere, and of dance and marching bands, demonstrated that, however deficient Americans might be in understanding, they liked music and wanted to hear it almost constantly.

The widespread enthusiasm for what was called "jazz" at the opening of the decade confirmed the assumptions of some critics about the essential barbarity of American taste in music. Paul Rosenfeld spoke for such devotees of "high culture" when, in 1929, he described jazz as "an extraordinarily popular drug-like use of the materials of sound"—in short, "just another means of escape." Jazz, offering "mere beat," violated the sonority of instruments and pandered to cheap, illusory desires. At the other extreme were those to whom jazz was the one genuine native American music, a form which, in its improvisation and syncopated rhythms, expressed both the individualism of Americans and the complexity of modern industrial society. The controversy over the legitimacy of jazz as musical art, which had begun long before 1930, perhaps reached its peak during the Depression decade. Although the controversy far outlived the Great Depression, there seems to be little doubt that in the thirties jazz enthusiasts, buttressed to some extent by the "total culture" conceptions of cultural anthropologists, made substantial progress toward gaining critical acceptance for their music.

The nature of the jazz form underwent significant alteration in the thirties. "Hot jazz," which had gravitated from Chicago to New York to become a principal ingredient in the "Harlem renaissance" of the twenties, began to lose popularity about the time of the crash of 1929. Conceivably the eclipse of hot jazz in the early Depression years was related to the evaporation of the hedonistic prosperity of the twenties; in any case, many jazz ensembles broke up and erstwhile "jazzmen" found themselves playing soothing dance music in bands like those of Rudy Vallee or Guy Lombardo. Seemingly the "jazz age" was over.

About the middle of the decade, the jazz form took on new life, albeit under a new name—"swing." In a sense swing was but another name for jazz. The term, in fact, seems to have originated in the prudishness of the British Broadcasting Company. Not wanting to describe the offerings on one of its programs as "hot jazz," the BBC substituted the phrase "swing music." The new name caught on and became generic for all kinds of music featuring syncopation, improvisation, and a heavy beat. Moreover, swing represented a logical consolidation of developments in jazz over the previous two or three decades. Yet swing differed from the hot jazz of the pre-Depression years in several significant ways. The main distinguishing mark of swing, as opposed to hot jazz, was increased band size. Bigger bands made for smoother or "cooler" music, more complex arrangements, and more teamwork among band members. Although swing was largely an outgrowth of innovative arrangements in the twenties by the Negro musicians Edward "Duke" Ellington and Earl "Fatha" Hines, most of swing's leaders—Benny Goodman, the Dorsey brothers, Glenn Miller, Artie Shaw—were white. Goodman was the preeminent musician and band leader in the swing movement. His music combined precision and traditional harmony with hot jazz solo improvisations, such as those of drummer Gene Krupa. The result was a blend of music that toned down, refined, and even sterilized jazz—and greatly broadened its appeal.

The Swing Era lasted roughly ten years. Many jazz connoisseurs might spurn Goodman and his fellow-purveyors of swing, preferring instead to collect early records and listen to obscure groups in New Orleans, Harlem, and other wellsprings of jazz. But throughout the country radio blared swing, and "hep-cats" "jitter-bugged" to "boogie-woogie" melodies. Stripped of its racial and speakeasy connotations, jazz, as swing, became popular with millions of American who acquired a familiarity with the elements of the musical form without realizing it. After the Second World War swing would all but vanish and jazz would again take new directions. Even though the Swing Era was brief, it did much to weave jazz into the pattern of national life, and to make Americans aware of jazz as part of their cultural heritage.

Jazz, like functional architecture and abstract painting, suggested national vitality to some people, national decadence to others. For some the nationalist impulse in American art was a sign of growing cultural maturity; for others esthetic nationalism was reactionary, provincial, and stultifying. Such critical polarities pointed up the difficulty, even the futility, of trying to determine what was or should be "American art." As America left behind its continental apartness and moved into another world war, it seemingly also left behind its last and greatest period of esthetic nationalism. In time most American artists and critics would come to feel that the search for a uniquely American art was irrelevant. Perhaps, after all, it was the absence of a particular national idiom or style that truly defined Americanism in the arts.

Notes

1. The Roosevelt administration and Congress made federal support for public housing long-term policy in 1937 with the establishment of the United States Housing Authority. This agency, created as a public corporation under the Department of the Interior, made available low-interest loans to municipal governments for the construction of low-rent housing projects. By the end of 1940 nearly 350 projects had been initiated.
2. Impressionism, which had flourished in the United States after being imported from France around 1900, was virtually dead as a coherent movement in American painting by the end of the First World War.
3. Murals by Jose Orozco and Diego Rivera, who, along with David Siquieros, were the foremost Mexican muralists, aroused heated controversy in the United States during the thirties. Orozco's mural at Dartmouth College brought protests from alumni, while local citizens in Detroit attacked Rivera's work at the city's Institute of Art. Rivera lost his commission at Rockefeller Center when someone discovered a head of Lenin in one of his panels. Eventually the mural was destroyed. The incident prompted Archibald MacLeish to write his poem *Frescoes for Mr. Rockefeller's City.*
4. Ferde Grofé orchestrated *Rhapsody in Blue* for Gershwin.

Chapter IV

Varieties of Cultural Experience: Films, Radio, Journalism

In the 1930s, as today, people usually thought of the "mass media"—motion pictures, radio, and the daily and periodical press—not as forms of esthetic expression but as means of popular entertainment and factual communication. What was seen on the motion picture screen, heard over the airwaves, or read in the newspapers and magazines supposedly had little connection with or relevance to culture. During the thirties, however, both popular writers and scholars increasingly broadened their definition of culture to include the whole societal complex and all that was said and done within a society. To accept this definition of culture meant looking at every aspect of American life, however pedestrian, crude, or eccentric, searching every corner of the national existence for clues that helped create an understanding of what America really was.

One of the pioneer expositors of what came to be called "popular culture" was the journalist and critic Gilbert Seldes. In a widely read collection of essays in 1924, Seldes argued that one could not begin to understand esthetics in America simply by examining achievements in the traditional forms of expression, the "fine arts." It was necessary to consider what Seldes called the "lively arts" (and later termed "public arts")—such forms as vaudeville, jazz music, popular songs, comic strips, motion pictures, and (he subsequently added) radio. For Seldes and the growing number of writers who shared his viewpoint, the best in the various forms of mass entertainment was equal to the norm, and occasionally to the best, in the traditional literary, visual, and aural arts.

But if the films, radio, journalism, and other mass media emphasized the rich diversity of American culture, they also produced more and more standardization in American tastes and attitudes. People in every part of the country—in cities, towns, and rural areas—eventually saw the same motion pictures, heard many of the same radio programs, and read the same magazines and the same syndicated material in newspapers. Such universal, mass exposure to the same influences was both cheered and damned by critics of American art and society. That ten million people heard Toscanini direct the NBC Symphony in a Beethoven concert presumably was good; that other millions laughed at "Amos 'n Andy" on the radio or swallowed hard when Clark Gable embraced Jean Harlow on the theater screen presumably was bad. But whether or not cultural arbiters and social scientists approved, the close of a decade and a half of depression and war found Americans talking alike, dressing alike, and perhaps thinking alike as never before.

Films: The Struggle Toward Art

For many years, especially after motion-picture production was concentrated in southern California about 1912, the makers of American films had loudly claimed that they were artists and that the films they turned out represented true art. For the large majority in the traditional arts who disliked Hollywood films, the claim was false; for the huge numbers of Americans who enjoyed films simply as entertainment, the claim was inconsequential. At the same time that they called themselves artists, motion picture producers defended themselves from criticism on the ground that films were still in their infancy, that maturity took time. The fact was that the "movies," from their inception as primitive peep-show attractions in the 1890s, had been, for the people who produced them, primarily business enterprise. The great majority of films in this country, and perhaps abroad as well, had been made not with honesty, imagination, and serious intent, but with the goal of attracting ever-increasing box office revenues. Even Seldes, a tireless seeker after film art, had to admit that "the majority of [films] are so stupid, tasteless, and wearisome that no man of average intelligence could bear to look at them twice. . . ." By 1930, however, all but the severest skeptics acknowledged that on occasion the motion picture could attain the status of art. Besides the much-admired German and Russian films of the 1920s, a few American efforts had shown the film's esthetic possibilities, particularly D. W. Griffith's *The Birth of a Nation* (1915), a cinema milestone despite its blatant racism, and Charles Chaplin's whimsical, ironic, uproariously funny pictures. As Seldes wrote in 1929, "half a dozen people have, in the thirty years of the movie's existence, created perhaps a score of films which have interested men and women of intelligence. . . ."

The most important distinguishing feature of the motion picture is, of course, continual motion. This fact seems obvious enough, but it took a long period of development before film directors came to understand fully the two preconditions for film art: mastery of the movable camera, and perfection of the technique known as "montage"—the cutting and editing of film shot in any order so as to build scenes from individual shots, sequences from separate scenes, and a whole film story from separate sequences. By the late twenties it seemed that, however banal and escapist most Hollywood fare might be, the people who made motion pictures in America had learned these technical lessons well. The silent film, in technique if not in content, was on the verge of brilliant maturity.

Then, in 1928, came the first films with sound, the "talkies." The initial response of the giant Hollywood studios was to assume that the public wanted only to hear the voices behind the moving lips of their favorites. Consequently film-makers, forced to immobilize their cameras in soundproof boxes, made pictures that were little more than photographed plays. The result was virtual abandonment of the techniques developed so painstakingly over the decades. Several years passed before mobile cameras and microphones, together with the realization that sound had an expressiveness of its own quite apart from recorded speech, broke down the real technical dichotomy between silent "movies" and plodding "talkies." By the mid-thirties sound was fully integrated with motion in film technique, the term "movies" was again synonymous with all motion pictures, and color, first used throughout a full-length film in 1935, had opened new possibilities for the film art.

The Great Depression struck the motion picture industry just as Hollywood was beginning to understand the full implications of sound. The complete conversion to sound-film production by the early 1930s may have saved the movies financially, as some claimed, but the film industry nevertheless sagged under the impact of the economic crisis. By mid-June 1933 about one-third of the movie houses in the country had closed down. Although none of the major film companies went under, their executives and financial backers turned to various practices to try to stabilize an industry that, despite its fabulous profits, had always experienced business insecurity. The most pernicious new business practice was block-booking, under which distributing companies forced theater syndicates and local operators to accept a large number of second-rate films in order to get a few prime attractions. Since exhibiters ended up with more films than they could show individually, they began to offer "double features," which proved popular with youths and poorer people but annoying and distasteful to more prosperous and discriminating moviegoers. In 1940 the federal Department of Justice intervened to arrange a compromise between distributers and exhibiters whereby block-booking was limited to five films rather than the usual fifty.

The American motion picture industry had a long history of trouble with groups over the country who feared the effect of the films on the moral standards of Americans, especially young people. The film magnates had placated organized censorship bodies early in the twenties by hiring Will Hays, postmaster general in the Harding cabinet, to become "czar" of the industry and clean up Hollywood's offerings. Thereafter the quantity of sex in American films declined somewhat, although violence became more and more prominent. And guardians of the public's morals almost completely ignored the enervating cheapness, hypocrisy, and escapism in hundreds of films cranked out by the Hollywood "dream factory," as well as the distorted notion of America which the fantasies exported by the film companies gave millions of people in foreign countries.

In the early thirties the forces of censorship once again became militant, this time primarily in opposition to the cycle of "gangster movies" precipitated by Mervyn LeRoy's *Little Caesar* (1930). Besides the National Board of Review in New York and numerous other state and local censors, the powerful Legion of Decency, formed under the auspices of the American Roman Catholic hierarchy in 1934, demanded an end to films that glamorized crime or tended to excite lustful desires. The progressive Protestant monthly *Christian Century* even advocated making motion pictures a public utility and establishing a federal commission to police film content and control film exports. A spate of heavily statistical sociological studies reached the same general conclusion as that of religious and civic groups: Films, by their very nature, exerted a more powerful influence on young people than other media, and much of what came out of Hollywood was injurious to traditional youthful values and morals. As the Catholic bishop of Los Angeles and San Diego put it, "one hour spent in the darkness of a cinema palace, intent on the unfolding of a wrong kind of story, can and frequently does nullify years of careful training on the part of the church, the school, the home." To which Mark Van Doren replied, "This seems to me a very damaging statement about the church, the school, and the home. . . ."

The film content in question might seem pallid and prudish to a later generation watching "old movies" on late television, but the mounting protest against license and lasciviousness in the early thirties represented Hollywood's second great censorship crisis. Faced with the prospect of national Catholic boycotts, local and statewide bans, and even federal legislation, the Motion Picture Producers and Distributors Association announced in 1934 that it would live up to the restrictions on content in its twelve-point "Production Code" of 1930. With capitalized and italicized emphasis, the Code proclaimed that "The motion picture, because of . . . the trust placed in it by the peoples of the world, has special *MORAL OBLIGATIONS*." Once again Hollywood set out to police itself; once again the clamor for censorship died down. The career of the voluptuous Mae West, whose "hot" roles had made her the top female box office attraction of 1933–1934, cooled down considerably, while Hollywood switched from glorifying gangsters to glorifying the Federal Bureau of Investigation and its gun-wielding "G-men." James Cagney made a smooth transition from bad killer to good hired killer. For the rest of the decade, however, social scientists and social critics continued to debate the behavioral effects of movies; the Legion of Decency continued to review individual films and issue formal approvals or disapprovals; and local moralists remained watchful.

The persistent controversy over what films should or should not contain pointed up the general confusion regarding their proper role in American life. Some asserted that the motion picture—regardless of its mass audience, its exposure to children and adolescents, and its darkened, larger-than-life setting—constituted an art form, and that as a consequence its creators must work unfettered by community mores. Others wanted only to insure that films had no deleterious effect on the norms of moral and social behavior. Still others, like Charles and Mary Beard, assumed that films should have "constructive significance," that they should be "conducive to the development and preservation of those virtues essential to the health of a democratic republic." To the Beards, therefore, the socio-political content of Hollywood productions was of central importance. Too few pictures, they felt, helped create a climate for collective social and economic reform; too many fortified political conservatism or, in the late thirties, contributed to the growing militarism of the country under the Roosevelt administration. Even Hollywood—perhaps especially Hollywood—lacked a clear conception of what the movies were supposed to be. "Theatrical motion pictures," the Motion Picture Production Code stipulated, "are primarily to be regarded as ENTERTAINMENT." Yet the Code also acknowledged that "Motion pictures are very important as ART."

In the midst of such disagreements over definition and purpose, compounded by the fundamentally commercial nature of motion picture production in the United States, it was perhaps surprising that anything worthwhile came out of Hollywood in the thirties. The single greatest limitation on the development of the film art was the fact that 85 million Americans, of all ages, social strata, and educational levels, attended movie houses each week. The existence of this mass audience was responsible for censorship crusades; the glut of Hollywood films (and thus block-booking); the wasteful "star system"; the weakness of film directors; and, with the exception of Seldes in the thirties, James Agee in the early forties, and a handful of others, the absence of capable and conscientious film critics serving both to improve the taste of movie patrons and enlarge the conceptions of movie-makers.

The star system meant that film producers paid huge salaries to men and women with audience appeal but little real dramatic talent, then offered pictures on the apparently correct assumption that moviegoers were more interested in seeing their favorites in juxtaposition than well-made films. Directors, who should have been the dominant figures in the whole creative process, usually had to accept these public favorites whether they wanted them or not. Hampered by commercial pressures and restrictions on content, most Hollywood directors found it impossible to do pictures according to their own tastes. Some did many mediocre films so that, occasionally, they might do something on their own. As Lewis Jacobs wrote in 1938 in his excellent history of American films, "The art of moving pictures is so dependent for its livelihood on commerce that directors enjoy less freedom than artists in any other media." And the German-born director Ernst Lubitsch, drawn to Hollywood in the twenties by the superior physical facilities there, mused, "The American public—the American public with the mind of a twelve-year-old child, you see—it must have life as it ain't." Yet Lubitsch himself turned out dozens of slick, pseudo-sophisticated, "life-as-it-ain't" films.[1]

Despite the numerous handicaps under which serious filmmakers labored, the film art in America advanced notably during the thirties. The documentary film came into its own in a decade that saw a demand for heightened realism in both art and social thought. Newsreels, first shown regularly in movie houses during the twenties, became increasingly popular with the advent of sound film, the steady technical improvement in documentary moving picture photography, and the renewed mass involvement in public affairs stimulated by the crises of depression and war. Of course, however informative they might be, newsreels were also commercial entertainment, produced by the film companies and sold to exhibiters as companion features, or "shorts." But the thirties also brought an outpouring of pure documentary motion pictures, a number of which were authorized and financed by federal government agencies to dramatize the economic and social problems under attack by the New Deal. The most interesting such efforts were Pare Lorentz's studies of drouth, floods, and soil erosion for the Farm Security Administration, *The Plough That Broke the Plains* (1936) and *The River* (1938). With musical scores by Virgil Thomson and stirring narrations by Lorentz, the two films were imposing combinations of art and reporting.

Although the Hollywood studios usually shied from themes with meaningful social content, a few pictures managed to retain some relevance to the collective strivings and struggles of the period. Chaplin, who wrote and directed as well as played in his films, showed that his pantomime skills were highly compatible with spoken comedy in *Modern Times* (1936), a biting depiction of the 'little guy' trapped by machine civilization. King Vidor's *The Citadel* (1938) dealt with injustices in the medical profession and implicitly favored socialized medicine. John Ford's *The Informer* (1935) was a masterful portrayal of a simpleton whose mistakes lead him to death at the hands of Irish revolutionaries. Less dramatically successful was Ford's much-amended film version (1939) of *The Grapes of Wrath*. Mervyn LeRoy, besides directing the most famous of the gangster movies, made two socially conscious films: *I Am a Fugitive* (1932), an attack on brutal southern chain gangs, and *They Won't Forget* (1937), a treatment of lynching based on the Leo Frank case in Georgia.

Yet it was always hard for screen writers and directors to handle controversial matters honestly, especially matters of international politics which raised the possibility of bans by foreign governments. Chaplin's *The Great Dictator,* for example, was delayed so long by Hollywood sensitivity to foreign opinion that its comic ridicule of Hitler seemed anachronistic by the time the picture appeared in 1940. And while the setting of *Blockade* (1938) was obviously the Spanish Civil War and the script, written by the leftist playwright John Howard Lawson, was plainly anti-fascist, none of the parties involved in the war—Spanish Republicans, Spanish fascists, Germany, Italy, the Soviet Union—were mentioned by name.

An upsurge of films with historical themes paralleled the increase of period fiction in the popular literature of the thirties. Film biographies, however free they might be with historical fact, proved popular. Probably the best such efforts were *Louis Pasteur* (1936), *Emile Zola* (1937), *Juarez* (1939), and *Abe Lincoln in Illinois* (1940), all of which simplistically celebrated democratic principles and denounced bigotry and reaction. "Westerns" and frontier sagas also drew great throngs of moviegoers. Ford's *Stagecoach* (1939) furnished a pattern for the successful western which less imaginative directors would copy for a generation. The most costly, most profitable, and most admired historical epic of the decade was David O. Selznick's *Gone with the Wind* (1939). Well acted and effectively photographed in the perfected Technicolor process, the film was, dramatically and technically, an impressive work. Yet like the huge, enormously popular novel by Margaret Mitchell from which it was drawn, the film version of *Gone with the Wind* perpetuated myths about the antebellum South, hardened racial stereotypes, and confirmed millions of Americans in their distorted image of the Reconstruction period.

The two most remarkable film accomplishments of the prewar years could scarcely have been further apart in purpose and content. The first was *Snow White* (1938), a feature-length cartoon film which climaxed a decade of spectacular progress by Walt Disney and his associates in techniques of film animation. Appearing in a year that saw an intensification of the Depression, the stalling of the New Deal, and the Munich crisis in Europe, *Snow White* was 'pure entertainment,' designed primarily for children. The film nevertheless introduced an enchanting array of cartoon characters; brilliantly exploited the two principal technical developments of the thirties, sound and color; and actually achieved what numerous subsequent movies by Disney and others claimed—"entertainment for all the family."

The second prewar triumph of American film-making was Orson Welles's *Citizen Kane* (1941). More than anything else done in Hollywood during the period, *Kane* was the creation of one man. The twenty-six-year-old Welles, already acclaimed as the "boy genius" for his feats in legitimate theater and radio, not only directed but wrote, produced, and played the lead in *Kane*. The script was based rather loosely on the life of the newspaper overlord William Randolph Hearst; undoubtedly many went to see the picture for that reason alone. But *Kane* was infinitely more than thinly veiled biography. Welles understood motion picture technique better than most established Hollywood directors, and he used camera angles, montage, sound, and lighting to achieve elements of realism and symbolism that were breathtaking for 1941—and were still admired a quarter-century later. *Kane* was perhaps the finest motion picture ever made in this country, assuredly the most significant American contribution to the film art since *The Birth of a Nation*.

For many years, however, *Kane* had little influence on film production in the United States. Welles himself continued to work in Hollywood, even after *The Magnificent Ambersons* (1942) was altered so radically by studio editors that he repudiated the film before its release. But most of the other people in the "film capital" continued to make pictures that were unimaginative in technique, superficial and trivial in content. As America entered the Second World War, James Rorty's indictment in 1935 was still valid: "Hollywood is organized and capitalized evasion of reality and of the problem of art (which is: to deal with reality and to tell the truth). It is a vast, departmentalized, delicately coordinated dream factory."

Radio: The Sound of Everything

The persistent frustration felt by exponents of motion picture art in America was shared by those who saw in radio an opportunity to develop a new art form. By the end of the thirties radio had become a seemingly indispensable means of mass entertainment and communication, but its esthetic potential, despite important progress, was as yet unfulfilled. Radio was handicapped by the same broad, interrelated problems as motion-picture production—an essentially commercial orientation and the necessity to serve a mass audience. After the First World War the national government, instead of retaining its wartime monopoly on wireless means of communication, had let private interests establish commercial broadcasting stations, sell receiving sets, and transmit with as much power as possible over whatever wavelengths they chose. Hundreds of local stations soon created a chaos of sound, virtually destroying the ability of radio owners to receive broadcasts free of interference. Finally, in 1927, Congress created the Federal Radio Commission to license radio stations, assign wavelengths, and regulate the power level of station transmissions. Meanwhile many local stations over the country were consolidated into two major networks, the National Broadcasting Company and the Columbia Broadcasting System.

The advent of regular network programming and the improvement of reception greatly increased the national radio audience in the late twenties, but the average price of radio sets was still about $100. Some 12 million homes had radios at the end of 1929. Technical developments after 1930 substantially decreased the size and complexity of radios, and thus their price. By 1940, despite the Depression, radios could be found in 28 million homes, representing 86 per cent of the population.

The necessity to reach and hold this mass audience placed severe restrictions on the quality of radio programming. Then, too, the practice of selling radio time to advertisers, which was firmly entrenched by 1930, meant that a steadily increasing portion of what came over the airwaves took the form of "commercials" proclaiming the wares of "sponsors." The Federal Communications Commission, having the means to influence radio programming through its power to grant or withhold original licenses and renewals, took an essentially negative approach to the problem of program content. Instead of setting qualitative standards, and thus presumably working to maximize the esthetic and educational potentials of radio, the FCC contented itself with insuring that radio offerings did not offend the moral and ethical values of the community. Occasionally there were cases in which the FCC refused license renewals on the basis of objectionable program content, but for the most part the networks and station operators obviated direct federal regulation by policing themselves rigorously. Despite the forebodings of a number of writers, there was never much danger in this country of the kind of state censorship over communications effected in Nazi Germany and fascist Italy; the FCC allowed networks and stations complete freedom to broadcast news reports and analyses and to air diverse political viewpoints. Artistic efforts in radio, however, remained constricted by many factors, not the least of which was the regulatory effect of the federal licensing power.

Sociologists and social psychologists in the thirties seemed even more interested in radio's effects on collective attitudes and behavior than they were in the effects of motion pictures. In general, scholars found that as an entertainment medium radio was inherently different from films, and that this difference acted as a built-in censoring device. Gordon Allport and Hadley Cantril observed that radio was designed for enjoyment within the home, whereas the movie was a means of escaping restraints associated with the home situation. As a consequence, radio was more directly concerned with morals in society. "The radio is a modern substitute for the hearthside," wrote Allport and Cantril, "and a family seated before it is obedient to its own conventional habits and taboos. The radio dares not violate those attitudes fundamental in the great American home."[2] Another team of investigators concluded that radio, because of its commercial character, had to skirt controversial social issues, cater to established thought patterns, and ignore specialized tastes and points of view. Radio thus acted as "a strongly conservative tendency in all social matters. . . ."

In short, radio had to entertain, even as it advertised or reported the news. During the Depression, Americans—whether because of technological progress, government restrictions on working hours, or unemployment—had more leisure time than ever before. Two or three evening hours of radio-listening became fixed in the daily routine of most families. The spurious Negro humor of "Amos 'n Andy" (played by two white men), the drolleries of Jack Benny, the sarcasm of the ventriloquist's dummy Charlie McCarthy, or the acts of the ambitious amateurs on Major Bowes's program, became even more prominent elements in American popular culture than the exploits of the motion picture idols.

Yet there were encouraging indications that radio might become something more than a device for mass diversion, that it might contribute significantly to the development of the traditional arts in

America. Certainly radio had a pronounced effect on American musical taste and musical production. As early as 1930, CBS began airing concerts of the New York Philharmonic Orchestra on Saturday evenings. NBC countered the next year with Saturday afternoon broadcasts of the Metropolitan Opera and later inaugurated the "Ford Sunday Evening Hour," which presented the Detroit Symphony in "light classical" concerts. Then, in 1937, NBC made both musical and radio history when it formed its own symphony orchestra and brought Toscanini back to the United States to direct the orchestra's Saturday evening concerts. The premiere of the NBC Symphony was much publicized, meticulously planned, and eagerly awaited; network officials even provided velvet programs for the studio audience so the rustling of cardboard would not bother the mercurial maestro. The premier concert reached a large and approving radio audience, most of which continued to listen faithfully over the next several years.

Besides these popular network broadcasts, about one-third of the remaining weekly radio time went to music, mostly popular ballads, "country and western" tunes, and jazz. The recording industry, dependent on the sale of phonographs before the mass acquisition of radio, expanded rapidly in the thirties under the ever-increasing demands of local radio stations for music suitable for broadcasting. Largely because of radio, swing became a national musical craze and the dominant form of jazz in the last half of the decade.

It was radio theater, however, that seemed to hold the greatest promise. Two interconnected attitudes produced an ambitious radio theater movement in the late thirties. The first was concern for decentralizing and democratizing the dramatic art, which also provided much of the impetus behind the Federal Theatre Project. It appeared that radio, like Federal Theatre, could help eliminate the commercialized isolation of theatrical activity in the largest cities and restore theater to the people. Radio could create a truly national theater, accessible to and enjoyed by all Americans free of charge. The second attitude emphasized the potential for developing a unique kind of theater in terms of radio's unique technical features. As a 'blind' medium, radio has to depend on the ability of the dividual listener, using his imagination, to create visual images for what is communicated to him solely through his auditory sense. Yet, as the exponents of radio theater realized, this apparent deficiency in relation to motion pictures or the legitimate theater could be radio's greatest advantage. Through the maximum utilization of sound, radio could, with relative ease and economy, create effects that were impossible in legitimate theater and extremely problematical in motion pictures. Thus, instead of merely adapting plays and movies for radio, Orson Welles, Norman Corwin, Arch Oboler, and others vigorously tried to create a theater fashioned to the sound medium, a dramatic form whose imaginative possibilities were theoretically limitless.

The brightest, most incisive efforts in radio theater came from three groups: the "Mercury Theatre of the Air," formed by Welles and John Houseman after they left the Federal Theatre Project in 1938; CBS's "Columbia Workshop"; and "Arch Oboler's Plays" on NBC. Mercury Theatre aired a number of ingenious productions, but unquestionably its most memorable offering was a dramatization of H. G. Wells's novel *The War of the Worlds* on October 30, 1938. The program, presented in the form of a special news report, seemed so authentic that millions of Americans became convinced Martians had actually invaded New Jersey. Repeated assurances to the contrary by Welles and CBS finally quelled a threatened national panic. The chief figure in the "Columbia Workshop" was Corwin, who wrote, produced, directed, and narrated many of its plays. Such prominent writers as William Saroyan and Archibald MacLeish also contributed to the Workshop. Aaron Copland did the musical score for MacLeish's *The Fall of the City* (1936), a powerful anti-fascist verse-drama which climaxes when the terrified city surrenders to an empty suit of armor. "Arch Oboler's Plays" offered highly experimental pieces by Oboler, acted by such well-known and capable performers as Charles Laughton, Bette Davis, and Walter Huston. All these radio theater groups pioneered in sound innovations, striving always for the maximum in aural description. Their efforts to achieve a new dramatic art may not have been wholly successful, but at least radio theater did many worthwhile things, and did them in radio's own way.

The flourishing state of radio theater, together with the solid network support and enthusiastic audience acceptance of the various formal music broadcasts, made the late thirties and early forties the golden age of radio as a contributer to the arts. Yet televison, still in the experimental stage at the time of Pearl Harbor, had already thrown its shadow over the future of radio. In the postwar years this new mass medium would radically alter radio's role in relation to both the traditional arts and popular culture.

Radio news broadcasting also reached its pinnacle beginning in the late thirties. Even before the series of crises that culminated in the dismemberment of Czechoslovakia at Munich, "newscasts" occupied nearly one-third of all program time. The dramatic events of September and October 1938 gave new stature to radio news reporting. The "on-the-spot" reports from the major European capitals and the broadcasts of the speeches of Hitler and Prime Minister Neville Chamberlain—relayed instantaneously across the Atlantic to the network studios, then transmitted over the nation—impressed upon Americans as had nothing before the nearness and relevance to America of Europe and Europe's troubles. Increasingly after Munich, people switched on the radio to learn the latest of what was happening in the world around them. It was perhaps understandable that, only two weeks after Munich, so many Americans took the Mercury Theatre's description of rampaging Martians for the real thing.

To some observers it seemed that reading habits might be severely affected as more and more families turned to radio. Ultimately the printed page might give way to the sound box as the principal source for entertainment and information. Such speculation lost much of its substance after the Rockefeller Foundation sponsored a Princeton University study, directed by the social psychologist Paul Lazarsfeld, on the relationship between radio and reading. Lazarsfeld and his associates found that, instead of impairing reading habits, radio actually had a great potential for making reading more fruitful. Most radio-listeners, especially the more educated ones, did follow-up reading after hearing news and other information programs. Thus while more leisure had made available more listening hours, radio apparently increased the amount of time devoted to reading.

If Americans were going to spend several hours each day listening to radio, then presumably radio should try to educate as well as inform, to analyze issues as well as report facts. A growing element within radio felt that, in addition to covering political conventions, campaigns and candidates, and offering itself for masterful exploitation by President Roosevelt, radio should present "public affairs" programs designed to handle national and international issues with thoroughness and finesse. One of the pioneers in such informative programming was George V. Denny, Jr., who organized for NBC a series called "The Town Meeting of the Air." Broadcast from Town Hall in New York with a format intended to capture the atmosphere of an early New England town meeting, the program featured Denny as moderator, two or more prominent guests arguing the issues, and a spirited period of questions from the audience. Town Meeting went on the air May 30, 1935. Its first topic posed a question that seemed exceedingly pertinent in the mid-thirties: "Which Way America—Fascism, Communism, Socialism or Democracy?" Offering such speakers as Eleanor Roosevelt, Harold Ickes, Wendell Willkie, and Earl Browder, the program proved enormously popular and remained on the air for more than a decade. For a few years CBS tried unsuccessfully to compete with "The People's Platform," a series that had an even more unusual format: Lyman Bryson, a Columbia University journalism instructor, would invite four well-known guests to dinner; the network would air both the table conversation and a more formal discussion led by Bryson afterward.

Radio's continually broadening coverage of news events, the appearance of more and more programs of news analysis and discussion, and the popularity of a growing number of radio "commentators" like Lowell Thomas, H. G. Kaltenborn, and Edward R. Murrow—these and other signs pointed to the development of a new kind of journalism in the early forties. But while radio journalism may have altered significantly the news-getting habits of Americans, it could only complement, not replace, the more traditional forms of American journalism—the country's newspapers and magazines.

Journalism—New and Newer

Since the late nineteenth century, virtually all daily and most weekly newspapers in the United States have been financially dependent on selling space to advertisers, not selling issues to readers. The Depression, bringing drastic drops in advertising revenues, forced a number of dailies to consolidate and drove out of business dozens of local weeklies. The seeming paradox of a steadily growing population served by a steadily decreasing number of newspapers had been present for decades. But the Depression, then mounting operating costs during the Second World War, greatly accelerated the trend toward the concentration and consolidation of newspaper publishing. By 1945 only 117 cities in the United States, less than one in twelve, had a competitive newspaper situation; that is, were served by more than one newspaper publishing company. In ten states no city had competing dailies; in twenty-two states all cities lacked competing Sunday papers. While the total circulation of the nation's daily newspapers in 1945 was 48 million, an all-time high, some forty per cent of this circulation was noncompetitive.

Such statistics disturbed numerous social critics in the thirties and forties. The longtime liberal journalist Oswald Garrison Villard expressed the anxieties of many in 1944: "The outstanding fact in any survey of the American press is the steady and alarming decrease in the number of dailies." Villard feared, as did others, that the concentration of the newspaper business into ever-fewer hands not only curtailed the citizen's alternative sources for information and editorial opinion, but raised the prospect of ultimate government control of the news, "under which republican institutions could not possibly flourish."

The forebodings of people like Villard derived from certain idealistic assumptions about the nature of the democratic process in the United States. The typical 'good citizen'—the kind of bald, bespectacled, mustachioed little man depicted in so many political cartoons—was supposed to study a diversity of viewpoints, arrive at his own decisions dispassionately and objectively, and then join with other similarly well-informed citizens in choosing public officials. In fact, such idyllic behavior had never characterized any significant portion of the electorate; rather, as a growing number of political science studies showed in the thirties, the American political process could be understood largely in terms of the complex interaction of various "pressure groups," aggregations of people acting together out of some common interest, frequently an economic one. In the context of pressure-group politics, the traditional concept of an atomized electorate, dependent on free access to information and opinion in a competitive press, lost much of its meaning. More Americans than ever read newspapers in the Depression years, but apparently there was not much relationship between the political stance of newspapers and the way their readers voted. A large majority of dailies opposed Roosevelt's bids for reelection in 1936, 1940, and 1944, yet most Americans continued to vote for him.

Various other circumstances suggested that the diminishing number of newspapers was less a threat to American freedoms than people like Villard supposed. The increasing effectiveness of radio in reporting events obviously lessened the importance of dailies as disseminators of 'hot' news. Then, too, it was doubtful whether most readers bothered with the editorial page at all. Those who did and who found their newspaper's opinions disagreeable could, and probably would, seek other judgments in a multiplicity of weekly and monthly magazines ranging over the intellectual and political spectrum. Besides, as John Cowles, director of the Associated Press, contended in 1938, most dailies were reasonably fair in their presentation of the news, taking care to separate reporting from commentary. Cowles discounted the prospect of the eventual organization of the country's dailies into giant national syndicates. Only two such syndicates—the Hearst and Scripps-Howard chains—existed in 1938; the Hearst empire was shrinking steadily, while Scripps-Howard permitted its members a large amount of local autonomy. Cowles concluded, "The threat of any nationwide newspaper monopoly is a phantom." This proved to be not only an accurate assessment of the contemporary American newspaper situation, but a sound prophecy for the coming generation.

However, both optimists like Cowles and pessimists like Villard usually overlooked the fact that, especially in towns and smaller cities, more and more radio stations were coming under the ownership of newspaper companies. The local communications monopolies that resulted from the tie-up of radio broadcasting with newspaper publishing posed more serious threats to a free press than did the consolidation of newspapers alone.

The thirties registered few changes in the form of American newspaper journalism, but rather a continuation of trends that had been underway for a decade or more. By 1939 the typical daily newspaper was an omnibus publication carrying an unprecedentedly large amount of advertising, pictures, sporting news, comic strips, and "women's features." News of national and international significance constantly competed for headlines with "human interest" stories, which were often sentimental, sensational, bizarre, even grotesque. According to various press surveys, the outstanding news stories of the decade, in terms of reader interest, were not such epochal events as the beginning of the New Deal, the Great Plains drouth, or the German invasion of Poland, but (1) the kidnapping of Charles Lindbergh's infant daughter and the arrest and trial of the kidnapper, 1932–1936; (2) the birth of the Dionne quintuplets in Canada in 1934; and (3) the abdication of King Edward VIII of Great Britain in 1936 and his subsequent marriage to an American divorcee. The most notable exception to what had become the dominant style in American newspaper publishing was the *New York Times,* which continued to present "all the news that's fit to print" soberly and compendiously. After 1930 the *Times,* through its comprehensive coverage and judicious analysis, solidified its reputation as America's finest daily newspaper.

The mass-readership newspaper, originating in Europe and the United States in the late nineteenth century, reached its logical extreme in the English and American "tabloids." The distinguishing mark of the tabloid was its size, which was about half that of the normal paper. Designed for quick reading in the cramped confines of subway, trolley car, or commuter train, the tabloid offered an alluring combination of sex, scandal, sports, and crime. Such "jazz journalism," as Simon Bessie called the tabloids, became enormously popular in the 1920s, especially in New York City. The most notorious of the tabloids, the *New York Daily Graphic* ("Daily Pornographic," said its critics), went under during the Depression years. But the *Daily Mirror,* featuring Walter Winchell's gossip column, and the *Daily News* increased their circulation in the New York area. In 1938 Bessie found that, contrary to a widespread notion among intellectuals, the tabloids appealed to people from every level of society, not just uneducated workers. It seemed that the typical tabloid reader was a middle-class New Yorker. Bessie also noted that over the years the tabloids—with their emphasis on pictures, human-interest items, and the sensational—had exerted considerable influence on the makeup of the larger dailies.

Writing in 1939, Charles and Mary Beard lamented the passing of the kind of crusading "personal journalism" which had characterized the newspaper exploits of Joseph Pulitzer, William Randolph Hearst, and other colorful editors and publishers in the late nineteenth century. The Beards were partly right; with the exception of the Hearst syndicate, Robert R. McCormick's *Chicago Tribune,* and perhaps one or two other dailies, newspapers no longer carried the clear imprint of one man's personality and ideas. Most papers were corporatized, bureaucratized operations whose editorials were conceived and written by committees, not by recognizable individuals. By the 1930s, however, a new kind of personal journalism, expressed in the writings of a number of nationally syndicated newspaper columnists, had developed in America. The most popular columnists included the vitriolically rightist Westbrook Pegler and Boake Carter, the soberly conservative David Lawrence, the aggressively internationalist Dorothy Thompson, the muckraking team of Drew Pearson and Robert S. Allen, and the leftist Heywood Broun, who endorsed the Popular Front and sparked the formation of a labor union for newspaper reporters. Without doubt the most-respected, if not the most popular, columnist of the decade was Walter Lippmann, who moved into vigorous opposition to the New Deal after 1935. There was no way of determining the influence of Lippmann and the other political columnists on political behavior, but that they reached many more people every day than the oldtime editors dreamed possible was undeniable.

If anything, the Depression hit the periodical press—weekly, biweekly, monthly, and quarterly magazines—even harder than newspapers. Possibly one of the major longterm results of the Depression was a substantial lowering of the literary quality and intellectual content of American magazines. The weekly *Saturday Review of Literature* and the monthlies *Harper's* and *Atlantic Monthly*, offering an admirable balance of social and political analysis and art criticism, came out of the decade on fairly sound financial footing. So did the *New Yorker*, which catered to urbane (if not necessarily urban) tastes. On the other hand, such informative, well-designed magazines as *North American Review*, *Scribner's*, *Century*, *Outlook*, *Vanity Fair*, *World's Work*, and *Literary Digest*, which for many years had served a limited but significant readership, ceased publication in the thirties. Meanwhile the *American Mercury*, the principal spokesman for discontented young intellectuals in the late twenties, began a slow metamorphosis—from a monthly offering primarily literary and social criticism to one increasingly political in content and rightist in outlook. The *Nation* and the *New Republic* remained the leading leftist political magazines, while the Marxist *New Masses* gained in respectability and influence, at least until the Nazi-Soviet Pact of August 1939. "Little magazines," for the most part financially shaky quarterlies devoted to fiction, poetry, and criticism, rose and fell even more rapidly in the thirties than in the twenties; the outstanding little magazine begun in the thirties was the radical but anti-Stalinist *Partisan Review*.

The two leading mass-readership magazines in 1930, the *Saturday Evening Post* and *Collier's*, increased their circulation and remained reasonably prosperous in the Depression decade, although both had to give more space to advertising. Their weekly issues presented articles on a great variety of subjects, together with pieces of mostly bland fiction. Editorially, the *Post,* under George Horace Lorimer until 1937, was consistently anti-New Deal, while *Collier's,* edited by William L. Chenery, took a political stance slightly left of center.

If the *Post* and *Collier's,* as well as most other magazines, had to take on more advertising, the pocket-sized *Reader's Digest* became a phenomenal success in the thirties while steadfastly refusing to advertise. Established in the late twenties by DeWitt and Lila Wallace to reprint, often in condensed form, articles of popular interest which had originally appeared in a wide range of periodicals, *Reader's Digest* built its circulation to somewhat less than one-half million by 1930. The next decade and a half brought an amazing enlargement in the magazine's circulation—to two and one-half million in 1937, to four million in 1941, and to more than nine million by the end of 1945. Each monthly issue was translated into numerous different languages, plus a braille edition. In 1933 the *Digest* began publishing original articles (though the innovation was not acknowledged for several years), and in the late thirties the Wallaces began placing in other magazines articles designed for subsequent republication in the *Digest.* By 1943 less than half the articles appearing in the *Digest* were "straight" reprints.

Students of American society puzzled over the startling success of the *Reader's Digest.* The explanation probably lay in the appeal of the magazine's comforting, homespun 'philosophy,' which John Bainbridge described as "a tidy compound of two ageless aphorisms: 'Money isn't everything' and 'What does it matter as long as you've got your health.' " Such chronic optimism—reiterated in short, easy-to-read articles which dealt with everything from medicine to military affairs, from politics to poultry—proved particularly attractive to that most anxiety-ridden portion of the populace, the vast American middle class. Appropriately postmarked at Pleasantville, New York, the *Digest* spooned up tasty bites of canned information while it reassured Americans that their institutions were sound and their nation secure.[3] The nearly perfect formula made the "little wonder," as Bainbridge called the *Digest,* into an American institution.

The other great success story in American magazine journalism during the thirties consisted of the publishing ventures of Henry Luce. In 1926 Luce, only a few years out of Yale, and his classmate Briton Hadden had founded *Time: The Weekly News-Magazine.* The two young entrepreneurs designed *Time,* according to the magazine historian James P. Wood, "for a hypothetical man who is assumed to have no other source of information of current events. *Time*'s purpose [was] to provide him with all the important news of the week, background enough to make the news intelligible, and enough comment to direct his opinion." Thus *Time* not only tried to give comprehensive coverage to national and world news, but freely —and often recklessly—interpreted what was happening. Its studiously irreverent tone and its own unique "Timestyle," which featured inverted sentences, cryptic captions, and a superabundance of puns, made it especially popular with the younger members of the professions in America. Its political outlook, which was more skeptical than conservative, may have irritated some readers, but most people liked its useful overview of the news, presented within a growing variety of departments. *Time*'s weekly circulation rose steadily during the 1930s, until it stood at about one million by the time of Pearl Harbor. Its success and influence inevitably prompted imitative competitors. *Newsweek,* established in 1933, strived for thoroughness, which was *Time*'s greatest virtue, while insisting on objectivity, which *Time* explicitly disavowed. *U. S. News,* founded the same year as *Newsweek* and edited by David Lawrence, confined itself to national affairs until it joined with another magazine to form *U. S. News-World Report* after the Second World War.

After Hadden's death in 1929, Luce built Time, Inc. into the largest and most powerful journalistic enterprise in America. In January 1930, only three months after the stock market crash, Luce launched *Fortune,* a big, handsomely illustrated, and expensive monthly magazine designed for a limited clientele of business owners and executives. Within a few years *Fortune* was making sizable profits, thereby confounding the predictions of many in the publishing business. By the late thirties *Fortune* had outgrown its original strictly business orientation and was offering long, thoroughly researched, and well-written articles on a great variety of contemporary economic and social topics. Then, in the fall of 1936, Luce and associates brought out the first issue of *Life,* the most successful weekly in American publishing history. The essence of *Life* was pictures—photographs, reproductions, and drawings whose primary purpose was not to illustrate, but to provide an almost self-contained descriptive process and learning experience. Luce felt that nothing he published should just entertain; all his magazines should educate. Thus *Time* and *Life* should be complementary, one giving the news in words, with interpretation, the other giving the news in pictures, with dramatization. "Together," wrote Wood, "they make what is, in effect, a national tabloid weekly newspaper." Within three years after its appearance, *Life* had a weekly circulation of perhaps three million and a total readership (or 'viewership') of many millions more.

The striking popularity of *Life* as a picture magazine—and also the lesser but notable success of its bi-weekly competitor *Look*, initiated early in 1937—confirmed the critical role photography had assumed in the evolution of American journalism and, indeed, in all American life. Simon Bessie concluded that "by 1938 . . . the average citizen acquired most of his news through the medium of pictures." The mass enthusiasm for "camera journalism"—whether in newsreels, newspapers, or magazines—related to the widespread desire to "see things as they are," to get at the "real America." It seemed that almost everyone who called himself a writer was roaming up and down the country, trying to document what Americans were thinking and doing in the midst of the Great Depression. Perhaps the most effective jobs of social reportage came from writers who worked with photographers and made maximum use of the camera as a descriptive device.

During the thirties, more than ever before, cameras focused on the unhappy truths of American existence—the bleakness of the urban unemployed, the helplessness of the rural poor, the ravages of dust storms, the violence of industrial labor disputes. The combination of skillfully underwritten commentary and skillfully composed pictures produced compelling results in such volumes as *You Have Seen Their Faces* (1937) and *Say, Is This the U.S.A.* (1941), both with text by Erskine Caldwell and photographs by Margaret Bourke-White; *These are Our Lives* (1939), put together by workers for the Federal Writers' Project; or *Land of the Free* (1938), a collection of Farm Security Administration photographs for which Archibald MacLeish wrote a moving poetic accompaniment. In these and a number of other works, observed Alfred Kazin, "the words and pictures were not only mutually indispensable, a kind of commentary upon each other, but curiously interchangeable."

A stunning climax to the wave of photo-textual documentaries came in 1941 in the form of James Agee's and Walker Evans's *Let Us Now Praise Famous Men.* Starting out to gain material for a magazine series, Agee and Evans lived in Alabama with three white tenant families during two months in the summer of 1936. Agee became so enmeshed in the lives of the families that his finished prose contribution was far more than just another detailed, candid examination of rural poverty. To be sure, his lengthy text, rigidly segregated from Evans's pictures, did provide a minute analysis of what life was like for those in hopeless tenantry. But in these poverty-stricken Alabamans and their children, Agee also saw glimmerings of the fundamental nobility in all mankind. What resulted was a documentary that went far beyond documentation and told as much about Agee as about his ostensible subjects. Finally published in book form after much difficulty, *Let Us Now Praise Famous Men* was both unique journalism and brilliant literature, one of the most powerful personal statements by an American in the twentieth century.

In a multitude of ways, motion pictures, radio, and the press of the thirties served to entertain and divert the American people, and to make their experiences both more varied and more standardized. The mass media also informed and educated, however inadvertently or meretriciously they might do the job. If much of what came from films, radio, and journalism reflected the crassness, cheapness, and inanity of life in the United States, there was also much that suggested youthful strength and promise, and that pointed up the multicolored vibrance of American culture.

Notes

1. Because the central creative instrument in film-making is the camera, and because almost all films are composed not sequentially, but in montage, the director is a much more important figure in motion pictures than in the legitimate theater. On the other hand, the script writer is much less important to film-making than the playwright is to the theater.
2. Present-day readers of the controversial social psychologist Marshall McLuhan will, of course, recognize the similarity between the conclusions of Allport and Cantril on radio in the thirties and what McLuhan has written about the nature of television, which he describes as a "cool medium" (as opposed to the "hot medium," motion pictures).
3. Since early in its history, *Reader's Digest* has actually been published at Chappaqua, New York. But, significantly, the Wallaces retained the postmark of Pleasantville, the original place of publication.

Chapter V

Science and Scholarship in an Age of Depression

The two most striking characteristics of the intellectual development of Western society over the past hundred years are the astonishing expansion of knowledge and the consequent specialization and intensification of scholarly inquiry. In the last decades of the nineteenth and the first decades of the twentieth century, the portion of the population composed of trained, professional scholars began to expand tremendously in the European countries, while in the United States such a group actually came into existence for the first time. By 1930 the formal, systematic pursuit of knowledge in the United States was almost exclusively the domain of men and women supported by the rest of society to carry on research in their highly specialized "disciplines." Most of these people also held teaching positions in academic institutions, where they were expected to impart some understanding of their specialities to undergraduate and graduate students.

The Great Depression worked severe hardships on this corps of professional scholars and on their scholarship. While relatively few American institutions of higher learning had to close their doors permanently, almost every college and university in the nation endured financial crises. Privately supported institutions were hit hard by slumping alumni contributions; public colleges and universities saw their appropriations slashed in the face of critical reductions in state and local revenues brought on by the Depression. As enrollments declined nearly everywhere in the early thirties, so did income from tuition and student fees, although by the end of the decade more Americans than ever were in college. The economic crisis forced the large non-profit foundations, which had become bulwarks for academic research by 1930, to cut back sharply on their programs of monetary grants and awards. Foundation money remained scarce for the rest of the thirties. Overall, the Depression meant less money for libraries and other research facilities, for new buildings, and for the maintenance of faculties. For thousands of faculty members, the Depression meant cuts in salaries that were already low, stabilization in rank, or outright dismissal. A considerable number of ambitious young people emerged from graduate training with high expectations for academic or commercial employment, only to end up working for the WPA.

Despite Walter Lippmann's admonition that the wise scholar should "build a wall against chaos, and behind that wall, as in other dark ages of the history of man . . . give his true allegiance not to the immediate world, but to the invisible empire of reason," professional scholars generally displayed a heightened concern with social issues and action in the midst of the decade's domestic and international crises. It was largely this new sense of purpose that helped make the 1930s an extraordinarily fruitful time for the social science disciplines. Even some people in the natural sciences, however, felt moved to ask questions of themselves and each other about the relationship between science, the Depression, war, and the direction in which American society was heading.

Perplexity and Progress in Science

By 1929 the fortunes of American science were inextricably bound up with the condition of the national economy. The Depression seriously disrupted the structure of scientific research, not only in industry and universities but in the federal government as well. The research budgets of some government agencies were substantially curtailed in the early Depression years and did not regain pre-Depression levels until the late thirties. The New Deal, preoccupied with the problems of the Depression, had relatively little money left for federally sponsored science. Even so, in many ways and under various programs, research activities fostered by the Roosevelt administration promoted the growth of scientific knowledge. The federal government began financing research on non-infectious diseases in 1937, when Congress authorized the establishment of the National Cancer Institute under the Public Health Service. The Department of Agriculture set up a series of regional laboratories to carry on research into the basic problems of agriculture, another group of laboratories to work toward the maximum utilization of agricultural products, and a central agricultural research installation at Beltsville, Maryland. The Department of the Interior and the Tennessee Valley Authority conducted important programs in the conservation of soil, water, timber, and wildlife. "In a very loose sense," observed the foremost historian of federal science, "the TVA was a gigantic experiment in applied science."

Yet such activities, however valuable they might be, hardly touched the questions that were uppermost in the minds of a considerable number of scientists and science enthusiasts: What role could science play in relation to the Depression? Could science help pull the country out of the economic morass? Roosevelt, soon after coming into office, set up a Science Advisory Board headed by Karl T. Compton, physicist, president of the Massachusetts Institute of Technology, and a forerunner of the kind of scientist-adviser-promoter who would become central to government operations during and after the Second World War. The board had a broad responsibility for organizing and supervising existing government science activities. But Compton saw the Board as only the first step toward a much-enlarged program of government financing and encouragement of science, with federal research money channeled through the seventy-year-old National Academy of Sciences or the National Research Council, an advisory group which dated from the First World War. To Compton, science could be the key to economic recovery. Government-sponsored research would produce new inventions and techniques, which in turn would accelerate industrial production and distribution. Such a national research effort would also reabsorb the thousands of scientists and engineers thrown out of work by the Depression.

The kind of "New Deal for science" envisioned by Compton and a number of his fellow-scientists never became a reality in the prewar years, in part because of Roosevelt's reluctance to spend money on anything except immediately productive projects. But certain conceptual difficulties also help explain the failure of attempts to link recovery and science in a large government research program. One group of government officials and advisers, led by Compton, wanted to concentrate research money in the natural sciences; another, typified by Secretary of Agriculture Henry A. Wallace, wanted to make the social sciences equal to the natural sciences in both financial support and prestige within government. These conflicting attitudes were evident in the operations of the National Resources Board, whose Science Committee superseded the Science Advisory Board in 1935. The membership of the Science Committee was drawn from the Social Science Research Council and the American Council on Education as well as from the National Academy of Sciences. Rivalry quickly developed between the natural and social scientists, and the Committee was never able to mobilize support in the natural sciences for a broad-based program of government-sponsored research. The need for such a program and for some central coordinating agency to oversee scientific activity was evident from the Science Committee's excellent study of the whole American research establishment, issued by the National Resources Committee as *Research—A National Resource* (1938).[1]

The report recognized that while the United States was preeminent in applied science—the application of scientific principles to achieve technological development—it trailed several European countries in basic research, or 'pure science.' American scientists, of course, were well aware that throughout its history the United States had borrowed and applied formulas, concepts, and principles developed in other countries; that this nation had produced only a handful of men whose research contributions were internationally acclaimed; and that American science and engineering still lacked a solid grounding in basic research. The vast majority of Americans, however, did not really comprehend the distinction between scientific research and engineering development. Proud of their country's technological achievements, they mistook the long American tradition of invention for a meaningful historical record in basic science. Thus to the layman the foremost American 'scientist' was Thomas A. Edison, a brilliant inventor with little understanding of or interest in science.

In view of this American tendency to confuse science with invention and technology, it is understandable that many people saw the

Great Depression as a consequence of science gone out of control. Research scientists, inventors, and engineers were indiscriminately blamed for contributing to the social catastrophes of the twentieth century. Besides making war indescribably horrible, 'science' had supposedly created machines and processes in industry and agriculture that dehumanized and displaced workers and produced more than people could consume. In the Depression years some Americans even sanctioned the 1927 proposal of Bishop Edward Arthur Burroughs, of the Church of England, for a ten-year "moratorium on science" to give social institutions time to catch up with, assimilate, and control the momentous discoveries of the previous fifty years. What was needed, according to a writer in *Science* magazine in 1935, was "a slowing up of research in order that there may be time to discover, not new things, but the meaning of things already discovered." Perhaps the "science crop" should be "ploughed under" as the New Deal's farm program had ploughed under the cotton crop.

If runaway science had helped bring on the Depression, then it was foolish to think that a bigger research effort in the natural sciences, presumably financed by the federal government, could promote economic and social recovery. America and the whole Western world needed not more control of physical processes by the natural sciences, but more understanding and drastic alteration of social processes by the social sciences. Objectivity, precision, and a systematic approach—the components of the scientific method—must be carried over into the conduct of government and economics. "If democracy is to save itself," announced Waldemar Kaempffert, science editor of the *New York Times,* "the scientific outlook, the scientific method of detached appraisal of facts and situations must become part and parcel of the common mind." Somehow the enormous distance between man's technical development and his social institutions—what Thorstein Veblen had called "cultural lag"—must be bridged.

Needless to say, the New Deal, for all its vaunted experimentalism, did not bridge the distance. At the close of fifteen years of unprecedentedly severe economic crisis and unprecedentedly destructive world war, the cultural lag seemed greater than ever. The decade of the 1930s was probably the last in which a significant number of social theorists truly believed in the strict applicability of the techniques of science to collective human problems. On the other hand, the thirties marked the first time Americans seriously questioned the doctrine that human progress inevitably resulted from the increase of scientific knowledge and technological change. Some critics began to insist that scientists acquire a greater sense of social responsibility, a greater concern with the human consequences of their discoveries. Scientists, said Secretary of Agriculture Wallace, "have turned loose upon the world new productive power without regard to the social implications." Henry M. Wriston, president of Brown University, warned of new disasters "unless men of science understand the social significance of their work and are actuated by the warm emotions of the humanities."

The fact was that a social conscience was irrelevant to basic research, whose tasks were to formulate hypotheses, to subject hypotheses to experimental verification, and to establish first principles which might or might not have practical applicability. A social conscience became important in that broad area where applied science, invention, and engineering converged to produce technological development. For it was really technology, not science, that mechanized agriculture, automated industrial processes formerly performed by men, and invented ever-deadlier ways of warfare. It was not the creation of means in the form of new knowledge, but the utilization of those means, that transformed society. Roosevelt recognized this when, in 1936, he publicly asked more than one hundred engineering schools and colleges to consider whether their courses of study were sufficiently "balanced . . . so as to give coming generations of engineers the vision and flexible technical capacity necessary to meet the full range of engineering responsibility." Roosevelt's implied call for a more humanistic orientation had little effect on academic engineering training in the United States. And, aside from the Technocracy movement of 1932–1933, with which as many non-technical people as engineers were identified, the engineering profession was not notably stirred by a feeling of social responsibility in the thirties and forties.

While laymen became increasingly skeptical about the benefits of scientific and technical change and demanded more social awareness among natural scientists, some scientists began revising their notions about the character of science, the nature of the universe, and even the meaning of human existence. After 1930 American science received the full impact of various concepts developed by European scientists over the previous three decades; of particular significance for scientific thought were the General Theory of Relativity and the principle of uncertainty or indeterminacy in physics. These and other new propositions in science caused serious readjustments regarding the workings of the universe and the causal relationship between events in the physical world. A distinct element of doubt appeared in much popular literature on science in the thirties and even in the writings of a few prominent scientists. To the science popularizer George W. Gray, Albert Einstein's Theory of General Relativity meant a universe with "no hitching posts," "a cosmos in which space by itself and time by itself have ceased to exist. . . ." According to the Uncertainty Principle, if a physicist tries to calculate the position of an electron, its velocity becomes incalculable; an effort to determine its velocity leaves its position indeterminate.[2] When generalized to cover the whole problem of conception, measurement, and description, the Uncertainty Principle seemed to raise critical questions about the efficacy of the scientific method. Scientists, wrote Herbert J. Muller in 1941, "no longer pretend that science offers reality, the whole reality, and nothing but reality. They acknowledge that its abstractions are in fact abstractions, not complete descriptions, and its concepts valid only for limited purposes." As the mathematician Tobias Dantzig put it, science "has recognized the anthropomorphic origin and nature of human knowledge. . . . it has recognized that man is the measure of all things, and that there is no other measure."

The decline of absolutism in scientific thought was accompanied by an apparent willingness to make room for supernatural elements in the cosmos and in human life. The writings and statements of several esteemed British scientists, of Einstein, and of the American physicists Robert K. Millikan and Arthur H. Compton contained a striking humility, a frank recognition of the limitations of science, which many religious people found at least mildly comforting. As Compton said, "It is . . . only because the world in a physical sense is not wholly reliable that we can have any human meaning."

Of course such sociological and epistemological discussions did not greatly trouble the majority of American natural scientists. Like specialists in other fields of learning, natural scientists worked hard, accomplished much, and philosophized little. The thirties was a period of remarkable transition for American scientific research. Until the late thirties substantial numbers of young American scientists, particularly physicists, continued to go to England, Germany, Denmark, and other countries to study under such men as L. M. Rutherford, Werner Heisenberg, and Neils Bohr. Genetics was about the only field in which, by 1930, American achievements were sufficiently impressive to cause Europeans to come to this country for graduate and post-graduate study. After 1933, however, the spread of totalitarianism and war in Europe brought much of the Continental scientific community to the United States. From Germany and Austria alone came some 1,880 prominent scientists, most of whom were Jews fleeing the systematic Nazi campaign against "non-Aryans." The refugees included a considerable number of Nobel Prize winners. By 1939 three of the world's foremost physicists—Einstein, from Germany; Bohr, from Denmark; and Enrico Fermi, from Italy—were working in the United States. The heavy immigration of European scientists between 1933 and 1945 was a central factor behind the ascendancy of American science in the postwar decades.

Numerous accomplishments during the 1930s, however, signaled the growing maturity of scientific activity in the United States. Although the principal contributions in physics, such as the splitting of the uranium atom in 1939, continued to originate in Europe, American-born physicists made notable research gains. Millikan, who settled at the California Institute of Technology in the thirties, moved from work on electrons to research on the density, composition, and source of the enigmatic cosmic radiation permeating Earth's atmosphere. While Millikan climbed mountains and sent balloons into the upper atmosphere, Arthur Compton of the University of Chicago remained equally busy on globe-circling cosmic-ray studies. In 1932 Harold C. Urey of Columbia University discovered the element deuterium, or "heavy hydrogen." A few years later Arthur Dempster of the University of Chicago established that uranium contained three isotopes, of which one, U-235, seemed to have enormous destructive potential. Not surprisingly, several Americans were actively interested in the engineering aspects of experimental atomic physics. At CalTech in 1932, Ernest O. Lawrence devised a cyclotron, one means of generating sufficient voltage to "smash" atoms; at the Massachusetts Institute of Technology the next year, Robert van de Graff designed an electrostatic generator to achieve the same purpose. By 1940 the continuing progress of indigenous research—together with the immigration of European nuclear physicists and Roosevelt's 1939 decision, prompted by a letter from Einstein warning of German progress, to place all nuclear physics research under government control—had set the stage for the all-out drive to create an atomic weapon during the Second World War.

In astronomy the most spectacular findings of the thirties were those of Edwin Hubble of the Mount Wilson Observatory in Arizona. After viewing and photographing regions of the universe never before investigated, Hubble in 1932 made the staggering announcement that, if his assumptions and calculations were correct, the radius of curvature of the Universe should be about 3,000 million light years. In chemistry the outstanding American name was Linus Pauling, also of the California Institute of Technology. Applying the principles of quantum mechanics in physics to chemistry, Pauling formulated his famous theory of the chemical bond. The work of Pauling and other chemists indicated the extent to which chemical research was expanding into physics and biology, thus making it ever harder to distinguish between the sciences.

Meanwhile various teams of biologists over the country built on the discoveries of Hermann J. Müller of the University of Texas, who in the late twenties had induced mutations in fruit flies by exposing them to heavy amounts of radiation. Other biologists radically altered theories of nutrition, developed vitamins, and thus created a national craze for dietary supplements. Still others explored the process of cellular development, showing that cells were dynamic growth mechanisms which were critically affected by the actions of surrounding cells. And the late thirties also saw the inception of work that, during the war, would lead to the first tentative disclosures regarding deoxyribonucleic acid (DNA), the mysterious "life substance" which apparently determines the formation of genes inside chromosomes.

Finally, medical research continued to improve prospects for body and mind; the most striking results involved the use of new drugs to treat both organic and emotional disorders. By the end of the decade Americans were somewhat more familiar with the nature of mental illnesses and somewhat more willing, through their philanthropies and public health programs, to provide for psychological research and the treatment of mental patients. Even so, the fact remained that most Americans lacked adequate medical care of any kind in the thirties. President Hoover's Committee on the Costs of Medical Care reported in 1932 that more than half the population spent less than $15 a year on medicine. Almost half of the counties in the nation had no registered general hospital. During the New Deal years, field workers for the Tennessee Valley Authority, the Farm Security Administration, and other agencies found hundreds of thousands of undernourished, disease-ridden Americans, especially in the rural South. Portions of the New Deal's social security legislation, together with the expansion of state and local programs, improved the public health situation a bit; the increasing participation of Americans in private group health insurance plans helped even more. Yet a generation later the United States would still lack a comprehensive, publicly financed medical care program.

Humanistic Studies: Scientism and Relativism

While the tribulations of the 1930s produced an upsurge of social consciousness among both natural and social scientists, the period also witnessed the growing estrangement of technical philosophy from the immediate problems of human society. By 1930 the discipline of philosophy was just that—a distinct field of academic scholarship with its own set of assumptions, techniques, and terminology. The rise of science in the nineteenth century and the increasing specialization of intellectual activity had relegated philosophy, once the crown of learning, to the level of the numerous other academic disciplines in American and European universities. Meanwhile philosophy had abetted the atomization of knowledge by adapting the scientific method to its own uses, dividing itself into sub-specialities (values, logic, epistemology, etc.), and separating itself from theology, which in turn acquired its own academic niche.

In the thirties technical philosophy continued to deal with the same broad questions about man and the cosmos with which philosophers had always been concerned. Because of its abstruseness, however, most formal philosophical writing seemed to have little pertinence to the upheavals of the period. In 1931 Benjamin Ginzburg of the *Nation* gave a typical activist's estimate: "Philosophy has become a museum specialty, a lifeless play of systems and concepts to which the public can point in derision." To Sidney Hook, one of the handful of political radicals with formal training in the discipline, philosophy had become indifferent to both old theological considerations and contemporary social problems. Current philosophical study, concluded Hook, offered neither "imposing systems in the grand manner [nor] paths to personal or social salvation, but, at its best, training in precision of analysis."

For most American philosophical scholars, George Santayana, the brilliant Bostonian who left Harvard in 1911 to pursue a life of quiet contemplation in Europe, exemplified the true man of philosophy. Most technical philosophers in this country at least implicitly subscribed to the distinction between "practical reason" and "speculative reason" drawn by Alfred North Whitehead, the British scholar who settled in America in the twenties. Practical reason, said Whitehead, worked to improve man's material condition, while speculative reason sought an understanding of all existence through disinterested curiosity. But for John Dewey, the most admired figure in American philosophy for four decades, the purely contemplative life and the separation of intellectual activities into materialism and metaphysics were flatly unacceptable. Dewey's pragmatic view of the world allowed no distinction between the functions of human intelligence; to Dewey all intelligence was synonymous with creative reason. The human intellect was an experimental device with which man, following the approach of the natural sciences, could transform his social and physical environment.

This optimistic, adventurous outlook, which Dewey called "instrumentalism," found expression in hundreds of books, essays, and speeches from the late nineteenth to the mid-twentieth century. Dewey ranged eruditely over the whole spectrum of learning—from psychology, educational theory, and formal logic to esthetics, politics, and economics. Intimately involved with the struggle for social reform during the progressive era, the twenties, and the Depression years, he was the American personification of the activist intellectual. "So faithfully did Dewey live up to his own philosophical creed," Henry Steele Commager has written, "that he became the guide, the mentor, and the conscience of the American people. . . ."

The Depression disaster sharpened Dewey's vigorous reformism. Whether he was denouncing the old acquisitive, selfish individualism in favor of a new cooperative individualism based on the scientific method, blistering his disciples in progressive education for their lack of purpose and direction, or explaining the Soviet Union as an experiment in economic collectivism from which Americans had much to learn, Dewey was in public view in the thirties more than ever before. A few of the causes with which he willingly identified himself looked a bit unseemly to some of his non-Marxist admirers. In the late thirties, for example, he became involved in an effort to rehabilitate Leon Trotsky, going so far as to head a committee which went to Mexico to investigate the Stalin regime's charges of treason against the exiled revolutionary. To the idealistic hero in one of Mary McCarthy's stories, this episode "was like finding your father in bed with a woman." Yet always uppermost in Dewey's thinking was the necessity to link philosophy with science in the reconstruction of society. Although he occupied a prestigious chair in the philosophy department at Columbia University, Dewey had no patience with the scholarly aloofness of his professional colleagues. As he wrote in 1946, "The net result of neglect with issues that are urgent and of preoccupation with issues that are remote from active human concern explains the popular discredit into which philosophy has progressively fallen."

If Dewey's calls to activism got little response from the great majority of technical philosophers, neither did philosophical Marxism. Despite its attractiveness for many scholars in other academic disciplines, Marxism, as Hook noted, "produced barely a ripple on the surface of American philosophy." Hook's work in the thirties comprised about the only effort by an American to make Marxism the basis for a technical philosophical system. Nor, at the other extreme, did the "medieval revival"—which looked back to the thirteenth-century teachings of Thomas Aquinas and had its most effective advocates in the Frenchmen Étienne Gilson and Jacques Maritain—make much headway among philosophers in this country, although Thomism powerfully influenced educational theory in the thirties. "Idealism," inspired by the great German philosopher Hegel and nobly disseminated in this country by Josiah Royce, had been the dominant strain in American philosophical scholarship for several decades.[3] By 1930, however, idealism had lost much of its academic popularity and respectability. On the other hand, pragmatism, despite the boldness and vitality of the principles propounded by Charles Sanders Peirce, by William James, and later by Dewey, had never won a large number of followers in technical philosophy, perhaps because pragmatism adamantly shunned absolutist system-building. Pragmatism's impact was greatest in political, economic, legal, educational, and historical thought.

"Naturalism"—the assumption that the natural world is the whole of reality and that truth can be arrived at exclusive of supernatural explanations—was the prevailing tendency in American philosophical thought by the 1930s. More a predilection than a philosophy, naturalism took such divergent expressions as Dewey's reform-minded instrumentalism and Santayana's serene doctrine of "essences," which appealed especially to the disillusioned esthete. But in 1930 the ruling form of philosophical naturalism in academic circles was an austere system of ideas known as "realism." Influenced largely by Whitehead's and Bertrand Russell's three volume *Principia Mathematica* (1901–1913), realism demanded a rigorously disciplined attitude and the fusion of logic and mathematics in an effort to achieve an objective knowledge of reality, of the world as it exists apart from men's muddled conceptions of it. The realist movement in America originally developed, shortly before the First World War, as a reaction against the recondite excesses of philosophical idealism. By the mid-thirties, however, the realists had themselves become so entangled in epistemological subtleties that their arguments began to sound sterile to some scholars. The times seemed propitious for the injection of some new influence, one that would satisfy both the academic insistence on detached, speculative inquiry and the need for a reorientation of philosophical thinking.

The new influence received most of its impetus from a group of central European philosophers who formed, in the 1920s, what was known as the "Vienna Circle." The basic proposition put forth by these Europeans, and accepted and elaborated by a growing number of Continental, British, and American scholars in the late twenties and early thirties, was that assertions which are both theoretically and practically unprovable are meaningless. The philosophical movement that developed around this proposition came to be called "logical positivism" or, more frequently, "logical empiricism." Both terms connoted the movement's highly inductive and experimental attitude. What had to be done, said the logical empiricists, was to set criteria for distinguishing meaningful statements and questions from meaningless ones; otherwise the search for experimentally verifiable reality was futile. Repudiating all forms of deductive, dialectical, or transcendental thought, the logical empiricists set out to shift the emphasis in philosophy from the objectivity of data to the clarity and accuracy of language. Through the use of precise analytical techniques, especially mathematical symbols, they hoped to arrive at conceptual purity, thus providing a foundation for the refinement of knowledge in all fields of learning.

The naturalist and experimentalist tendencies which already pervaded American thought created a climate in which logical empiricism found ready acceptance, especially among the younger generation of academic philosophers. By 1945 the new system was well established in the philosophy departments of many American colleges and universities, although exposition and interpretation of logical empiricism's basic ideas still accounted for much of the scholarly literature in this country. Logical empiricism imparted a new freshness and vitality to philosophical scholarship in the United States. Yet, paradoxically, this extreme manifestation in philosophy of faith in the methodology and attitudes of science came at a time when a fair number of natural scientists were voicing their skepticism about the possibility of absolute objectivity and precision. Moreover, it seems safe to say that logical empiricism, with its exceedingly technical analyses, made the discipline of philosophy still less comprehensible to non-specialists. Dewey's description of the new movement was an indictment of its asocial precepts: "It converts the practical neglect by modern philosophies of political and moral subjects into systematic theoretical denial of the possibility of intelligent concern with them. It holds that the practical affairs of men which are of highest and deepest significance are . . . by their very nature incapable of intellectual adjudication. . . ."

While logical empiricism apparently diminished the social relevance of technical philosophy, semantics, another new intellectual movement of the thirties, had an unmistakable sense of mission. Semantics, like logical positivism, was preoccupied with clarifying the meaning of words and concepts, and to a considerable extent the two movements drew on the same sources. Logical empiricism and semantics both thrived on a general susceptibility to relativist thinking, to which the new theories in physics, pragmatism in social thought, and even a reaction against government propaganda campaigns and business advertising, all contributed. The keystone in the development of semantics, however, was a huge book entitled *Science and Sanity,* published in 1933 by Alfred Korzybski, a Polish count with training in engineering, mathematics, and psychiatry. Korzybski's thesis was that Aristotelian logic, which formed much of the basis for Western thought, had become inadequate for the twentieth-century world; thus "in the structure of our languages, methods, 'habits of thought,' orientations, etc., we preserve delusional, psychopathological factors. . . ." The difficulty of linguistic communication explained much of the human predicament; and the basic problems in communication stemmed from "identification," the tying of words, used at varying levels of abstraction, to feelings or emotional responses rather than to concrete things or situations. Identification led to the "enslavement" of man by his "habitual language." What Korzybski proposed was a "non-aristotelian system" of language, which by combining linguistics, mathematics, and psychiatry would eliminate the handicap of identification "in all known fields of human endeavors, in science, education, and all known phases of private, national, and international life." The result would be nothing less than a revolutionary science of human communication, to which Korzybski gave the name "General Semantics."

The work of Korzybski and other students of word meanings in the thirties sparked considerable interest on the part of scholars and the educated public in the United States. Kenneth Burke made the symbolic and connotative nature of words the basis for a series of complex studies in esthetics.[4] Both Dewey and Charles A. Beard took semantics as a point of departure in their discussions of mental conditioning as an impediment to social reform. But it was the ubiquitous Stuart Chase, an intellectual faddist with a gift for elucidating complicated subjects, who made the outstanding effort to popularize semantics and use the new 'science' as a tool for social change. In *The Tyranny of Words* (1938), Chase argued that the failure of individuals and groups to communicate properly led to a "misinterpretation of the environment in which we live," which in turn "endangers the survival of the species. Bad language [is] a powerful anti-survival agent." Chase discussed faulty communication in relation to philosophy, law, politics, and especially economics. The main problems, he felt, were the confusion of a word and the object for which it stands; the use of the same word in different contexts, thus giving the word different meanings; and the use of abstract terms which become more "loaded" and less directly relevant to objects the further one gets from the "referent," or the situation the abstraction represents. The resulting word tyranny constantly frustrated efforts to promote human understanding and enormously complicated even the everyday affairs of society. The way out of the entanglements of men and nations was to untangle human communications by applying the principles of semantics.

More than anyone else, Chase was responsible for a short-lived semantics vogue in the late thirties. "It's just a matter of semantics" became an expression heard frequently over cocktails at literary and academic gatherings. The champions of semantics seemed to believe that all man's dilemmas could be banished if people could just agree on word meanings. Critics were quick to point out the superficialities and oversimplifications of the arguments presented by Chase and other interpreters of Korzybski. S. I. Hayakawa of the Illinois Institute of Technology tried to answer these criticisms as well as to counteract the excesses of some of his fellow-semanticists in *Language in Action,* a readable, cautiously worded book published in

1941. But by the time Hayakawa's book appeared the popular excitement over semantics, as well as most of the revolutionary fervor of the movement, had subsided. The argument that human conflict could be explained primarily in terms of confused language began to sound a little silly as the country moved toward war with fascist totalitarianism. In the forties scholars like Hayakawa, Irving Lee, and Wendell Johnson subordinated the earlier messianic attitude to the task of giving semantics acceptable credentials as a social science. In 1943 the International Society for General Semantics, formed the previous year, began publishing *ETC.: A Review of General Semantics,* with Hayakawa as editor. As a field of technical study, semantics would gain maturity and solidity over the next quarter-century; but its appeal as a social panacea would remain muted.

The rise of semantics in the thirties was another variation on the theme of science as a tool for social improvement. The whole idea of "social science" implied—if it did not dictate—conscious social service. In response to the Great Depression, workers in all the social science disciplines—in law, economics, political science, sociology, and anthropology—showed more willingness to put their scholarship to the service of American society. All the social sciences were heavily influenced by relativist thinking, which rejected grand generalizations and focused on immediate circumstances and considerations. Yet relativism in the social sciences usually did not mean diminished faith in the efficacy of the scientific method. The great majority of social scientists continued to believe that the qualities of objectivity, exactness, order, and predictability associated with the natural sciences could be carried over into the study of the aggregate problems of Americans.

In legal thought, for example, the thirties saw the triumph of what Dean Roscoe Pound of the Harvard law school called "sociological jurisprudence," which emphasized both the changing socio-cultural setting for statutes and decisions and the feasibility of creating a science of the law. Derived from the opinions and writings of Supreme Court Justices Oliver Wendell Holmes and Louis Brandeis, formulated primarily by Pound, and rooted in the soil of pragmatic social reformism, sociological jurisprudence rejected the mechanistic, obstructionist legal conceptions prevalent in the late nineteenth century. What Pound and other reform-minded scholars wanted was a legal system based on facts, not theories; on change and growth, not rigidity; and on the needs of the whole society, not the propertied interests of a few. As Pound wrote in 1908, "We have to rid ourselves of this sort of [traditional] legality and to attain to a pragmatic, a sociological science."

By 1930 Pound's ideals had been largely realized, at least in legal theory and instruction. Although the term sociological jurisprudence had given way to "legal realism," "functionalism," or "relativism," the pragmatic approach dominated the curricula of the nation's foremost law schools. Perhaps the most influential law professor was Harvard's Felix Frankfurter, who came to the United State Supreme Court in 1939 after a quarter-century of teaching that what was important was the specifics of legal controversies and the circumstances in which both judicial and administrative decisions were made. Yet judicial absolutism and popular veneration of judges and the federal Constitution remained powerful elements in American life; the furor over Roosevelt's efforts to enlarge the Supreme Court in 1937 proved that. Many Americans, wrote a liberal lawyer after the Court fight, still "tended to treat the Supreme Court like a phonograph which reproduces with high fidelity a record inscribed by the Philadelphia Orchestra in 1787."

Some exponents of legal relativism, driven by the logic of their position and by a fervor to dispel archaisms, denied that there could be any moral or philosophical basis for legal systems. At one extreme was the legal psychoanalysis of Jerome Frank, who argued in *Law and the Modern Mind* (1930) that the popular craving for certainty and the apotheosis of judges represented an extension of the postnatal reliance on the father and a manifestation of the innate desire to return to the security of the womb. In view of the Uncertainty Principle announced by physicists, said Frank, "it is surely absurd to expect to realize even approximate certainty and predictablility in law, dealing as it does with the vagaries of complicated human adjustments." At the other extreme was the legal scientism of Edward S. Robinson, who contended that a system of law must be grounded in scientific principles, and nothing else. The law could have no interest but facts, concrete situations. "Solemn men who go about the world preaching that there is something more to be relied on than facts," he wrote, "are doing what they can to prevent the world from catching up with science."

The most controversial expressions of legal relativism came in Thurman Arnold's witty, sardonic *The Symbols of Government* (1935) and *The Folklore of Capitalism* (1937). Both volumes unmistakably revealed Arnold's debt to the semantics movement, although at no point did he use the term. Arnold focused on what he called "the traps which lie in definitions and polar words." In prose that was alternately ironic, sarcastic, and indignant, he tried to explain the operation of American social institutions in terms of their symbolic, ritualistic character. The element of ceremony, said Arnold, was especially pronounced in the way the public viewed economic processes. He indicted Americans in general, but especially lawyers, law professors, and economists, for clinging to conservative assumptions that had long since ceased to have any relation to economic realities. It was obvious that American social mythology frustrated efforts to deal with the problems of American industrial capitalism. But since there was little prospect for raising the level of public intelligence, Arnold suggested that reform-minded judges and administrators find ways to make socially constructive decisions while also seeming to confirm the people in their misconceptions.

The cynical, elitist tone of Arnold's writings, especially *Folklore*, alienated some readers, including the septuagenarian Pound. Alarmed by the excesses of legal relativism, Pound declared that law must have its moral objectives, that justice must have "right guidance." Then, too, Arnold's ridicule of the antitrust laws seemed questionable when, in 1938, he became chief of the antitrust division of the Justice Department, the spearhead of the Roosevelt administration's campaign against corporate monopolies. Finally, it can be argued that in attacking law professors and professional economists, Arnold was swinging at straw men. In fact, a large portion of American law professors and even many practicing lawyers shared Arnold's views, while in the discipline of economics the kind of obsolete notions Arnold disdained were fast losing their intellectual respectability.

In the 1920s, for the first time, professional economists had assumed a significant public role. Sought out by the press, by corporations, and to some extent by government, economists willingly issued predictions regarding the status and prospects of the booming economy. Almost all of them foresaw an unbroken plain of future prosperity. As prophets, of course, they performed badly, and in the post-crash period they thrashed about in search of formulas for recovery. The scope and intensity of the debate among economic thinkers in the early thirties pointed up the growing acceptance of public responsibility by the economics profession. The scholarly interchange produced fairly general agreement on the need for monetary and credit reforms, at least temporary deficit financing, the readjustment of private debts, insurance for bank depositors, the divorce of commercial from investment banking, and government regulation of the securities market—all of which became law or policy during the New Deal years.

"The time cannot be far distant," wrote Rexford G. Tugwell in 1932, "when the absurdity of amateur muddling will begin to have such patent consequences as will become apparent everywhere. . . . will not sheer necessity dictate the staffiing of [the federal government's] permanent organs by economists?" The New Deal answered Tugwell's question by bringing professional economists into government in unprecedented numbers and giving them a central function in the shaping of policy. Experience with the National Recovery Administration, the Agricultural Adjustment Administration, the Reconstruction Finance Corporation, and a host of other government agencies provided academicians with practical experience in dealing with the raw materials of economics and substantially enlarged the scope of their scholarship.

The period from 1929 to about 1939, one of preeminent concern with economic problems, produced a flowering of American economic thought and striking transformations in the presuppositions of economists. The Depression shattered the remnants of the doctrinaire, mechanistic school whose notions of limited government and 'natural' economic processes had dominated the discipline during its emergence in the late nineteenth century. The great majority of professional economists came to assume a major role for the central government in restoring and maintaining the nation's economic health. Although orthodox Marxism had little appeal in academic circles, virtually everyone accepted some sort of economic collectivism. As the economist Broadus Mitchell wrote in 1938, "Capitalism is on the defensive. Collectivism is no longer treated in footnotes, as a dangerous or engaging proposal, as a change or minor variant, but occupies the text." "Institutional economics," which minimized theory and principle and concentrated on the evolving nature of economic systems and the actual workings of their components, reached its apex in formal economic thought in the thirties. The conception of the American economy as matured, overbuilt, and in need of central management to harmonize production with consumption levels was strongest among institutional economists, and thus so was support for comprehensive national planning. Tugwell, Adolph A. Berle, and Gardiner G. Means were perhaps the outstanding institutionalists in the Roosevelt administration. Berle evidently wrote most of Roosevelt's 1932 Commonwealth Club speech, which contained a ringing call for national planning.

The Depression converted many minority viewpoints on economic issues into respectable majority opinions. The most significant conversion concerned the meaning of deficit spending by the federal government. In the pre-Depression years almost all economists assumed that, ideally, the government should always balance its expenditures with its revenue. In the thirties, however, more and more economists came to feel that, in time of stagnation, government could greatly stimulate private investment and consumption, and thus promote economic revival, by slashing taxes on personal and corporate incomes and deliberately, if temporarily, foregoing a balanced budget. Deficit spending was only a portion of the complex of ideas and theories called "Keynesianism," after John Maynard Keynes, the British economist whose books and essays were enthusiastically read by American professional economists in the thirties. Above all, Keynesianism emphasized the central role of government fiscal policy in achieving sustained prosperity and the critical importance of continuous growth under capitalism.

Actually, various American economic theorists antedated Keynes in their advocacy of massive spending and the use of public credit to rejuvenate the economy. As early as 1931, for example, John Maurice Clark, discussing the "multiplier" effect of expanded foreign trade, looser credit, and public works expenditures, observed, "It is not orthodox arithmetic to take one from ten and leave eleven and one-half, but it seems to be possible in economics, if the ten represents income at the worst point of a depression and the one is a new 'effective demand' for goods." Within the Roosevelt administration, Marriner Eccles, chairman of the Board of Governors of the Federal Reserve System, consistently put forward the thesis that spending was the key to recovery. Roosevelt never fully accepted the theories of Eccles, Keynes, or any other advocate of systematic deficit financing. At the end of the New Deal period, in 1939, the triumph of Keynesianism in government policy was still a quarter-century in the future. Yet the new theories were rapidly gaining influence and popularity among economic scholars; the "Keynesian revolution" in economic thought was well underway.

If the study of economics seemed to have the greatest pertinence and utility for Depression America, the study of governmental processes, usually termed "political science," was a solid second. The major trends in the field of political science during the thirties were the direct participation of more and more scholars in government, the continuing expansion of collective research, the quantification of research data, and an emphasis on the reality, as opposed to the theory, of political behavior.

One of the consequences of the New Deal's general receptivity to new ideas was increased interest in the application of scientific techniques to the administrative operations of the federal government. As has been mentioned, Secretary of Agriculture Wallace, in particular, wanted to encourage the participation and enlarge the influence of social scientists in Washington. Under his aegis, the Department of Agriculture became not only the focal point of government activity in the natural sciences, but also the main employer of social scientists —agricultural economists, demographers, sociologists, administrative experts. Throughout the New Deal bureaucracy, however, political scientists worked on a great variety of projects. For the most part, political scientists made the studies and formulated the plans for Roosevelt's proposal to reorganize the executive branch, which Congress passed in emasculated form in 1939.

With rare exceptions, the political scientists in government during the thirties worked anonymously and in groups. In working as 'teams,' they were following not only institutionalized procedures in government and corporate life, but also the trend toward cooperative research in all the social science disciplines. A continuing faith in the scientific method partly explained the growth of team efforts among social scientists. "The 'subjective' imagination of the individual scholar," one political scientist has written of the mood of the thirties, "became suspect to the true social scientist—except possibly as a source of hypotheses to be tested. Solitary work became almost a morbid symptom; it showed a lack of importance, professional fraternity and true scientific method." Yet the practical needs of the evolving social sciences furnished the main reason for the growth of scholarly collaboration in the thirties. Students of political behavior, for example, saw the necessity for working with larger and larger amounts of data, handling the data more systematically, and generalizing from the data more cautiously. In the days before the advent of computer-programming, quantitative research usually required a number of workers simply to collate and analyze the material.

Closely allied to investigations by political scientists of such problems as legislative voting patterns and the makeup of political parties was the rise of public opinion research. As it became more systematic in the thirties, opinion research commanded veritable armies of data-gatherers. The crude polls of the *Literary Digest* magazine—which, after calling all the "Smiths" in the New York telephone directory, arrived at the disastrous conclusion that Alfred M. Landon would defeat Roosevelt in 1936—were soon superseded by much more sophisticated and reliable opinion surveys based on carefully chosen representative samples. By 1940 the foremost polling organizations were *Fortune* magazine, whose surveys were directed by Elmo Roper, and the American Institute of Public Opinion, headed by George Gallup.

The development and refinement of reasonably accurate polling techniques constituted a boon to all the social sciences, but the polls revealed almost nothing about the mental processes behind the answers of interviewees. In the thirties a number of political scientists, intrigued by the ways in which group behavior was influenced by business advertising, government propaganda, and other methods of mass persuasion, concentrated on the psychological bases of the American political system. The center for such research was the University of Chicago, where the social psychologist George Herbert Mead, before his death early in the thirties, provided a brilliant theoretical framework for studies in group behavior. The fusion of social psychology and political science produced a spate of impressive studies, of which the finest examples were Peter Odegard's *The American Public Mind* (1930) and several books and essays by Harold D. Lasswell. Strongly influenced by Freudian theories of psychoanalysis, Lasswell defined politics as the "study of influence and the influential." Political behavior, he felt, could be explained in terms of the exercise of power by elite groups in society. His *Psychopathology and Politics* (1930) and *Politics: Who Gets What, When, and How* (1936) were pioneering analyses of how the political process actually operated through the machinations of organized interest factions or "pressure groups." Lasswell's work, by calling attention to the realities of politics in an urbanized, concentrated society, where the economic motive was supreme, gave a new orientation to the study of American democracy.

In all fields of social study, the kind of bold, unorthodox interpretations that marked Lasswell's work were exceptional. Telling what, with minimal explanation of how and why, accounted for the great bulk of scholarly activity in the social science disciplines. Reportorial scholarship, which featured detailed description, the accumulation of masses of statistical evidence, and the exercise of extreme caution in presenting conclusions, was perhaps most fully enthroned in the field of sociology. The grand "social philosophies" of such American sociological pioneers as William Graham Sumner, Lester Frank Ward, and Edward A. Ross had lost favor with scholars intent on creating a true science of society. The long-term goal of sociology continued to be the establishment of principles or laws of social behavior based on proven hypotheses, but the goal seemed to grow more distant as specialized study revealed the enormous complexity of human organization. Thus in the thirties, especially for American sociologists, "social science" meant not the formulation of first principles but quantitative research—the use of the scientific method to compile mountains of data on the workings of society.

The Great Depression, fundamentally a social crisis, greatly stimulated the development of sociological research in the United States, although sociology had come into its own well before the crash of 1929. In the twenties urban sociology had been the outstanding area of social study. The most famous work was that directed at the University of Chicago by Robert E. Park, whose students made Chicago the most closely examined city in the world. According to the schema developed by Park and his "ecological school" of sociologists, the city was an organism in which, over time, the movement of social groups between evolving "natural areas" of settlement could be observed. After 1930 urban sociology continued to attract large numbers of scholars, and the theories of the ecological school continued to guide most urban research. Yet the finest work came from people who had not been directly involved with the Chicago group. Caroline Ware examined one of Park's hypothetical natural areas in her unique and fascinating study of Bohemian sub-culture in New York's Greenwich Village. The husband-wife sociologist team of Robert S. and Helen Lynd, whose *Middletown* (1929) had been a groundbreaking investigation of the small city transformed by industrial development, revisited their subject (Muncie, Indiana) to see what effects the Depression had had. In *Middletown in Transition* (1937) the Lynds, partially influenced by Marxist theory, emphasized class structure and the concentration of economic power. Meanwhile W. Lloyd Warner of Yale University and his associates began their massive investigations of "Yankee City" (Newburyport, Massachusetts), another small industrial city but one importantly different from Middletown.

While urban sociology continued to flourish, many sociologists moved into hitherto uncharted areas of research. Quantitatively, perhaps the most impressive sociological achievement of the decade was the report of the Research Committee on Recent Social Trends, appointed by President Hoover before the Depression to make an intensive survey of American society. *Recent Social Trends,* appearing in two fat volumes in 1933, made available a huge reservoir of information on both pre- and post-crash America. The Depression prompted renewed interest in the economy and social traits of the American South, where most Negroes still lived, where poverty, for both blacks and whites, was most persistent and widespread, and where the consequences of the Depression were most disastrous. John Dollard, with a background in social psychology, brilliantly probed the psychoanalytical implications of small-town class and interracial relationships in *Caste and Class in a Southern Town* (1937). Many of Dollard's findings received exhaustive documentation in *An American Dilemma* (2 vols., 1944), the monumental study of American Negro life directed by the Swedish sociologist Gunnar Myrdal, whose research group compiled most of its data in the thirties. The plight of the South also provided the main impetus for the development of rural sociology, which, at least in the quantity of its scholarly literature, soon came to rival urban studies. Regional sociology, a southern academic curiosity before the Depression, became a thriving field of specialization at universities throughout the nation. The center for such research, however, remained the University of North Carolina, where Howard W. Odum and his co-workers in sociology produced a series of epochal volumes, and where Rupert P. Vance imaginatively combined the approaches of geography, sociology, and economics into the new field of "human geography."

In the thirties sociology, like nearly every other academic discipline, continued to splinter and sub-divide into new areas of specialized research. At the same time, however, sociology increasingly shaded into and even merged with other fields of social study. Human geography, for example, had virtually the same concerns as the sociological speciality of human ecology. And certain new attitudes and orientations in anthropology made that discipline nearly indistinguishable from sociology.

The two outstanding developments in anthropology after 1930

were the triumph of relativism in the study of social evolution and the rise of "cultural anthropology," whose main concerns were not simple, "primitive" societies, but modern, complex ones. The thesis of the relativists was that all human organizations, however strange and backward they might seem through Western eyes, must be considered on their own terms, outside the framework of Western history. The anthropologist must study any society pragmatically, trying to determine what social institutions best suited the needs and fulfilled the goals of the group under consideration. Such an approach meant abandoning the Western-oriented anthropology of Lewis Henry Morgan, whose linear evolutionary scale—which described man's progress from "savagery" to "barbarism" to "civilization," with the Anglo-Saxon nations held up as the civilized ideal—had conditioned American anthropological thought since the 1870s. Following the lead of Franz Boas of Columbia University, scholars like Ruth Benedict, Margaret Mead, and Melville J. Herskovits refused to measure cultural values by Western standards of 'progress,' recognized the genius inherent in all human social organization, and demonstrated that African and South Pacific societies, though lacking Western technological prowess, had contributed durable and valuable social inventions. The disposition in anthropology to emphasize the relativity and plurality of cultural achievement, together with new discoveries in genetics concerning the hereditary process and the tendency throughout the social sciences to stress environmental over hereditary factors, gave added intellectual substance to the mounting attack on Caucasian assumptions of racial superiority.

Although originally used only in the study of small, primitive societies, the relativist approach, which defined culture as the totality of a people's ideas, attitudes, institutions, as well as their esthetic expressions, seemed a promising way to deal with the complex social groupings of the West. The field of cultural anthropology resulted from the application of anthropological relativism to contemporary Western society. The foundation of cultural anthropology was the conception of culture as a whole, as a total social expression, in contrast with the traditional notion of "high culture," or the activity of a limited number of intellectuals and artists. Although cultural anthropology was still in its infancy at the close of the thirties, Margaret Mead and others were rapidly delineating its contours. Mead's *And Keep Your Powder Dry,* published shortly after Pearl Harbor, was a pioneering effort to utilize the techniques of the new sub-discipline in studying American national character.

History was the one area of social study in which, during the thirties, relativist ideas seemed to conflict with scholarly confidence in the scientific method. The unique consequences of relativism for American historical thought can be explained largely in terms of history's traditionally anomalous position as both social science and literary art. In their zeal to establish their professional autonomy in the late nineteenth century, historians in the United States had divorced the study of history from philosophy on one side and from literature on the other. Their objective was a "science of history," to be achieved as a result of dispassionate, rigorously empirical inquiry into the past. In the first decades of the new century, the second generation of American professional historians hurried toward their goal of strict objectivity, brushing aside the complaints of literary people, including "amateur historians," that scientific history neglected the esthetics of historical writing. At the same time, historians became quite sensitive to attacks on history's 'unsystematic' character by scholars in the social science disciplines, where the historical approach had fallen into disrepute. As John Higham has shown, much of the historical profession came to feel a kind of scholarly inadequacy. The result was a movement called the "New History," which aimed to give history closer identity with more methodological fields of social study like sociology, political science, and economics. Hence historians joined in the formation of the Social Science Research Council in 1923 and enthusiastically endorsed and contributed to the fifteen-volume *Encyclopedia of the Social Sciences* (1930-1935). Edited by E. R. A. Seligman, an economist, and Allen Johnson, a historian, the *Encyclopedia* became a monument to the ideal of integrative social science. Throughout the 1920s and for most of the next decade, the "schism" in American historical scholarship persisted, with the majority (devotees of scientific history) striving to emulate the social sciences, and with a minority (traditionalists) clinging to the concept of "literary history."

Early in the thirties, however, an element of apprehensiveness entered American historical thought. Carl Becker of Cornell University and Charles A. Beard, two of America's most eminent historians, questioned whether history could ever approach the ideal of objectivity set by the natural sciences. History, they pointed out, deals with the most complex and unpredictable of subjects, human behavior. The historian must always work with a fragmentary record, and his image of the past is inescapably blurred and distorted by a superimposed image of the present. Was not historical truth thus always relative to time, place, and circumstance? Was not the past really a creation of the present? In his 1931 presidential address to the American Historical Association, Becker declared that since "Everyman" was his own historian, the task of the scholar of history was to square the image of the past with the needs of the present. Everyman must be confirmed in his "useful myths." Beard refused to countenance Becker's extreme relativism. "If all historical conceptions are merely relative to passing events," he said in his AHA presidential address two years later, "then the conception of relativity is itself relative." Beard nevertheless denied that the historian could "describe the past as it actually was, somewhat as the engineer describes a single machine." For Beard, writing history must be "an act of faith" in which the scholar, realizing his limitations, makes his choices according to a modest belief that something true can be learned about the past. Whereas Becker emphasized the limitations of history in relation to science, Beard made subjectivity a virtue, arguing that the historian should inculcate human values in history. In Beard's view, history must be emancipated from scientific determinism.

The rejection of scientism and positivism in historical writing by Becker, Beard, and their followers in the thirties constituted what Cushing Strout has termed "the pragmatic revolt in American history." Apparently the theories of relativity and uncertainty in physics had little if any relationship to the growth of relativism in historical thought. The relativism of Becker, it seems, represented a logical extension of certain elements in American pragmatism and in one of pragmatism's offspring, the New History. Becker's thinking was greatly affected by John Dewey's denial of absolute moral values and his willingness to define truth in terms of its usefulness for science, as well as by the New History's emphasis on the need for making the study of the past directly relevant to contemporary problems. By contrast, Beard seems to have arrived at his reassessment of history mainly from reading the European historical theorists Benedetto Croce and Karl Heussi. Neither Beard nor Becker truly understood contemporary scientific thought; if they had, they might not have become preoccupied with demonstrating the 'unscientific' nature of history. Both advocates and critics of scientific history failed to recognize that their arguments were based on obsolete notions of science. At the time Becker and Beard issued their relativist manifestoes, scientific thought was undergoing a reorientation necessitated by the twentieth century developments in physics. The historical relativists, as Strout has said, "were not sufficiently aware that the dream of science . . . had been discarded by scientists themselves." Perhaps the natural scientist, no less than the historian, had to perform an act of faith.

Of course, as was the case with natural scientists, the vast majority of historians went about their work without giving much serious consideration to its theoretical basis. "The fluid, unsystematic character of the historian's enterprise," Higham has noted, "rarely permits him to go directly from a general theory to a particular proof." Even a full acceptance of relativism did not compel the historian to give up his quest for objectivity, order, and precision. For the scientific method, as Beard affirmed, "is the only method that can be employed in obtaining accurate knowledge of historical facts, personalities, situations, and movements." Most historians, like most physicists, came to realize that carfully determined probability was almost as good as absolute certainty.

The 1930s was an extraordinarily productive period for American historical scholarship. The public demand for fiction and films taking historical themes had a counterpart in the popularity of historical biography. The cynical, "debunking" spirit which dominated American biographical writing in the twenties gave way after 1930 to a more sympathetic, frequently more admiring attitude, perhaps related to the phenomenon of national discovery and reaffirmation in the arts. As a rule, the best biographies continued to come from non-academic writers who practiced careful scholarship but willingly offered interpretations and value judgments. Among the decade's outstanding biographies, all written by journalists or former journalists, were Carl Sandburg's lyrical *Lincoln, the War Years* (4 vols., 1939), Douglas Southall Freeman's four-volume life of Robert E. Lee (1934–1935), Marquis James's two volumes on Andrew Jackson (1933–1937), Henry F. Pringle's study of Theodore Roosevelt (1931), and Allan Nevins's *Grover Cleveland* (1932) and *John D. Rockefeller* (2 vols., 1940).[5] The foremost cooperative achievement of the period in biography was the *Dictionary of American Biography* (21 vols., 1928–1944), begun under the editorship of Allen Johnson and continued under Dumas Malone.

"Progressive History," which viewed the American past largely as a story of incessant struggle by farmers, workers, and other forces of democratic reformism against the vested interests of industrial and commercial enterprise, was ascendant in the thirties. While only a handful of historians wholly accepted Marxist theory, the Depression did heighten the appeal of economic history and leftist-oriented economic interpretations. Beard's writings, which focused on economic motives and the conflict of economic groups, remained influential throughout the decade. Still more didactically leftist were Matthew Josephson's studies of late-nineteenth-century business and politics, *The Robber Barons* (1934) and *The Politicos* (1938). Scholars continued to write the history of the American frontier, which a generation earlier Frederick Jackson Turner had placed at the center of the national experience. Although the frontier interpretation was increasingly reexamined, revised, and rejected in the thirties, Walter Prescott Webb brilliantly utilized a Turner-like environmental analysis in *The Great Plains* (1931), published the year before Turner's death.[6]

Turner's other great insight, the critical role of sections in American history, continued to influence scholars. The South, still the most distinctive section of the nation and still something of an economic and cultural frontier, commanded an unprecedented amount of attention from historians. The Southern Historical Association came into existence in 1934; within a few years its quarterly, the *Journal of Southern History*, had become one of the foremost scholarly publications in the country. The rising interest in southern history was bound up with the public and scholarly popularity of Civil War studies. More than ever, historians debated the causes and consequences and refought the battles of the war. If some scholars drew lessons in collective courage and perseverance from the war itself, others damned the prewar generation, North and South, for "blundering" into a conflict that could have been avoided, while still others described the healing of the nation as it traveled the postwar "road to reunion."

Social history, which developed out of the New History's concern with social science, contemporary relevance, and the 'whole past,' became a thriving speciality for historians after 1930. Additional volumes in the History of American Life series, initiated in the twenties under the editorship of Dixon Ryan Fox and Arthur M. Schlesinger, continued to reveal the fertile research possibilities in such little-explored areas of national history as urbanization, education, family life, and recreation. And for the first time a significant number of professional scholars began studying American intellectual history, whose development was inspired primarily by the philosopher Arthur O. Lovejoy of Johns Hopkins University. In 1940, under Lovejoy's aegis, the *Journal of the History of Ideas* was founded.

The new interest in the history of ideas provided additional evidence of the growing specialization of historical research and, more broadly, the accelerating application of the tools of science to humanistic study. Yet the fact that historians in the thirties were more willing than ever to describe what Americans had thought and felt, as well as what they had done, suggested a general inclination to explore the nation's traditions and values. In *The Course of American Democratic Thought* (1940), a landmark contribution to the history of American ideas, Ralph H. Gabriel saw the unity and continuity of attitudes, not conflict and division, as the key to the national experience. Throughout their history, said Gabriel, the great majority of Americans had agreed on three major assumptions: the worth and dignity of the free individual, the existence of fundamental principles underlying the affairs of men in society, and the mission of the United States to promote freedom and human dignity both at home and abroad.

It was doubtless more than coincidental that Gabriel's book, which subordinated conflict to stability, came at a time when the United States was edging into another global war. The years of continual domestic and international crisis prompted many writers in many fields to seek a common ground of experience, not only for Americans but for all mankind. In both American educational theory and religious thought, the search for fundamental values involved a reexamination and a rejection of certain precepts about the efficacy of science for human society.

Notes

1. It will be recalled that the National Planning Board, set up in 1933, experienced periodic name changes in the thirties, becoming the National Resources Board, the National Resources Committee, and finally the National Resources Planning Board.

2. The development of the Uncertainty Principle is usually associated with the German physicists Werner Heisenberg and Erwin Schrödinger and the Dane Neils Bohr.
3. The meanings in philosophy of such terms as "naturalism," "idealism," and "realism" are, of course, radically different from their meanings in literature.
4. Burke was usually identified as one of the "New Critics" in literary criticism. All of the New Critics were intensely interested in word usage and language structure as keys to literary meaning.
5. Although Freeman held a Ph. D. in history and political science from Johns Hopkins, he served as editor of the Richmond *News Leader* throughout the thirties. Nevins, who never bothered to get the Ph.D., worked as a newspaperman until 1931, when he became professor of American history at Columbia.
6. Webb himself denied that he had ever read Turner before writing *The Great Plains,* but he acknowledged the influence of a variety of other theorists, including William Graham Sumner and the economist L. M. Keasbey, one of his professors at the University of Texas.

Chapter VI

Storm and Stress in Education and Religion

The national and international upheavals of the thirties and early forties called into question established patterns of thought and action in all fields of human endeavor. In American educational and religious thought the Depression experience and the renewal of global war accentuated social consciousness and social action and, at the same time, helped create a demand for a return to the fundamental values Americans had supposedly obfuscated or abandoned in their pursuit of material advancement through science. Some educational theorists reexamined the interrelationship between the individual, the educational process, and American society, while others attacked the traditional American commitment to the scientific method and intellectual specialization. A growing number of American theologians coupled their call for the greater involvement of organized religion in society with a reinquiry into the nature of man and social organization. Out of this period of storm and stress in education and religion came attitudes that supposedly provided a more realistic assessment of human intellectual and spiritual prospects.

The Depression and American Public Education

The consequences of the Great Depression for public education in the United States were disastrous. Total school expenditures declined for the first time in the twentieth century. Public education, almost exclusively a local and state enterprise in 1930, buckled under the impact of plummeting public revenues. Schools closed in thousands of communities throughout the country, while numerous others shortened their terms. By 1933 some 200,000 certified elementary and high school teachers were unemployed. Many of those who kept their jobs received payment in tax deficiency warrants or scrip. The condition of public schooling in the impoverished southern states became particularly desperate. At one time early in the thirties, four of every five schools in Alabama were inoperative.

Yet, in the midst of American education's worst financial crisis, school enrollment skyrocketed, especially at the high school level. Between 1926 and 1932 the national high school enrollment increased about two and one-half times, to an estimated 8,719,000. The growing realization of the economic value of formal education, the raising of the age level under state compulsory attendance laws, and the curbs on child labor written into the National Recovery Administration's industrial codes, all help to explain this enormous expansion of the number of boys and girls remaining in high school. But the principal explanation was the Depression itself, which convinced millions of young people that they would be better off staying in the free public schools than joining the multitudes of jobless Americans.

Various New Deal programs helped alleviate the nation's educational maladies. The Public Works Administration constructed some 12,700 new school buildings during the thirties. The Civilian Conservation Corps, besides putting several million young men to work on a great variety of outdoor projects, conducted classes in its camps in both vocational and general education. Between 1933 and 1935 the Federal Emergency Relief Administration's adult education program hired more than 40,000 unemployed teachers to hold classes for semiliterate adults. This program was continued and enlarged under the Works Progress Administration, which also organized thousands of nursery schools and made grants to the states for school construction, school lunch programs, and the purchase of vocational education and recreation equipment. Meanwhile the National Youth Administration, set up in mid-1935, a few months after the WPA, provided part-time work to help hundreds of thousands of youths stay in high school and college. The NYA also offered guidance, training, and placement services to its employees.

These federal programs brought the national government into the field of education to a greater degree than ever before. The amount of actual federal participation in the educational process at elementary and high school levels remained minimal. Even so, the New Deal's efforts, by bypassing both state and local authorities and the professional education establishment, added fuel to the longstanding controversy over the role of the federal government in public education. In 1938 the President's Advisory Committee on Education inferentially called for "federal aid"; two years later the White House Conference on Education made federal grants to the states a central item in its recommendation for a broad-based attack on the problems of educational finance. Such suggestions ran head-on into the hoary American principle of local control over educational affairs, a principle that was invoked most loudly in the thirties and forties by the National Education Association, representative of the majority of public school administrators and teachers. The NEA's powerful Educational Policies Commission forthrightly condemned all proposals for "federalization." "If the schools are to serve democracy," the Commission proclaimed in 1938, "they must be kept in close touch with the people locally. . . . the schools will fail of their purpose unless they reflect the interests, the ideals, and the devotion of the community which they serve."

The NEA assumed, as did most Americans, that in educational matters democracy was synonymous with local authority, and that there was something intrinsically dangerous about the centralization of educational policy. In fact, as many teachers in the NEA could attest, the question of comprehensive federal subsidy for education had little to do with the maintenance of democracy and educational freedom. Various writers in the thirties—most notably the historian Howard K. Beale in *Are American Teachers Free?* (1936)—described the numerous restrictions state governments and local school boards imposed on the freedom of teachers. During the thirties legislators, state boards of education, and trustees seemed to shift the emphasis in their supervision of teachers' conduct from matters of personal morality to matters of public expression. After 1930, twelve states joined Rhode Island, which as early as 1917 had required its teachers to swear their loyalty to both state and federal governments. Some states also outlawed teachers' unions and compelled students to salute the national flag. In numerous cases teachers were fired by local boards because of political activism. The bans on free expression spread to colleges and universities, both public and private. On many campuses trustees and administrators censored student newspapers, barred controversial speakers, and dismissed leftist-oriented faculty members.

The mounting incidence of controversies involving students' rights and academic freedom was symptomatic of a heightened social concern among both students and faculty in the Depression years. Most observers agreed that students seemed more interested in politics and public problems, less occupied with horseplay and social activity. The foremost student political organizations were the American Youth Congress, which amalgamated more than one thousand student groups in 1934, and the Marxist-dominated American Student Union, founded in 1935. The Youth Congress endorsed the New Deal and maintained an isolationist stance toward foreign policy. The Student Union, although its national membership never exceeded 12,000, wielded power on many campuses. In April 1936 the Student Union mobilized a massive antiwar demonstration in which a half million students walked out of their classes to proclaim that they would never support their government in another war.

Progressivism and Collectivism

The Great Depression, a financial setback for American education and a powerful stimulant to political activism on the part of teachers and students, also prompted educational theorists to reconsider the relationship between education and the welfare of society. In the 1920s the collection of ideas and attitudes called "progressivism" had become dominant in American educational thought and in much of educational practice, especially at the elementary school level. The citadel of progressive education was Teachers College of Columbia University, established in the 1880s, and greatly expanded in the twentieth century under the approving eye of John Dewey in the neighboring philosophy department. Teachers College boasted the outstanding educational thinkers in the country and provided the spark behind the flourishing Progressive Education Association. Inspired largely by Dewey's writings and by his early experiments in the Laboratory School at the University of Chicago, the exponents of educational progressivism strived to make the learning process duplicate the child's life experience as nearly as possible. Minimizing formal subject matter, the progressivists tried to create conditions under which the child could set his own goals and discover his own interests. The pragmatic union of learning with the child's physical and social environment would develop a full personality, qualities of leadership, and habits of cooperative behavior.

Dewey saw the school as the key to the achievement of social democracy in the United States. The school should produce well-rounded individuals who recognized the necessity for social cooperation. Dewey's ideal, therefore, was a balance between the needs of the individual and the exigencies of collective living. But over the years various disciples of Dewey, in an effort to work out the practical applications of his broad teachings on education, reached conclusions that Dewey refused to countenance. Dewey, according to Lawrence Cremin, never envisioned the utter elimination of subject matter; he wanted to develop "a new body of subject matter, better ordered and better designed, that would begin with the experience of the learners and culminate with the organized subjects that represented the cumulative experience of the race." By contrast, William H. Kilpatrick and other theorists in the twenties denied that specific objectives and subject matter could be determined in advance. They conceived of an almost completely individualized learning process in which the child would actually create his own subject matter. The result would be what Harold Rugg, in a classic exposition of the progressivist outlook in the twenties, called "the child-centered school."

By 1930 Dewey had become severely critical of what he considered dangerous excesses in progressive theory. The child-centered school, he felt, was as bad at one extreme as the traditional teacher-centered schools had been at the other. The absence of well-defined subject matter led to pedagogical chaos and learning without meaning, while the lack of purposeful guidance on the part of teachers produced egotism, impertinence, and insufficient respect for the rights of others. Without a sense of direction, the school failed to impart to the children a proper social awareness and responsibility. Thus in their efforts to cultivate individual expression, the new progressive schools only perpetuated the same old anarchic, destructive individualism which underlay the economic and social inequities of American society.

What was needed was a "new" individualism based on the use of social intelligence to promote collective welfare. Instead of child-centeredness, said Dewey, education must have life-centeredness.

After the economic collapse, Dewey's assault on child-centeredness gained an increasing number of supporters and active participants. Perhaps the most influential educational progressivists who turned against the trends of the twenties were two friends and admirers of Dewey at Teachers College, George S. Counts and Boyd H. Bode. In the twenties Counts had been a close student of the emerging educational system in the Soviet Union. He contrasted the classless character of Soviet education with the widespread lack of opportunity for schooling in the United States. Like Dewey, Counts saw the free public school as a tool of democracy. And to Counts, as to Dewey, democracy was not simply a political process or a form of government; it was a system of human freedom and responsibility grounded in economic planning and cooperation.

In 1932 Counts formally challenged his fellow progressivists to reform their thinking about the purposes of education. *Dare the School Build a New Social Order?* he asked in a pamphlet that precipitated heated discussions within and without the Progressive Education Association. "The weakness of Progressive Education," he declared, "lies in the fact that it has elaborated no theory of social welfare, unless it be that of anarchy or extreme individualism." The child-centered school derived from "an ideal of rugged individualism evolved in a simple pioneering and agrarian order at a time when free land existed in abundance. . . ." Now that form of individualism buttressed "a system which exploits pitilessly and without thought of the morrow the natural and human resources of the nation and of the world." Counts argued that child-centered education, with its aversion to the imposition of objectives and social ideals, ignored the simple fact that society would inevitably impose some preconceptions on its system of education. Thus educators must make sure that the goals of learning were the right ones; that the school furthered progress toward "a planned, coordinated, and socialized economy managed in the interests of the people."

Counts's peroration in behalf of economic collectivism and a school system dedicated to social reconstruction prompted the formation of various study committees affiliated with the Progressive Education Association. Yet the PEA refused to adopt the kind of far-reaching leftist policy pronouncements envisioned by Counts. His ideas actually got a more sympathetic hearing within the American Historical Association. Counts was a member of the AHA's Commission on the Social Studies, which, between 1932 and 1941, published a seventeen-volume report on the status of social-studies teaching in the public schools. Counts's *The Social Foundations of Education* (1934) was the ninth volume of the report. The basic assumption behind all the volumes, he said, was "that the public school may be expected to make a genuine and positive contribution to the solution of the numerous social problems confronting the American people." Once again he called for the abandonment of individualistic economic practices in favor of collective social reform. The social studies, he maintained, should give boys and girls a devotion to the ideals of democracy, an understanding of contemporary social problems, and a realization of the virtues of a planned economy. Counts also wrote, in consultation with Charles A. Beard, the Commission's *Conclusions and Recommendations* (1934). The teaching of social studies in the public schools, this document proclaimed, must recognize "that the age of individualism and *laissez faire* in economy and government is closing and that a new age of collectivism is emerging."

That same year, 1934, Counts, Bode, and other leftist educational theorists at Teachers College established a quarterly called *Social Frontier.* Holding fast to the interrelated ideals of "community-centered" education and democratic collectivism, *Social Frontier* regularly carried articles by Dewey and by Kilpatrick, who had put aside most of his individualistic theories of the twenties in favor of socially directed learning. Such widely divergent figures as Lewis Mumford, Charles A. Beard, Lawrence Dennis, and Earl Browder also contributed to the journal. *Social Frontier* ran into financial troubles in the late thirties and appealed to the Progressive Education Association for official sponsorship. The PEA finally took over the journal in 1939, but only after its name was changed and its board of editors was reorganized to give it a more 'moderate' orientation. The sanitized version, called *Frontiers of Democracy,* continued under PEA auspices until 1943.

The reform-minded progressivists were animated by a fervent conviction that the social attitudes and practices of Americans could be transformed through their schools. "Progressive education stands at the parting of the ways," Bode wrote in 1938. "If progressive education can succeed in translating its spirit into terms of democratic philosophy and procedure, the future of education in this country will be in its hands." One of the critical failings of the collectivist movement in educational thought was an inability to translate its spirit into practical procedure. The progressivists never managed to delineate how, short of outright indoctrination, teachers were supposed to instill the new collectivist outlook in children. And the bugaboo of indoctrination scared numerous administrators and teachers, not only in the Progessive Education Association, but also in the much larger and more influential National Education Association, whose members were always hypersensitive to local and state political pressures. Both George Counts and the NEA's Educational Policies Commission wanted to make free public schooling available to every boy and girl in America, and both Counts and the NEA wanted community-centered education. But while Counts and other collectivists conceived of the community-centered school as an instrument for basic social reform, the NEA contended that the school should both reflect and respond to its immediate or local environs. Local control, which in practice often meant right-wing supervision of instructional content, remained a vital part of NEA policy. Paradoxically, the Great Depression produced a social climate in which one of the fundamental tenets of progressive education, the necessity for shaping the school to the needs of American society, inspired both crusading collectivism in theory and reactionary localism in practice.

Progressive education, as a general approach to pedagogy and as a coherent movement, reached its peak about 1938, the year the Progressive Education Association had its largest membership. There is little doubt that the close of the thirties found progressivism weaker than it had been before the Depression. The theoretical debate over child-centeredness versus community-centeredness, carried on by people who shared a faith in progressivism's first principles, eventually worked to weaken the solidarity and vitality of the movement. More damaging than the internal differences among progressives, however, were the attacks on certain underlying assumptions of progressivism mounted outside the fold.

The Demand for Fundamentals

Despite the enthusiasm for progressive ideals in academic circles throughout the country during the first quater of the twentieth century, a few educational theorists held out for traditional learning principles. Even in the heyday of progressivism in the twenties, William C. Bagley of Columbia Teachers College had disdained the "education as life" syndrome. In the mid-thirties Bagley became more militant, leading a small but vocal group of colleagues in the formation of an "Essentialist Committee." Bagley and his associates wanted to switch the emphasis in teacher preparation from methodology to the acquisition of subject matter, and to offer children systematic, formal instruction in such fundamental subjects as English, history, and mathematics. To the Essentialists, the prospective teacher had to know what to teach before he could know how, and what pupils learned was more important than how they learned. Discipline and obedience, they added, were indispensable elements of the learning process.

In focusing criticism on progressive-dominated teacher-training programs and their preoccupation with form rather than substance, the Bagley group presaged the nationwide assault on progressive education that would follow the Second World War. In the thirties and early forties, however, it was not training and techniques, but the whole line of American educational development in the twentieth century, that provoked the most acrimonious, publicized, and far-reaching controversy among educational thinkers. Intellectual specialization, the child of modern science, was the main target of a movement that was favorably described as "liberal education," pejoratively labeled "neo-Thomism," and properly termed "general education."

Science, with its emphasis on precise analysis, concrete facts, and practical consequences, underlay not only the triumph of progressive education in the public schools, but prevailing theory and practice at all educational levels in the United States. The appearance of such 'practical' subjects as bookkeeping, typing, shorthand, cooking, and manual training in public school curricula in the late nineteenth century demonstrated the early acceptance by state and local school officials of the idea that publicly supported learning should serve the material needs of American society. The transformation of public school education was already well underway by the time Dewey, G. Stanley Hall, and others provided a philosophical basis for specialized, immediately useful learning.

The post-Civil War decades also saw the establishment in many American colleges and universities of the elective system, which resulted directly from the application of the techniques of science to all areas of knowledge. Under the elective system the student could choose with almost complete freedom from a rapidly increasing number of courses in a steadily widening range of disciplines. After 1900 a reaction set in against the seeming aimlessness of the elective system; nearly all institutions ultimately settled on a compromise whereby the student had to concentrate in particular "major" and "minor" fields of study, but could also elect a certain number of courses from other fields. Yet, despite the general retreat from the pure elective system, the ideal of practical 'service' continued to permeate American higher education. The University of Wisconsin, with its numerous extension courses, its large commercial and vocational programs, and its close working relationship with the state government, was only the most spectacular manifestation of the operating philosophy that prevailed in the great majority of colleges and universities, whether publicly or privately supported. By 1930 the pragmatic, multi-functional approach to primary, secondary, and higher education in America seemed triumphant.

It was precisely this "service-station conception" of learning, as Robert Maynard Hutchins called it, that ired and alienated the people who formed the general education movement. Dissatisfied with educational utilitarianism, convinced that high schools and colleges were not providing balanced learning, and fearful that the humanistic subjects would be extinguished by the demand for vocational and professional training, professors and administrators at various colleges and universities determined to restore values, tradition, and rationality to education. Like the leftist theorists within progressive education, the generalists wanted to give purpose and direction to American learning. But whereas Dewey, Counts, or Bode wanted to accentuate the scientific, utilitarian orientation of learning by making the school an instrument for democratic collectivist reform, the generalists assumed that the cultivated mind was an end in itself and that the specialized, empirical approach to knowledge was antagonistic to a true "liberal" or broad-based education. Thus they wished to make a "common learning," anchored in the permanent, unvarying principles of the Western humanistic tradition, the foundation of education in America.

After 1930 progressive educational thought continued to concentrate on elementary and secondary education, although such new or rejuvenated colleges as Bennington, Black Mountain, Sarah Lawrence, Bard, and Rollins did adopt the progressivist "open-ended" approach, allowing the student broad initiative in choosing a plan of study. The generalists, on the other hand, focused on transforming American higher education. Their objective was to separate liberal education, which they identified with the traditional liberal arts college, from both the diffused and disordered secondary school and the specialized university. Presumably one result of separating general from specialized learning would be to improve the quality of American universities, which Abraham Flexner, formerly an executive with the Carnegie Foundation and the General Education Board, found severely deficient when he compared them with English and German universities in 1930. Flexner observed that the European ideal of the university was "an organism, characterized by highness and definiteness of aim, unity of spirit and purpose." American institutions, trying to serve every interest, ended up emphasizing almost everything except pure scholarly research, which should be their preoccupation. "No sound or consistent philosophy, thesis, or principle," he lamented, "lies beneath the American university of today." Although Flexner did not endorse the general education movement, his criticisms of the lack of unity and purpose in American higher education fortified the arguments of the generalists.

The outstanding figure in the general education movement was Robert M. Hutchins, who in 1929, at the age of thirty, left the deanship of the Yale law school to become chancellor of the University of Chicago. Hutchins brought to Chicago a passionate desire to counteract the atomization of learning. He wanted to achieve a synthesized body of study which would impart a grasp of the "eternal intellectual verities," the first principles of beauty and truth that governed man, nature, and society. In the early thirties Hutchins disseminated his critique of American education and his proposals for reform in a number of magazine articles and lectures, which he brought together in 1936 in two books, *No Friendly Voice* and *The Higher Learning in America.*

Hutchins's conception of the nature of learning was basically metaphysical. He declared that "the heart of education will be, if education is rightly understood, the same at any time, in any place, under any political, social or economic conditions." The main shortcomings of the higher learning in America were its overspecialized pursuit of material ends and its "confused notion of democracy," according to which educators assumed that every person who came to college should be able to acquire an education that prepared him for some serviceable role in society. As a result, the higher learning was in a condition of chaos, which could be eliminated only "by removing the elements which disorder it today, and these are vocationalism and unqualified empiricism."

Hutchins wished to rebuild the modern college curriculum around the medieval system of study known as scholasticism, which, combining logic, philosophy, and theology, derived mainly from the teachings of Thomas Aquinas. Thus Hutchins's critics often referred to his proposals as "neo-Thomism." Substituting mathematics for theology and adding some study in the natural and social sciences, Hutchins offered the formal learning of the Middle Ages as the model of academic wisdom. He summed up his arguments for a return to scholasticism in a neat syllogism: "Education implies teaching. Teaching implies knowledge. Knowledge is truth. The truth is everywhere the same. Hence education should be everywhere the same."

Hutchins mustered sufficient support from the trustees and faculty at Chicago to inaugurate a succession of far-reaching changes. Besides abolishing intercollegiate football (and thereby gaining the lingering enmity of students and alumni), the young chancellor and his followers did away with the system of course credit hours in favor of comprehensive examinations in various broad areas of knowledge. Then, according to the recommendations of a study group led by Mortimer Adler, professor of legal philosophy at Chicago, and by Stringfellow Barr and Scott Buchanan from the University of Virginia, the program for the bachelor of arts degree underwent radical reorganization. The new program was designed to fulfill the ideal of the genuine liberal arts college. Students could begin the four-year B.A. course of study after two years of high school if they scored satisfactorily on entrance examinations; qualified high school graduates could finish the bachelor's degree after only two years at Chicago. The B.A. curriculum conformed to the principles of scholasticism and was supposed to instill "the arts of reading, writing, thinking, and speaking. . . ." Its foundation was a prescribed reading program consisting of one hundred "great books of the Western tradition," drawn from literature, science, history, and philosophy. The student was expected to read the one hundred volumes during his four years in "The College," as undergraduate studies at Chicago came to be called. At the end of the Bachelor's program, students who showed an aptitude for research and original thought could begin graduate work in the University proper.

The Chicago reforms sparked much lively discussion, some enthusiastic endorsement, and many vigorous criticisms from scholars and administrators over the country. Those who were concerned about the future of the humanities and who conceived of education as primarily a matter of gaining maturity, habits of rational thought, and an appreciation of the Western cultural heritage, applauded the changes instituted at Chicago and copied at St. John's College, Annapolis, Maryland. There Barr, as president, and Buchanan, as dean, built the entire academic program around the Great Books idea. A writer for the monthly *Catholic World* commended Hutchins's plans "for getting rid of the choking growth of empiricism, and for drinking in strength-giving fundamental principles." Walter Lippmann tacitly sanctioned the generalist movement when he lamented that American education, in failing to transmit "the Western culture which produced the modern democratic state," had produced youths with "no moral and intellectual discipline." Lippmann called for "a thorough reconsideration of [American education's] underlying assumptions."

Many other observers agreed with the generalists' broad criticisms, even if they did not accept the specific solutions offered by the Chicago group. Efforts to 'save the humanities' actually antedated the changes at Chicago, although Hutchins's labors gave some impetus to what became a nationwide academic reform movement in the thirties. Between 1928 and 1940 at least thirty American institutions of higher learning, from small liberal arts colleges to large state universities, installed interdisciplinary courses, usually offered in the first two years of study, with titles like "Humanities," "Civilization," or "Western Culture."

The general education movement, especially the scholasticism of Hutchins and his cohorts, was anathema to Americans who saw education as the means to a practical social intelligence. If, to the generalists, specialized learning betrayed the Western cultural heritage, to pragmatic educational and social theorists the effort to create a "common learning" betrayed the scientific outlook, which had furnished the key to man's progress over the centuries. John Dewey wrote that Hutchins's first principles were "more than irrelevant and futile. They are literally terrible in their distraction of social intelligence and activity from genuine social problems and from the only methods by which these problems can be met." To Charles and Mary Beard, the notion of a common learning "merely stopped a bit short of taking over the Roman Catholic view of the universe and the function of the university learning. . . ."

But the most systematic and effective rebuttal of the generalist educational scheme came from one of Hutchins's own faculty at the University of Chicago. In a widely read pamphlet entitled *The Higher Learning in a Democracy* (1937), Harry D. Gideonese, associate professor of economics, agreed with Hutchins that American higher education lacked cultural unity and consistency. But, said Gideonese, universities in this country accurately expressed the diversity, specialization, and devotion to material considerations that characterized American society as a whole. Thus a metaphysics of learning, based on the assumption that knowledge was fixed, could hardly serve as an effective antidote to the admitted commercial and vocational excesses in many American institutions. The consequences of Hutchins's formula were inevitably retrogressive and authoritarian. Instead of returning to medieval metaphysics, Gideonese maintained, modern higher education, building on the "intellectually distinctive characteristics of the modern world—scientific methods and results," must blend science and the humanities into a philosophy suitable to a democratic society.

In the 1930s the general education movement failed to alter the course of higher learning in America, just as the collectivist movement within progressive education failed to transform American public schools into agents for basic social change. The generalists did not understand—or at least refused to acknowledge—that intellectual specialization had produced the vast accretions of human knowledge over the previous century, and that, conversely, the growth of knowledge perforce intensified specialized study. Hutchins, Adler, and the others at Chicago invited ridicule with their attempts to distill wisdom into a list of one hundred books, while the broader interdisciplinary movement they helped generate did little to stem the tide of academic parochialism. For, as Isaac L. Kandel has noted, "the notion that intellectual integration could be prompted by the mechanical process of substituting disjecta membra of a variety of fields of knowledge for the fields themselves was fallacious from the start. . . . areas of knowledge have developed as tools and methods for understanding the world; as disciplines, in short." Before long the interdisciplinary approach to learning began to look very much like a discipline unto itself.

The debates over general versus specialized education in the thirties represented only the first shots in a battle that would gain new intensity during the war years and rage far into the postwar period. By Pearl Harbor, however, it was evident that, of the various parties involved in the struggle, progressive education had suffered the worst wounds. Besides their own internal theoretical disagreements and incessant external criticism of their techniques and assumptions, the progressivists had to endure a growing disposition on the part of some writers to blame all the defects of society on the shortcomings of the public schools. For example, Hans Elias, a refugee German academician, contended in 1940 that the adoption of the progressive approach in German schools before 1930 had prepared the way for the capitulation to Naziism. By destroying respect for authority in children, "liberalistic education" created a subsequent yearning among adults for the strong man who would provide the compulsion and subordination lacking in childhood. Elias implied that the same attraction to authoritarianism might develop in the United States. The abandonment of firm discipline under progressivism, said a writer in the *Saturday Evening Post,* amounted to the substitution of "lollypops for learning." The *American Legion Magazine* even suggested that the progressive education movement was dominated by radicals, Socialists, and Communists, who were guilty of "treason in the textbooks."

Yet it was not just the adherents of pragmatism and functionalism in education who found themselves on the defensive in the early forties. The whole set of optimistic assumptions about the nature of man and man's ability to work toward human perfection by using the tools of science seemed less comfortably ensconced than in the years before the economic disaster and the renewal of global war. In American religious thought the decade of the Great Depression witnessed an upsurge of social consciousness among theologians and practicing ministers, but, at the same time, the steady erosion of the intellectual and spiritual accommodation between religion and science constructed so confidently in the late nineteenth and early twentieth centuries.

Institutional Religion in the Depression Era

Some observers of American life expected the discouragement and despair of the Depression years to produce an extensive renewal of religious fervor in the United States. Statistics on the size of American religious groups are notoriously unreliable for any period, but it does appear that the total membership of churches in the United States actually declined rather considerably in the thirties. The sociologist Hornell Hart estimated in 1942 that organized religion had lost 27 members for every 1,000 Americans between 1930 and 1940; church attendance had dropped twelve per thousand. Even so, the vast majority of Americans evidently continued to believe in traditional Christian teachings. In a 1936 poll by the American Institute of Public Opinion, 64 per cent replied affirmatively to the question, "Do you believe there is a life after death?" Six years later *Fortune* pollsters found that 82 per cent of those questioned thought "there is a God who rewards and punishes after death." The most surprising thing about the *Fortune* poll was that 45.5 per cent of the non-churchgoers affirmed a belief in a god of judgment.

The relationship between science and religion was less abrasive in the thirties than at any time since Darwin's evolutionary theories began to reach Americans in the post-Civil War years. Various notable natural scientists voiced their belief in some kind of plan, purpose, or transcendent power beyond the comprehension of science. No less a figure than Albert Einstein said that the work of science must be inspired by "a cosmic religious sense." Einstein expressed his own "deep faith in the rationality of the structure of the world." James H. Leuba, A Bryn Mawr College psychologist, found in 1933 that large numbers of American scientists believed in spiritual immortality and in a personal god who responded to prayer. Leuba added, however, that such beliefs were strongest among physicists and chemists, "the scientists who know least about living matter, society, and the mind," as opposed to biologists, psychologists, and social scientists.

Probably the majority of American Protestants in the thirties maintained a fundamentalist outlook, which meant that they continued to regard the Bible as the literal, revealed word of God. Yet the organized Fundamentalist movement, which in the twenties had plunged into state politics in an effort to eradicate Darwinian evolution from the public schools, lost most of its political potence. The decline of organized Fundamentalism, according to Norman F. Furniss, resulted from a combination of factors: internal financial troubles; the death of Fundamentalism's prophet, William Jennings Bryan, in 1925; diversion of attention from anti-Darwinism to the revived prohibition issue after 1928; and the gradual percolation of scientific knowledge throughout the population. Then, too, Fundamentalism, by securing the passage of anti-Darwin laws in several states, actually accomplished much of what it wanted. Perhaps the most important factor weakening Fundamentalist fervor, however, was the Depression itself, which drew social energies to basic economic issues.

The decline of the Fundamentalist movement was symptomatic of the general lessening of doctrinal differences among the major Protestant denominations. Beginning in the late twenties, Protestant theologians, ministers, and laymen tended to subordinate their relatively minor points of disagreement to their broad common beliefs. The result was a succession of notable mergers among Protestant groups. In 1929 the Congregationalists merged with the Christian Church. A decade later the northern and southern branches of the Methodist Episcopal Church, divided since the 1840s, reunited and also absorbed the Methodist Protestant Church. The American Reformed Church combined with the Evangelical Synod of North America in 1940. An effort to merge Presbyterians and Episcopalians in the late thirties, however, foundered on the mutual animosities of High Church Anglicans and intractable Calvinists. And northern and southern Baptists not only remained disunited, but actually appeared to grow further apart as the century progressed.

If most Protestants seemed to be seeking a common ground in the thirties, they also seemed less hostile toward their fellow-Americans in the Roman Catholic faith. Anti-Catholic sentiment, which reached a hysterical zenith after the First World War, slackened in the late twenties and early Depression years. Anti-Catholicism revived somewhat after 1936 as a result of the Church's support of the Franco fascists in the Spanish Civil War. But the Knights of the Ku Klux Klan, whose national power between 1920 and 1925 had been built largely on religious nativism, remained small and ineffectual throughout the Depression decade.

Among American Jews, meanwhile, the Conservative movement, launched early in the century in an effort to make religion the focus of Jewish cultural identity, continued to make progress. Rabbi Mordecai Kaplan of the Jewish Theological Seminary in New York was the principal spokesman for Conservative Judaism and for the concept of "Jewishness," which viewed Judaism as a religious civilization, not simply as a religious faith. Kaplan and his followers wished to bring together all American Jews—Reform, Conservative, Orthodox, and non-religious—in a broad community which recognized a common cultural heritage. The philosopher Horace M. Kallen, with his advocacy of "cultural pluralism"—the creation of a social climate in which diverse ethnic and religious influences could have free expression within the framework of American democracy—provided a useful scholarly rationale for the rise of Jewishness. Paralleling the drive for Jewish cultural consciousness, however, was growing anxiety among American Jews over Nazi persecutions of Jews in Europe and the apparent increase of anti-Semitism in the United States.

The issue of Judaism, as a religion, versus Jewishness, as a way of life, was still being debated by American Jewish leaders at the time of Pearl Harbor. But by the end of the war, according to Nathan Glazer, "the idea that the Jews in America could continue as a group defined not primarily by religion but by secular culture and quasi-national feeling . . . was recognized as impossible." In the postwar years most Jews in this country lost interest in the creation of cultural unity, partly because of the Nazi terror, partly because of the establishment of the independent state of Israel, but mainly, says Glazer, because of the mounting economic gains and social aspirations of American Jews. Judaism emerged alongside Protestantism and Catholicism as one of the three great religions of America, part of the new national religiosity which, as Will Herberg has shown, came to be synonymous with the "American Way of Life."

The Depression disaster compelled all three religious faiths to reexamine their relationship to American society and to concern themselves more directly with the collective sufferings of Americans. In 1932 the Central Conference of American Rabbis, spokesman for Reform Judaism, drew up a "program of Social Justice" which called for "a more adequate distribution of the profits of industry." That same year Pope Pius XI, in his encyclical *Quadrigesimo Anno,* condemned the spread of Marxist ideology and affirmed the sanctity of private property, but at the same time gave his general approval to programs for achieving economic reform according to Christian principles. Two American Catholic leaders used the encyclical as a rationale for their vigorous social activism. Father John A. Ryan, professor of moral philosophy at Catholic University, called for an advanced system of economic planning built around the government ownership of public utilities and key industries and the decentralization of policy making in corporate councils of workers and managers. Although Ryan's scheme bore much similarity to the economic theory, if not the practice, of Italian Fascism, Ryan was a staunch supporter of the New Deal and had little use for Benito Mussolini. On the other hand, Father Charles Coughlin of Royal Oak, Michigan, whose weekly radio broadcasts reached several million listeners, coupled demands for welfare legislation, government control of big business, and monetary inflation through silver coinage with praise for Mussolini, vitriolic attacks on Roosevelt, and open anti-Semitism.

Protestantism: Social Gospel to Neo-orthodoxy

In the 1930s most Americans still regarded themselves as Protestants; Protestantism remained the most powerful religious influence in American life. The Great Depression rekindled the spirit of political participation and economic criticism which, in the early years of the century, had come to be called the "Social Gospel." Socially conscious Protestant ministers had played an active role in the many-sided reform movement called progressivism before the First World War. In the prosperous postwar decade, however, Social Gospel ministers gave less and less attention to "Christianizing" and "humanizing" industrial capitalism. Rather, most of them focused on implementing the great American experiment in moral regeneration, nationwide prohibition of intoxicating beverages. The economic crash and sagging public revenues armed anti-prohibitionists with a powerful argument for "repeal." Largely because of the mistaken assumption that the revenue problems of local, state, and national governments could be relieved by legalizing and taxing liquor, Congress early in 1933 submitted the Twenty-first Amendment to the Federal Constitution. By the end of that year nationwide prohibition was dead, and so was one of the most compelling goals of the original Social Gospel movement. For many clergymen, however, the prohibition issue had already become inconsequential alongside the critical need for the involvement of the Protestant churches in the drive for economic and social reconstruction.

As early as the fall of 1931, the twenty-three-year-old Federal Council of Churches, speaking for more than thirty Protestant denominations, urged "social planning and control of the credit and monetary systems and economic processes for the common good." More specifically, the Federal Council advocated a system of unemployment and retirement compensation, a "living wage" for all workers, shorter working hours, the right of labor unions to bargain collectively with management, the abolition of child labor in industry, and "economic justice" for American farmers. In short, the

1931 program of the Federal Council presaged most of the significant legislation enacted under the New Deal between 1933 and 1938. The forthright response to the economic collapse by the Federal Council and by such leading Protestant clergymen as John Haynes Holmes, Harry Emerson Fosdick, and Ralph W. Sockman made the Depresison decade the high tide of the Social Gospel influence in American Protestantism.

A fairly large number of ministers came to occupy positions on the political spectrum that were notably to the left of the Federal Council's Social Gospel precepts. Some of the more radical divines came together in 1930 to form the Fellowship of Socialist Christians, which proclaimed its allegiance to the Socialist party of Norman Thomas, himself a former Presbyterian minister. For four years the Fellowship published the stridently leftist *World Tomorrow.* Early in 1934 the magazine polled 100,000 Protestant clergymen throughout the nation on their political beliefs. Of the 20,870 who returned their questionnaires, 95 per cent endorsed some marked departure from orthodox capitalism, about three-fourths favored a "drastically reformed capitalism," and nearly one-third described themselves as socialists. *World Tomorrow* exuberantly concluded that "Among all the trades, occupations, and professions in the country, few can produce as high a percentage of Socialists as can the ministry." But another and perhaps more revealing way of viewing the survey was that, since less than 21 per cent of the ministers polled bothered to respond, political apathy or aloofness continued to be the prevailing mood among the leaders of the nation's Protestant congregations.

In 1936 the Fellowship of Socialist Christians began publishing a new journal called *Radical Religion.* The name of the publication indicated the Fellowship's growing disdain for the half-hearted methods of political liberalism, as embodied in the New Deal, and the desire for a more basic—a more "radical"—approach to the troubles of the Depression era. Yet the term "radical religion" also signaled an incipient transformation in American Protestant thought, the outcome of which would be a partial return to the basic beliefs of the Protestant Reformation together with the desertion of the idealistic assumptions that underlay the Social Gospel. The name most commonly applied to the new theological movement was "neo-orthodoxy."

The rise of neo-orthodoxy came as a reaction against theological liberalism, which had been the prevalent influence in American

Protestant thought during the first three decades of this century. Liberalism was not so much a systematic theology as it was a collection of ideas and attitudes which had evolved in response to the development of science and the individualistic, utilitarian, and materialistic elements in American culture. Liberalism represented an effective adjustment of religious beliefs to the growth of scientific knowledge. Liberal theologians looked forward to man's continual improvement, if not his ultimate perfection, which would be achieved as a result of the spread of Christian love by religion and the spread of knowledge of the physical world by science. Since man was basically moral and well-meaning, selfishness, greed, and conflict in human society resulted from ignorance and could be overcome through education in the principles of goodwill, brotherhood, and justice. History was the process by which man became more generous, more moral, and more 'civilized.' Thus history was the story of man's inexorable progress and of the gradual revelation of God's value, meaning, and purpose.

In the 1920s theological liberalism had helped confirm the majority of American Protestant ministers in their uncritical relationship to a society dominated by bourgeois materialism and complacency. But liberalism, with its pragmatic, open-minded approach to the problems of individuals and society, also furnished the impetus for the revived Social Gospel spirit in the early post-crash period. The economic sickness of the thirties could supposedly be treated with a combination of detached analysis, moral suasion, and government intervention. What Reinhold Niebuhr sardonically but accurately called the "Social Gospel-John Dewey amalgam, with its faith in the politics of love and reason," continued to characterize the Protestant approach to social issues.

The course of events in the twenties and thirties severely weakened the authority of Protestant liberalism. As Herbert W. Schneider has said, the optimistic structure of American Protestant thought simply could not withstand a succession of spiritual tremors which began with the collapse of Woodrow Wilson's dream for an American-led League of Nations, continued with the failure and eventual abandonment of national prohibition, intensified with the coming of the Great Depression, and climaxed with the unparalleled savageries of the Second World War. Meanwhile American religious thinkers gained increasing exposure, through translations, to such new influences as the brooding, pessimistic writings of the mid-nineteenth-century Danish philosopher Soren Kierkegaard and the contemporary neo-orthodox movement in European Protestant thought, expressed most forcefully in the works of the Swiss theologian Karl Barth and the Germans Emil Brunner and Paul Tillich.

Although they differed significantly among themselves, Barth, Brunner, and Tillich shared a distaste for liberalism, the worship of science, and the idea of inexorable progress. They returned to the basic Biblical doctrine of original sin, to the image of man as sinner confronted by a transcendent, omnipotent God. Their theological constructs began with the word of God, not the intelligence of man; with God's self-disclosure, not man's discovery; and with the redemptive act of God in Christ's death, not the ethical framework of Jesus's teachings. At the same time, however, the new theology recognized the value of a rigorously critical Biblical scholarship, rejected a literal reading of the Bible, and maintained a broad intellectual tolerance of diverse religious faiths. Thus the new theology was "neo-orthodox" in that it involved a renewal of the Reformationist, especially the Lutheran, outlook; it was also "post-liberal," peculiarly a product of the dilemma of twentieth-century man.

Americans received a challenging introduction to neo-orthodox theology in 1932, when Reinhold Niebuhr, of Union Theological Seminary in New York, published *Moral Man and Immoral Society.* Niebuhr had been an early enthusiast for the reform objectives of the Social Gospel. In the late twenties, however, partly as a result of his frustrating personal experiences as a pastor in the brutalizing industrial environment of Detroit, Niebuhr was drawn to the theocentric theology then exciting European Protestant intellectuals. Deeply troubled by the gross economic disparities in American capitalist society and convinced of the inadequacy of moderate reform, Niebuhr came to question not only the social efficacy of the Social Gospel, but whether the kind of Christian idealism shared by most Protestant ministers was truly Christian and Protestant. The conclusions he reached recognized the dialectical relationships between man, the hopeless sinner, and God; and between man, striving to achieve a moral social order, and society, which inevitably corrupted its members.

The fact that Niebuhr, a leader in the Fellowship of Socialist Christians, came to neo-orthodox theology primarily through his involvement with social and political issues gave his writings a distinctly American orientation and an immediate relevance to the Depression period. As Richard Kroner has noted, Barth and Brunner were primarily "academic and theoretical dogmatists," whereas Niebuhr was "not interested in purely theoretical questions, but in the solution of urgent social and political problems." *Moral Man and Immoral Society* was basically a study not in theology, but in political behavior and ethics. Rejecting the Social Gospel synthesis of religion and politics, Niebuhr made the two mutually exclusive and mutually critical. Love, the ideal of liberalism, could be approximated only in the moral relations between individuals. The furtherance of individual morality was the proper province of religion. But love was never attainable in the social order. The best that man could hope for in the way of social morality was "proximate justice," whose realization was the proper function of politics. Thus Niebuhr's goal was "a society in which there will be enough justice, and in which coercion will be sufficiently non-violent to prevent [man's] common enterprise from issuing into complete disaster." Justice was impossible under a capitalist economy, which only accentuated the self-seeking, egotistical—in short, the "sinful"—elements in man's nature. Marxism, Niebuhr felt, offered the only effective way to achieve the "uneasy balance of power" that marked the limits of society's capabilities.

With *Reflections on the End of an Era* (1934) and *An Interpretation of Christian Ethics* (1935), Niebuhr became more explicit both in his Marxism and in his description of the human predicament. Man's primary sin, said Niebuhr, was the sin of pride. Pride manifested itself in the quest for glory, the worship of science, and faith in the rational power of the human intellect. Because of pride, man refused to recognize the inevitable tragedy of his imperfect existence and the necessity to seek salvation in the transcendent, redemptive grace of God. Social organization lured man into thinking that he could be omnipotent, that he could reach beyond his finite self. "Individuals," he wrote, "may be saved by repentance, which is the gateway to grace. . . . But the collective life of mankind promises no such hope of salvation, for the very reason that it offers men the very symbols of pseudo-universality which tempt them to glorify and worship themselves as God."

Niebuhr thought the era of hopeful "bourgeois liberalism" had ended with the collapse of the economic system in America. Capitalism was a "spent force" and so was the Social Gospel. The politics of the future must recognize that political choices were always no more than choices between evils. To secure proximate justice meant acknowledging the existence of social conflict and the necessity for the use of coercion to protect men from each other. There was an obvious paradox in the fact that Niebuhr, who placed the concepts of sin and redemption through grace at the center of theology, also embraced Marxism, a doctrine of materialism that envisioned the ultimate disappearance of man's interest in a transcendent power. To Niebuhr, theocentrism and Marxism were not incompatible; they were, in fact, logically interrelated. Because he thought Soviet-style Communism excessively autocratic and thus destructive of social "equilibrium," he adopted a tough-minded, practical socialism which, beginning in 1936, he expounded as editor of *Radical Religion*. In 1940 Niebuhr resigned from the Socialist party in protest against its pacifist and non-interventionist policy toward the European war, but he seems to have retained his conviction that socialism offered the best way to check the sinful elements in the social order.

Niebuhr's writings are crucial for understanding both religious and political thought in America since the thirties. More than any other American theologian, he explained, analyzed, and elaborated on the ideas of the European neo-orthodoxists. Niebuhr helped to create a favorable climate particularly for Tillich, whose Christian Existentialist theology reached a steadily widening audience after he immigrated to the United States and joined Niebuhr at Union Seminary in 1933. By the end of the decade the neo-orthodox movement in America, which had begun, primarily in the work of Niebuhr, as a critique of Social Gospel politics, had become a thoroughgoing attack on the whole bright, comfortable structure of theological liberalism. Niebuhr himself—especially in *Beyond Tragedy* (1938) and in his Gifford lectures at Edinburgh University, published as *The Nature and Destiny of Man* (2 vols., 1941–43)—seemed to be moving away from political and ethical analysis toward a more formally theological examination of the problems and possibilities of individual and collective salvation.

Yet Niebuhr never fully went over to the formal logic and abstractionism of Continental neo-orthodoxy. He continued to be heedful of the concrete historical and contemporary consequences of man's religious attitudes, and he continued to draw primarily from the American experience in forming his conclusions. He remained on the political left after leaving the Socialist party to support American aid to the anti-fascist powers. After the war, in the context of stiffening international rivalry between the Soviet Union and the United States and the wholesale disaffection of American leftists from Marxism, Niebuhr helped organize the liberal, anti-Communist Americans for Democratic Action. On his odyssey from qualified Marxian Socialism to staunch anti-Communism, Niebuhr marked the trail for many American radicals, who drew on his writings in constructing a new political position, one that supported both the forceful "containment" of Soviet power abroad and the continuation of broad welfare programs at home. Thus Niebuhr had a central role in the reorientation of American leftist thought which took place between the 1930s and the 1950s—between the decade of Depression, New Deal, and Popular Front, and the decade of prosperity and Cold War. The new 'hard-nosed,' 'realistic' politics of the postwar years in America owed much to the new theology and to its foremost American expositor.

Neo-orthodoxy came to dominate Protestant thought in the United States in the postwar period. In the prewar and wartime years, however, both theological and secular liberals carried on a vigorous counteroffensive against the new religious ideas, denouncing Niebuhr and his American and Continental contemporaries as "reactionary," "irrational," and "obscurantist." A Harvard theologian described the creed of the Radical Religionists as: "We must move theologically to the right, politically to the left, back to sin and on to Moscow." In a 1943 symposium in *Partisan Review,* such leading intellectual figures as John Dewey, Ruth Benedict, and Sidney Hook indicted neo-orthodox theology, along with fascism and neo-Thomist philosophy, for contributing to "a new failure of nerve" among contemporary intellectuals in Europe and the United States.

Such criticisms missed the point of neo-orthodoxy, at least as it was expressed in Niebuhr's work. In fact, Niebuhr and other American theologians came to the new religious ideas because they felt man needed something to hold on to, something to steel his nerve in the midst of the accelerating calamities of the twentieth century. Like the proponents of general education, the Radical Religionists found the traditional American faith in science and progress inadequate for meeting the challenges at home and abroad in the thirties and forties. Niebuhr and his co-religionists were basically nationalists, as were Robert M. Hutchins and his associates in the general education movement. In quite different ways, these two groups of religious and educational thinkers tried to give purpose and meaning to the disordered lives of Americans in an age of Depression and war. Their efforts took on new relevance as the nation found itself being drawn into the currents of conflict in Europe and Asia.

Chapter VII

Defining the American Cause

In the spring of 1935 Walter Millis, a young and talented staff writer for the New York *Herald-Tribune*, published a book entitled *Road to War: America, 1914–1917*. Millis's thesis was that the administration of Woodrow Wilson had allowed itself to be maneuvered into such a position after 1914 that it was unable to turn back from war with Germany. Millis stressed four main themes: (1) Wilson had begun with the erroneous assumption that the United States should wield a major influence in world affairs. (2) The administration had doggedly insisted that the German government must conduct its submarine warfare according to this country's outworn notions of neutral rights; at the same time, Wilson and his advisers tolerated flagrant Allied interference with American commerce in central Europe. (3) British and French propagandists had been amazingly successful in persuading Wilson and much of the American public that Imperial Germany represented a direct threat to the United States, and that there was an inherent moral difference between the German and Allied causes. Thus Americans came to believe that the defeat of the blood-thirsty "Hun," who had supposedly raped his way across Europe, was vital to the preservation of democracy and "civilization" everywhere. (4) Because of the sale of hugh quantities of arms and munitions and the extension of loans and credits to the Allied governments, American business interests had acquired a heavy investment in an Allied victory. To Millis, only one conclusion seemed warranted: American entry into the war had been a ghastly mistake.

Revisionism and Isolationism

Millis's book marked the crest of the wave of "revisionist" writing on the causes and consequences of the First World War which appeared in the 1920s and 1930s. First, Continental and American scholars reexamined the problem of Germany's responsibilty for the outbreak of war. A number of them found that the Imperial government was no more culpable than Great Britain, and perhaps considerably less so than France or Russia. Hence the critical "war guilt" clause written into the Treaty of Versailles, they implied, was no more than a rationalization for the vengeful peace terms which the Allies, with the weak-kneed acquiescence of Wilson, dictated to the helpless Germans. Then, beginning with C. Hartley Grattan's *Why We Fought* in 1929, American writers questioned the wisdom and even the honesty of Wilson's official pronouncements and actions leading up to April 2, 1917, when he went before Congress to ask for the declaration of war. Grattan's work reflected growing popular suspicions that America had been duped into war by wily propagandists and profiteers. These suspicions were fed by such writings as Harold D. Lasswell's detached, meticulous analysis of *Propaganda Techniques in the World War* (1927) and by three strident exposes, all published in 1934, of the gigantic munitions combines in various countries—Helmuth C. Englebrecht's *Merchants of Death,* George Seldes's *Iron, Blood, and Profits,* and an anonymously written *Fortune* article, "Arms and Men."

The "merchants of death" thesis stirred so much controversy that the United States Senate established a special committee, headed by the Republican Gerald P. Nye of North Dakota, to determine the extent to which American bankers and armaments interests had actually influenced the policies of the Wilson administration after 1914. The testimony before the Nye committee, taken intermittently from the spring of 1934 to February 1936, revealed a great deal about profits, sales agreements, and corporate structures, but failed to prove the existence of any past or present conspiracy of politically powerful munitions-makers. Yet the hearings, accompanied by much fanfare in the daily and periodical press, doubtless confirmed millions of Americans in their determination not be to misled into another war.

Millis's *Road to War*, appearing at the height of public excitement over the Nye probe, was the first book to bring together the various lines of anti-Wilson criticism. His treatment was much more thorough than Grattan's, yet much more straightforward and readable than Charles C. Tansill's ponderous *America Goes to War* (1938). Millis drew much of his material from Lasswell, and he also used information gathered during the first series of hearings held by the Nye committee. The result was an impressive collection of facts, insights, and inferences, which seemed to demonstrate conclusively that America had erred in 1917. Bearing the implied message that the country must be careful not to err again, the book became a best seller and received almost unanimous praise from reviewers. William MacDonald in the *New York Times Book Review* expressed the critical consensus: "If it were possible to exact of every citizen a short course of required reading before anything more should be said or written about American participation in another European war, Mr. Millis's book might very well head the prescribed list."

The decade of the 1930s was a rare period in which the popular attitudes of Americans toward a particular historical problem corresponded closely to the most recent and most respected historical scholarship. "By 1929, the disillusionist theory of the war had become part of conventional American thinking," Selig Adler has written. "It found its way into high school and college classrooms via textbooks and teachers anxious to purvey the newest point of view. Historians who refused to follow the intellectual fad were derided as obscurantists." Seventy per cent of those polled by the American Institute of Public Opinion in January 1937 said they thought the United States should have stayed out of the First World War. When, as late as October 1939 (weeks after the German invasion of Poland), AIPO asked why the nation had entered the war in 1917, 34 per cent answered that "America was the victim of propaganda and selfish interests."

The widespread American revulsion against the past, against the heady idealism of the First World War, only partly explains why the collection of attitudes and emotions known as "isolationism" swept the country during the thirties. For various reasons, the complacency and detachment which had characterized American thinking about international affairs in the late twenties grew into a militant determination to stay out of foreign involvements in the succeeding decade. The enormity of the nation's economic problems overshadowed all other considerations for most of the Depression years. The Japanese conquest of Manchuria in 1931; the rise of the xenophobic, aggressive-sounding Nazis to power in Germany in 1933; Benito Mussolini's determination to establish an Italian Fascist empire by overrunning helpless Ethiopia in 1935–1936; the German reoccupation and remilitarization of the Rhineland in 1936; the full-scale invasion of China launched by Japan in 1937; and the crucial German-Italian intervention in the Spanish Civil War between 1936 and 1939—these and other potentially threatening developments beyond American shores created relatively little excitement in the United States alongside the Roosevelt administration's persistent efforts to cope with the Great Depression.

During these same years, Americans turned in disgust and disillusionment from Great Britain and France, whom they came to regard as untrustworthy debtors and unfit defenders of democracy. Most people in the United States were embittered when the British and French governments, beset by financial crises, defaulted on the payment of their debts to American creditors, then completely repudiated their legal obligations in 1933. To the average citizen, a debt was a debt, whether public or private, and the refusal of the British and French to pay what they owed only proved the incorrigible duplicity of America's erstwhile comrades-in-arms. Then, in a series of European Crises which began when Hitler pulled Germany out of the League of Nations and announced a program of general rearmament in 1933, the Allies acted with remarkable pusillanimity. During the Ethiopian war, Great Britain, France, and other League members not only continued selling to Italy strategic materials like coal, steel, and oil, but the British foreign minister and the French premier even tried to buy off Mussolini by offering him part of the African kingdom. When German troops marched into the Rhineland in 1936 and into Vienna two years later, following the annexation of Austria, the British and French protested weakly before accepting the new status quo. The Allies scrupulously embargoed all arms sales to the Spanish Republican government (as did the United States), while the Hitler and Mussolini regimes poured troops and their latest miltary machines into Spain to insure victory for Francisco Franco's fascist rebels.

What seemed to be the crowning instance of Anglo-French cold feet came in October 1938 at the Munich Conference, where Prime Minister Neville Chamberlain and Premier Eduard Daladier agreed to Hitler's demands for the inclusion of western Czechoslovakia, with its German-speaking minority, in the Third Reich. The Czechs, barred from the conference table, had no alternative but to accept the dismemberment of their country. For many of the millions of Americans who followed the central European crisis by daily and then almost hourly radio broadcasts, the Munich settlement left little doubt that the governments and people of Britain and France had no stomach for standing up to totalitarian aggression. And if the British and French refused to fight for their own freedoms and the integrity of small countries, then what possible interest could the United States have in Europe's mess?

Yet, even if the Allies had shown more backbone in dealing with the German and Italian dictatorships in the thirties, the American public would have been scarcely more susceptible to proposals for collective security. That large numbers of Americans saw a connection between war and the activities of private arms interests was evident from an American Institute of Public Opinion poll taken in February 1936. Eighty-two per cent of the interviewees thought the manufacture and sale of munitions for profit should be outlawed. Many American radicals coupled the merchants-of-death thesis with the Marxist-Leninist argument that militarism and war were inevitable concomitants of rival imperialist ambitions. At the other end of the political scale, conservative politicians and businessmen, already alarmed by the rapid expansion of government functions under the New Deal and the growth of executive power in the hands of President Roosevelt, feared that another war would deal a deathblow to free enterprise capitalism, which they thought coexistensive with true Americanism. Roosevelt, they were convinced, would seize the chance provided by a war emergency to regiment business under a socialist dictatorship.

For entirely different reasons, members of the non-Marxist left—whether they called themselves progressives, liberals, or radicals—were also certain that the involvement of the country in another war would be disastrous for the cause of American freedom and democracy. To leftist intellectuals like John Dewey, Charles Beard, Stuart Chase, George Soule, Grattan, or Oswald Garrison Villard, rearmament, the gearing of the economy for war production, and then war itself would shatter all hope for achieving economic and social democracy through peacetime economic planning. As Grattan put it, "The wartime dictatorship will be manned by the representatives of economic and social power. There is nothing like a war for revealing who really runs the country. The liberals go, the tough guys move in." However much leftists might criticize the New Deal's haphazard, sporadic efforts to bring recovery, they realized that it was at least a first step toward the kind of collective economic order they wanted. Beard, Villard, and the editors of the *New Republic* pointed out that in 1917 Americans had mistakenly tried to follow Wilson's admonition to "make the world safe for democracy," only to end up curtailing civil liberties and destroying progressive reform efforts at home. The task before Depression-wracked America, they contended, was to make this country safe for democracy by drastically reforming American industrial capitalism.

The conviction that foreign adventures and entanglements were incompatible with progress toward democracy at home was closely allied to the belief in a unique American mission, an idea that had been voiced by American leaders since the founding of Puritan New England. As Ralph H. Gabriel and other historians have shown, the doctrine of the "mission of America" had two basic meanings. One found expression in the spread-eagle expansionism of the nineteenth and early twentieth centuries, when Americans drove across North America and seized an overseas empire, justifying their conquests in terms of their "manifest destiny" to spread republican institutions and the white man's civilization to benighted peoples in farflung regions. But in its second meaning, the missionary doctrine held that Americans should strive to create a society offering a maximum of liberty and opportunity, one that would furnish a model for all humanity. Beginning fresh, without the contaminating history of the Old World, America would best serve the cause of human freedom by tending to its own affairs. The sufferings of the Great Depression gave new relevance and a new moral power to the traditional argument that, in Carl Becker's words, "The place to save democracy is at home." "If we can put our people to work," Becker wrote in the spring of 1938, "democracy will be safe enough here, and we can't save it in Europe by fighting for it there."

The Pacifist Persuasion

The American isolationist reaction of the thirties contained a deep strain of pacifism, cultivated by dozens of antiwar organizations whose combined membership, in the judgment of Merle Curti in 1936, was several million. The goals of the groups making up the American "peace movement" were varied and often contradictory. Some labored for the dying cause of international disarmament, which had seemed so promising in the twenties, and for the Kellogg-Briand Pact, whose ringing renunciation of war "as an instrument of national policy," signed by more than sixty nations in 1928–1930, proved in the thirties to be the proverbial scrap of paper. Some peace groups advocated peaceful international cooperation through the League of Nations, while others, insisting that the League was a British and French plot, continued to fight all proposals for American participation in the League or its sister organization, the World Court.[1] Various pacifist groups endorsed a constitutional amendment proposed by Representative Louis Ludlow of Indiana to require that, except in case of foreign invasion, a national referendum must be held before the country could go to war. Because of the qualifying clause concerning foreign invasion, the amendment would have neither crippled presidential conduct of foreign relations, as Roosevelt claimed, nor insured that the nation would remain at peace. The potential value of the "Ludlow referendum" was much more symbolic than practical, although conceivably the submission and ratification of such an amendment might have slowed somewhat the concentration of war-making power in the executive. One hundred and eighty-eight members of the House of Representatives voted to approve the amendment in January 1938, twenty-one short of a majority. Coming nine months before Munich and twenty months before Germany invaded Poland, the vote in the House probably marked the high tide of American neutralist-pacifist feeling in the Depression decade.

Pacifism was perhaps strongest among college and university students and socially conscious Protestant ministers. Doubtless many of the estimated half-million students who participated in the "peace strike" instigated by the American Student Union in the spring of 1936 were simply seizing an excuse to cut classes, but the fact that the Student Union could attract and hold the attention of so many youths at so many academic institutions revealed the extent of pacifist inclinations among the nation's college-age population. Within American Protestanism, the interdenominational *Christian Century* and *World Tomorrow*, published by the Fellowship of Socialist Christians, spoke for numerous clergymen in denouncing war as futile and contrary to the teachings of Christ. In 1933, in a book entitled *Preachers*

Present Arms, Ray Abrams caused red faces throughout the ministerial profession by skillfully and wittily juxtaposing some of the numerous antiwar pronouncements by American Protestant clergymen before 1917 with the florid blessings they bestowed on the nation's "holy war" in 1917–1918. In response to a *World Tomorrow* poll in 1934, thirteen thousand ministers, mostly Episcopalians, Presbyterians, and Methodists, replied that they would never again sanction American participation in a war.

As peace collapsed in Europe in the late thirties, many Protestant clergymen, especially Social Gospel supporters of the New Deal, struggled with questions of national security versus domestic social betterment and of international violence versus Christian principles of love and sacrifice. On the other hand, since political activism was less pronounced among Roman Catholic clergymen and since the Church had never condemned the use of force in international relations, American Catholicism was affected relatively little by the moral question of war. Indeed, some Catholic leaders in the United States openly sympathized with the fascist side in the Spanish Civil War because "El Caudillo" Franco promised to restore the privileges and power the Church had lost under the Republic. And while some Jewish religious spokesmen condemned all war in the early thirties, nearly all religious-minded Jews came to support American aid to the enemies of Nazi Germany by 1939.

In the 1930s, perhaps more than at any time in their history, the American people tended to think of 'war' as an abstraction, an evil force commonly symbolized by the cartoonist's figure of the burly Mars looming over a distraught world. The tendency to abstract war from its historical and contemporary context was evident from the popular reception and critical admiration of such grim antiwar writings as Irwin Shaw's play *Bury the Dead* (1936) and Humphrey Cobb's novel *Paths of Glory* (1935). Translations of *All Quiet on the Western Front* (1929), the powerful pacifist novel by the German, Erich Maria Remarque, were widely read in the United States, and millions crowded movie houses in 1939 to see the inevitable Hollywood version.

Americans had greeted the Kellogg-Briand Pact with such enthusiasm in the twenties because, by signing it, the nations of Europe supposedly repudiated the Old World conception of the purpose of war. The people of America usually distinguished between diplomacy, under which their nation pursued its legitimate objectives in the world, and war, which was always defensive. Although the United States had engaged in a sizable number of military conflicts in its relatively short national history, this country, so the story went, had never fought a war for selfish reasons, never used force "as an instrument of national policy." Aggressive warfare was something other countries practiced. Such views obviously ran counter to historical reality and to the grandiose rationalizations for American imperialism before the First World War. Nevertheless, in the 1930s the common feeling was that, as Beard and others argued, the interests of the nation must be separated from the interests of organized economic groups which might prod America into war. The true "national interest" dictated that America remain at peace.

Pacifism in the United States in the thirties was much more a reaction to contemporary events than a systematic outlook; Protestant ministers accounted for the great majority of true philosophical (or theological) pacifists. Until the fall of 1939, however, pacifism and isolationism were parallel, complementary, and largely interchangeable elements in American opinion. The outbreak of war in Europe altered the attitudes of Americans rapidly and significantly. After Poland fell, the Roosevelt administration secured a partial relaxation of the restrictions on American trade with belligerent countries which Congress had written into a series of neutrality acts beginning in 1935.[2] Roosevelt also got increased military appropriations from a Congress that was becoming increasingly apprehensive about Nazi and Japanese threats to American security. Roosevelt's eagerness to aid Great Britain and France against Hitler forced isolationists in and out of Congress to face up to the question of what isolationism actually meant. Most isolationists began to talk about building a military establishment that would make the Western Hemisphere impregnable to attack by a non-hemispheric power. Hence in the two years and three months from the German attack on Poland to the Japanese attack at Pearl Harbor, American isolationism became rather thoroughly militarized. By 1941 the alliance between isolationists and pacifists had broken apart, and few pacifists remained prominent in public life.

Popular Front Ambivalence

For a considerable portion of the American political left, however, it was the Popular Front movement organized in 1935, not the coming of war four years later, that first brought into sharp focus questions of isolationism versus internationalism, pacifism versus militarism. In locking arms with American Communists to form a united front against fascism, Socialists and non-Marxist leftists presumably endorsed the Soviet Union's new policy of seeking collective-security arrangements with the Western capitalist democracies. Some Popular Fronters, like Louis Fischer of the *Nation,* Archibald MacLeish, Reinhold Niebuhr, and Frederick L. Schuman, did join the Communists in advocating American economic and military aid to all nations threatened by fascist aggression. They admired the Soviet Union as the only major power willing to stand in the way of Nazi territorial ambitions, and they denounced Congress and the Roosevelt administration for embargoing trade with the Spanish Republican government, fighting for its life against national and international fascism.

Other supporters of the Popular Front, however, were unable to accept the full implications of leftist fraternity. The name of one of the largest Front organizations, the American League against War and Fascism, suggested the ambivalent nature of the whole Front movement. The League stood for united action to repel aggressive international fascism, yet it also denounced the growth of the American military establishment, which leftists feared would become a breeding ground for domestic fascism. For many leftists the principal fascist threat was an internal one, represented by munitions-makers, the disciples of Huey Long and Father Coughlin, and such smaller but more blatantly authoritarian groups as the Ku Klux Klan in the South, the Black Legion in the Midwest, and the German-American Bund and the Silver Shirts along the Atlantic coast. "Progressive" elements on the left must unite to thwart the forces of reaction at home. Thus, however illogical it might seem in retrospect, some Americans managed to give their sympathies to the leftist coalition at the same time that they retained their pacifist and isolationist convictions.

The Spanish Civil War—which Allen Guttmann has accurately described as a "wound in the heart" for much of America—placed non-Communist leftists in a painful predicament. They all wished to see the fascist revolt fail, but most could not bring themselves to support United States intervention in the war. The Spanish conflict was Europe's problem, cautioned such writers as Beard, Chase, Villard, Alfred Bingham, and the editors of the *New Republic.* To abandon the policy of strict neutrality set down by Congress in 1935, 1936, and 1937 and to heed the call for collective security would be to repeat the mistakes of 1914–1917 and destroy domocracy at home.

So the United States watched as the fascists stormed to victory in Spain. American leftists agonized over Spain's plight, and most of them applauded the Soviet Union for giving miltary aid to the Republic. But they also fretted and argued over the advent of Communist-inspired terrorism within the republican government and over the bloody purge of Stalin's enemies carried out in the form of the Moscow trials of 1936–1938. Then, in August 1939, came the Nazi-Soviet Pact. Overnight the official policy of the American Communist party changed from collective security to strict neutrality. The Popular Front collapsed, and, as war again convulsed Europe, non-Communist leftists searched the wreckage of the Front for some sort of coherent position.

In the aftermath of the partition of Poland by Germany and Russia, Bruce Bliven and George Soule of the *New Republic* vacillated from moral condemnation of the Stalin regime to grudging acceptance of Soviet *realpolitik*. The *New Republic's* editorial uncertainties continued as the U.S.S.R. extended its control over the Baltic states in the fall of 1939. Bliven and Soule did not become truly disenchanted with Soviet foreign policy until the Russian invasion of Finland during the winter of 1939–1940. Meanwhile anti-Front leftists like Villard and Beard could take some satisfaction that their warnings about the equally reprehensible nature of the Nazi and Soviet dictatorships had been confirmed. Now more than ever, they insisted, America must keep free of the European morass. Other leftists managed to retain their pro-Russian sympathies and thus endorsed the Communist neutrality line. Still others, like Freda Kirchwey and her associates on the *Nation,* MacLeish, and Niebuhr, called for all-out aid to Great Britain and France in their struggle against Naziism. Niebuhr resigned from the Socialist party because of its "utopian" persistence in labeling the European war a conflict of rival imperialisms. The trouble with Socialist utopianism, he wrote, was that it "creates confusion in politics by measuring all significant historical distinctions against purely ideal perspectives and blinding the eye to differences which may be matters of life and death. . . ." Even the *New Republic* eventually advocated military and economic assistance to the Allies.

Yet, as Frank A. Warren has pointed out, most American leftists who had supported the Popular Front never really faced up to the basic ideological questions they had avoided during the period of collaboration with the Communists. They continued to ignore the inherent contradiction between Communist totalitarianism and their own dedication to democratic processes. The image of Soviet Communism, though somewhat tarnished, remained brighter than that of fascism; Russia remained 'on the left,' fascism 'on the right.' The goals of the Soviet state continued to appear admirable, however dictatorial, cynical, and repressive its means might be. Thus when German armor smashed across the Soviet borders on June 22, 1941, non-Communist radicals easily revised their list of anti-totalitarian nations to include the U.S.S.R. As American Communists hurriedly switched to ardent interventionism, it again became possible to close ranks on the left.

The Refugee Contribution

If the Popular Front experience increased confusion on the political left about America's proper relationship to the war in Europe, the statements and writings of the "refugee intellectuals" who fled fascist tyranny in the thirties helped clarify the thinking of Americans. Coming mostly from Germany and Austria, the emigres represented virtually every field of learning and art. They continued their work in the United States under the auspices of the American Guild for German Cultural Freedom and other refugee organizations. As early as 1932 Columbia University set up a University in Exile, the members of which ultimately became part of the graduate faculty of the New School for Social Research, operated since 1919 in conjunction with Columbia. American cultural and intellectual life was greatly enriched by such figures as the novelist Thomas Mann; the theologian Paul Tillich; George Grosz, the leading German expressionist painter; the composer Paul Hindemith, who, after coming to Yale University, led in the creation of the Berkshire Music Festival; the architect Walter Gropius, whose New Bauhaus, established in 1937 in Chicago, helped promote functional building design in America; and the physicist Albert Einstein, who joined the Institute for Advanced Studies at Princeton University.

The refugee intellectuals did much to make the American people aware that Naziism was not just another despotic regime; that what had happened in Germany was a repudiation of the fundamental values of Western Civilization—a "revolution of nihilism," in the phrase of the ex-Nazi politician Hermann Rauschning. As the United States became a sanctuary for European rationalism in the thirties, some Americans came to feel that their country had an obligation to defend civilization against the atavistic designs of the fascists. That was one way of responding to Mann's prediction that "for the duration of the European dark age, the center of Western culture will shift to America." But another response was voiced by Richard Aldington, an English poet who settled in Connecticut in the thirties. America, said Aldington on Armistice Day, 1939, "has only one task—to preserve in peace those inheritances of European culture which the coming years will see destroyed in Europe. The only possible future for Europe is that it shall be recolonized in years to come with the civilization preserved in America intact." Two isolationist writers put it more succinctly early the next year: "The United States must recover its role as an impartial healer, and abandon that of unintelligent preacher."

The Dilemma and the Debate

Such contradictory responses to the destruction of free thought in Europe pointed up the larger dilemma the people of the United States faced after the fighting actually began in the fall of 1939. According to the increasingly numerous public opinion polls, three basic attitudes characterized the thinking of Americans from the outset of the war to the Pearl Harbor attack. The first was sympathy for Great Britain and France, which, as the war progressed, became almost unanimous. Parallel and equal to the overwhelmingly pro-Allied sentiment, however, was a fervent wish to keep out of war. As late as September 17, 1941, 87 per cent said "no" when asked by the American Institute of Public Opinion, "Should the United States go into the war now and send an army to Europe to fight?" The third characteristic American attitude in the post-Poland period was a sense of helplessness in the face of what was happening abroad. Shortly after the beginning of the European hostilities, AIPO reported that 56 per cent of its respondents thought the United States would eventually become involved; by the spring of 1941, 82 per cent were convinced that the nation would go to war. Bombarded by the propaganda of the interventionist Committee to Defend America by Aiding the Allies, by the isolationist America First Committee, and by various other groups, most Americans, as Harold Lavine and

James Wechsler observed in 1940, "seemed to be watching the enactment of a drama in which their role had already been fixed. . . . They waited, and the words rolled over them."

The battle of words continued right up until Pearl Harbor. The "Great Debate" on American foreign policy provoked some of the most florid oratory and some of the worst demagogy in the country's history. But if much of the debate of 1940–41 revealed American political discourse at its rawest, there were also a number of honest, often eloquent, efforts to define America's true responsibilities in a world in upheaval. The great majority of writers focused on the problem of developing a concrete, workable policy toward the war. But others, like Charles Beard and Lewis Mumford, combined their advocacy of specific measures with broader analyses of the purposes and ideals of American society. A third group, typified by Ralph Barton Perry and Carl Becker, tried to provide a well-reasoned ideological basis for American efforts to prevent a fascist triumph. Finally, such writers as Archibald MacLeish, Howard Mumford Jones, and Mortimer Adler, besides describing the fascist threat to American values and security, tried also to explain why their countrymen were so hesitant to confront the challenge of totalitarian power.

Until the spring of 1940 it seemed feasible to rely on French military power, to assume that, as Roosevelt had allegedly said early in 1939, "the American frontier is on the Rhine." Consequently the position of the Committee to Defend America by Aiding the Allies, and of nearly all interventionists, was rather severely limited. America should sell great amounts of war goods and materials to the British and French and might even eventually extend credits to the Allied governments, but beyond that the United States should not go. As Raymond L. Buell, a former president of the internationalist Foreign Policy Association, declared, "we should not go to war in the 1917 sense. . . . Under no circumstances should the United States send a huge expeditionary force to Europe." The subjugation of Denmark, Norway, Holland, Belgium, and finally France by the smooth-running Nazi war machine swiftly transformed interventionist thinking. As Germany, supreme on the Continent, launched its air offensive against the British Isles, "limited interventionism" was abandoned in favor of "all aid short of war." A few writers even began to advocate a war declaration against Germany.

In the midst of mounting support for stepped-up assistance to the British, Charles Beard tried to offer a reasonable alternative to what he rightly judged was the Roosevelt administration's determination to tie the future of America to the fate of Britain. Beard's *A Foreign Policy for America*, appearing in the early fall of 1940, was both a summation of his many writings on national and international affairs in the thirties and a response to the immediate crisis of approaching war. Three alternative approaches to foreign policy competed for the favor of the American people, said Beard. The first was imperialism, a doctrine of international entanglement rationalized in terms of America's worldwide economic interests and its supposed omnipotence. Beard dismissed imperialism as contrary to American ideals and as the cause for a succession of overseas failures in the past. The second alternative was internationalism, "which sees world peace as the fundamental objective for the Government." Beard thought the nation's experience with Wilson's visionary diplomacy should have demonstrated that it was impossible for America to strive for a peaceful international order without aligning itself with power blocs and becoming entrapped in foreign quarrels. There was only one sane foreign policy for America—what Beard called "continental Americanism." With characteristic emphasis on economic factors, Beard argued that wars resulted primarily from trade ambitions and rivalries. He assumed that it was possible for the United States, through extensive economic planning, to eliminate its dependence on international trade. The result would be an economic system able to function apart from the struggle for markets, investment opportunities, and raw materials. Withdrawing to its continental boundaries and concentrating its energies on the construction of a democratic social and economic order, the United States could become a beacon of freedom for decadent Europe and turbulent Asia. Continental Americanism, said Beard, recognized "the limited nature of American powers to relieve, restore, and maintain life beyond its own sphere of interest and control."

Beard's argument rested on some highly dubious assumptions about national and international economics, and about the ability of the United States to remain secure in the face of German domination of the Atlantic and the growth of fascist political and economic influence in Latin America. What was even more important, however, was the fact that Beard ignored the basic moral questions posed by the spread of Nazi power. To Beard, fascism differed from older forms of European imperialism only in degree, not in kind. It was

America that was fundamentally different, and, insofar as America had a moral responsibility in the world of 1940, it was to perpetuate the nation's democratic, anti-militarist traditions and to develop its full social potential.

Isolationists like Beard suffered from a tragic moral blindness, in Lewis Mumford's opinion. While certainly not the most influential, Mumford was at least one of the most thoughtful and articulate formulators of interventionist thinking. A vigorous champion of economic reform, functional architecture, and city planning throughout the twenties and thirties, he was a contributing editor to the *New Republic* from 1927 to 1940, when he resigned because the magazine refused to abandon its neutralism and pacifism. As early as May 1938, five months before the Munich debacle, he issued "A Call to Arms" in the *New Republic.* Terming fascism in Germany and Italy "codified and co-ordinated barbarism . . . whose deeply malignant character and cancerous spread have changed every problem of civilized political existence," Mumford exhorted Americans to "Strike first against fascism; and strike hard. But strike." Disgusted by the timorousness of the British and French, Mumford gave up on the prospect of collective resistance. On the other hand, isolationism was "nothing less than a declaration of submission to the forces that threaten . . . our own way of life" and an "encouragement to those obscene, irrational forces in the United States that favor fascism." Mumford advocated "a comprehensive Non-Intercourse Act," a complete severance of all diplomatic and commercial relations with Germany, Italy, and Japan. Such a non-intercourse policy, besides carrying great moral weight and hurting the fascist economies, would make it possible to "liquidate the skeleton army that the fascist states have already planted in this country." Like many writers on both sides of the foreign policy controversy, Mumford greatly exaggerated the size and influence of pro-fascist elements within the United States.

The course of the European war quickly demonstrated that, unless the British Isles were conquered, Great Britain would be able to maintain its centuries-old dominance in the Atlantic. This fact obviated Mumford's non-intercourse strategy, at least as far as Europe was concerned. Mumford eventually came around to vehement, if vague, support for collective security. His particular concern was awakening American leftists to the necessity for creating a "totalitarian democracy," one that would possess the military power to strike anywhere in the world, the political power to suppress fascist subversives at home, and the spiritual power to demand total sacrifices in the defense of American freedom.

Virulent fascism had spread so rapidly, Mumford wrote not long before he resigned from the *New Republic,* because the liberal ideology of the West, and especially of America, had become corrupted. Western liberalism consisted of two traditions. One was "ideal liberalism," which embodied the principles of personal responsibility, personal freedom, and personal expression. Ideal liberalism was a universal, moralizing force which antedated the rise of capitalism and science. The second, or modern, tradition was "pragmatic liberalism," a child of the eighteenth century and a product of "a rather adolescent pride in the scientific conquest of nature and the invention of power machinery." The main traits of pragmatic liberalism were a concern with abstract thought and the experimentally verifiable, an optimistic faith in human reason, and an insistence on the relativity of values. Pragmatic liberals minimized or rejected the role of irrationality and basic evil, and thus denied the need for coercion in human affairs. Because of their "open-minded" refusal to recognize normative values, pragmatic liberals were left ideologically and morally defenseless before the dark forces of fascism. Clinging to the "muddled nonsense" of economic determinism, they could not see that "it is not in Ricardo or Marx or Lenin, but in Dante and Shakespeare and Dostoevsky, that an understanding of the true sources of fascism are to be found." What American liberals must do, Mumford concluded, was "transcend the arid pragmatism that has served as a substitute for religion" and achieve "a recrystallization of the positive values of life, and an understanding of the basic issues of good and evil, of power and form, of force and grace, in the actual world."

Mumford's intellectual debt to Reinhold Niebuhr, though not explicitly acknowledged, was apparent in almost all his writings before Pearl Harbor. Both recognized the central fact of evil in human existence, and both grimly forecast a death struggle with Hitler's hordes. Both proclaimed that goodwill, reason, and the scientific method were inadequate in the irrational world of the twentieth century. For both, pragmatism became a pejorative.

For Ralph Barton Perry and Carl Becker, however, pragmatism retained its attractiveness. Neither Perry nor Becker accepted Mumford's distinction between age-old humanistic values on the one hand and confidence in the power of the human intellect on the other. The democratic faith that Americans must fight for was, they felt, a compound of reason, optimism, persuasion, and compassion. Perry, author of a magistral biography of William James, temporarily put aside his philosophical studies at Harvard to write a number of essays in which he described democracy as the social institution that best realized the universal human faculties of reason and conscience. Americans must resist attacks on their democratic ideology "on all fronts," at home and abroad. Becker, the brooding apostle of historical relativism in the early thirties, discovered that "to know the limitations of reason is to increase its power in the long run. . . . The fallacy is to suppose that because truth is in some sense relative it cannot be distinguished from error, or that the margin of error cannot be progressively reduced." American democracy must continue to be grounded in both reason and the "generalities that still glitter." For the essence of the American democratic faith, Becker wrote in the spring of 1940, was belief that the "good life" could be achieved by rational and humane means. The virtue of democracy was that "with all its faults it still provides the most favorable conditions for achieving that end by these means."

If Mumford's message seemed to be beamed mainly to American leftists, and if Perry and Becker tried to fortify the faith of all lovers of democracy, Archibald MacLeish spoke most effectively to the nation's allegedly apathetic artists and scholars. To be sure, MacLeish, who became Librarian of Congress in 1939 and thus a semi-official representative of the Roosevelt administration, addressed himself to a great variety of groups in the years before Pearl Harbor. His poems, essays, and speeches rang with militant declarations to all Americans. "There is Spain Poland China Bohemia," he cried late in 1939 in *America Was Promises*. "There are dead men in the pits in all those countries./ Their mouths are silent but they speak. They say/ *'The promises are theirs who take them.'* " The war was not "just another European war," he wrote two years later. It was the "American Cause" that was at stake. And the American Cause was freedom, "the single man's belief in liberty of mind and spirit; his willingness to sacrifice his goods and comforts and his earnings for its sake."

Yet MacLeish seemed especially eager to point out the responsibilities of the American literati in the fight against fascism. The need for social commitment on the part of the artist had been a persistent theme in his prose writings in the late thirties. During the Popular Front period he participated in the Communist-directed American

Writers' Congresses. After the Nazi-Soviet Pact and the conquest of Poland, he responded energetically and vociferously to the call for American intervention on behalf of Great Britain and France. When large numbers of his associates in the arts and letters refused to do the same, he tried to fathom the sources of their irresolution, aloofness, and cynicism.

In June 1940, in a widely publicized speech before the American Association for Adult Education, MacLeish singled out for criticism his own literary generation, the young writers of the 1920s. MacLeish admitted that the ideals for which Americans had fought in the First World War had gone unfulfilled, and that the disillusionment so many intellectuals felt in the postwar decade was understandable. But the ideals had been sound, said MacLeish, and in teaching that America was not worth fighting for, the writers of the Lost Generation had undermined the ability of their countrymen to meet the challenge of the fascist barbarians in the succeeding decade. Some of the nation's outstanding literary figures, like John Dos Passos and Ernest Hemingway, "must face the fact that the books they wrote in the years just after the war have done more to disarm democracy in the face of fascism than any other single influence." MacLeish suggested that writers, in their zeal to tell the truth, should pause to consider the long-term implications of the attitudes they helped instill in their readers. Perhaps because of their "great responsibility to the future," writers "must not weaken the validity of the Word even when the deceptions of the Word have injured them."

That same year MacLeish redrew his indictment to include virtually the entire literary and scholarly community in the United States. "The Irresponsibles" was the epithet he hurled at contemporary writers and academicians. Future historians, said MacLeish, would find it "strange—ironical and strange—that the great mass of American scholars and American writers made no effort to defend either themselves or the world by which they lived." Intellectuals simply refused to understand that the world crisis was essentially a cultural crisis, "a revolt . . . against the inherited culture of the West and against all common culture." MacLeish thought that in large part the irresponsibility of intellectuals resulted from the disappearance of the traditional "man of letters," the kind of person whose broad-ranging interests fused the functions of artist and scholar. In the twentieth century, intellectuals had divided themselves into two "cults"—scholars and writers. For different reasons, each group had abdicated its responsibility for preserving civilization from the fascist onslaught.

The scholar, who wanted only to pursue his own narrow concerns, was "the perfect type of irresponsibility. . . ." Insisting that he must maintain his objectivity and intellectual purity, the scholar behaved "as though the fire could not burn him because he has no business with the fire. . . . Whose business is it then? He will not answer even that. He has his work to do. He has his book to finish. . . ." The writer escaped his responsibility by trying to imitate the mood of the painter, "which is to say he thinks without responsibility to anything but truth of feeling." Ignoring antecedent, results, or judgments, the writer devoted himself to the thing observed and to depicting it truthfully. "The writer will write a bloody story about the expense of blood," MacLeish said. "He will present the face of agony as it has rarely been presented. But not even then will he take the weapon of his words and carry it to the barricades of intellectual warfare . . . where alone this fighting can be won." Committed to his art, "The artist does not fight."

Howard Mumford Jones, professor of literature at Harvard University, was even more specific in fixing the blame for the fact that patriotic fervor, which interventionists usually equated with support for collective security measures, had supposedly dwindled among Americans. The main culprits, in Jones's thinking, were cynical historians and European-minded writers. Jones disavowed propaganda and chauvinism, yet at the same time he castigated the practitioners of "scientific" history, who, in their quest for historical truth, had systematically destroyed the collection of myths, symbols, and traditions that underlay American nationalism. Charles Beard, with his tough economic analyses, had had an especially "unfortunate influence." Historians left only uncertainty as to "what it is that American democrats are to believe in during the coming struggle." If the nation had to go to war, Jones asked, "will it be emotionally inspired by the sound historic fact that the Lincoln administration is supposed to have favored the high-tariff crowd?" His verdict: "We debunked too much."

According to Jones, "European influences" in the nation's recent literary output had also undermined the American democratic faith. Jones condemned the three most powerful tendencies in modern literature—naturalism, Freudianism, and Marxism—as well as the rise of formal literary scholarship. The effect of the new literary tendencies had been to create a mood of fatalism, pessimism, and contempt for humanistic values. The exponents of "intellectualist criticism" assumed that "literature—true literature—is the property of a samurai class (the intelligentsia), which may ignore the vulgar herd." Thus the whole direction of American literature worked to alienate literature from the people and the people from their hopeful ideals of freedom and egalitarianism. Democracy, "battered and wounded and deserted by authors who should rally to its standard," survived only because "there is a vast deal more idealism and good will among ordinary Americans than ever gets pictured in the books that are written about them."

At any time of great social crisis, legitimate questions can be raised regarding the influence and obligations of intellectuals. Like most other people, scholars and artists tend to become transfixed by their own specialized interests and daily routines, so that they conveniently overlook the most glaring social evils. But in chastising novelists, poets, and scholars for weakening the patriotism and moral resolve of Americans, MacLeish and Jones came perilously close to saying that literature should accept and reinforce a nation's values, mores, and even its blunders. Their attacks on the scholars and writers of the interwar years contained strong hints of anti-intellectualism and the implication that scholarship and literature should voice some kind of official creed. When Mumford argued that American pro-fascists should be deprived of their constitutional protections, MacLeish was quick to point out the incongruity of trying to preserve freedom by curtailing freedom. Yet MacLeish and Jones proved equally unwilling to follow their line of reasoning to its logical conclusion. Their own arguments were infused with a dogmatism whose potential for intellectual stricture was all too clear during the bleak years of fascist conquest.

Mortimer Adler of the University of Chicago, a compatriot of Robert M. Hutchins in the general education movement, offered a somewhat more plausible, but no less dogmatic, explanation for the supposed scarcity of values, patriotism, and purpose among the prewar generation of Americans. The trouble was not the content of the literature produced in the United States and abroad, Adler wrote in the fall of 1940, because most people had never read the works of the outstanding contemporary writers. The trouble could be found in the nation's public schools, colleges, and universities, which glorified materialism, practical knowledge, and the scientific method. The skeptical attitudes cultivated by the American educational system steadily eroded the individual's sense of the common humanistic values of Western Civilization. Because the naturalistic frame of mind was so entrenched in the faculties and administrations of academic institutions, Adler saw little chance for reenshrining the fundamental truths in American learning. Ironically, the only ray of hope was the approaching war, which might, Adler thought, compel the American people to reeducate themselves in the virtues of democracy and reaffirm the heritage of the West.

In the two years following the attack on Poland, President Roosevelt was able, step by step, to win majority approval in Congress and in the country as a whole for policies that pushed the United States ever deeper into the war in Europe. By the late fall of 1941 war with Germany was imminent. The public opinion polls indicated that while the great majority of Americans continued to oppose a war declaration, they also applauded the undeclared war being waged by American warships and aircraft against German submarines in the Atlantic. The official and unofficial campaigns to convince the people of the United States that they should make common cause with all foes of fascism had been brilliantly successful.

There were serious flaws in the interventionist case. The argument presented by Mumford and others that all expressions of pro-fascist sentiment should be systematically suppressed had ominous overtones, as did the criticisms by MacLeish and Jones of recent American scholarship and literature. And one did not have to be a social scientist to realize the appalling paradox in America's portrayal of itself as the champion of freedom, democracy, and the dignity of man while it continued to oppress Negro Americans within a rigid caste system—although the contradiction was so engrained in the American experience that most people overlooked it. Nevertheless, to try to balance the cruelties and injustices of American society with Nazi atrocities was, as Mumford said, to "treat as equal a manure pile and a mountain because they had the same general shape and were both composed of 'dirt.'" The interventionist spokesmen of 1939–1941 were almost always vague and cryptic when it came to specifying the means by which the United States could stop the march of fascism without engaging in a full-scale war; at bottom the effort to formulate a policy based on "all aid short of war" was a product of naiveté and wishful thinking. But the basic message of interventionism was right: To understand and to fulfill the American Cause was to help destroy Naziism.

Asia and Abstractionism

Of course it was not Nazi Germany, but Imperial Japan, that forcefully terminated the Great Debate and resolved the war dilemma for Americans. The Pearl Harbor attack shocked and enraged the American people not only because it came without warning, but because few people really comprehended the depth of the Roosevelt administration's commitment to China and the fatal conflict between United States and Japanese aims in eastern Asia. Americans in the late fall of 1941 were, psychologically, facing eastward toward Europe. For more than two years their attention had been focused on the swiftly changing war on the Continent and in the Atlantic. To be sure, they read daily press accounts and saw grisly newsreel reports of the war being fought over vast areas of China, and they sympathized with the efforts of the Chinese to check the Japanese invaders. They saw Japan as one of the "predatory" countries, especially after Germany, Italy, and Japan signed their tripartite military alliance in September 1940.

Before Pearl Harbor, however, relatively few people in the United States gave their attentions primarily to the Sino-Japanese struggle. For some time after the Japanese began all-out military operations in China in July 1937, many millions favored neither side. In October 1937, the same month that Roosevelt suggested the United States should join other nations in "quarantining" aggressors, AIPO reported that 40 percent of its respondents professed complete neutrality. There was always a much greater disparity between popular attitudes and official policy toward the fighting in China than toward the European war. The Roosevelt administration obviously felt that the United States had vital interests at stake as well as a moral commitment to China, but in the initial stages of the China war most Americans felt otherwise. Roosevelt and Secretary of State Cordell Hull insisted that American lives and property in China must be scrupulously safeguarded, and in December 1937 they protested vigorously (and got an apology and an indemnity) when Japanese aircraft sank a United States gunboat in the Yangtse River. A month later, however, the polls showed that 70 per cent of the people favored a withdrawal of all American personnel from China.

Eventually, a large majority of Americans gave their moral support to China and endorsed the increasingly severe restrictions on Japanese trade put into effect by the Roosevelt administration. But it seems that the principal cause for the gradual stiffening of American attitudes toward Japan was not the course of the war in China, where the military situation really did not change much after 1938, but rather the series of startling Nazi triumphs that began with the Munich conference. "Only comparatively recently," observed one analyst in the spring of 1941, "has opinion favored a policy of determined pressure, and this opinion . . . seems to have been produced by the course of events in Europe, not in the Far East." By May 1939, according to AIPO, only 22 per cent of the people still claimed to be neutral in their feelings about the Sino-Japanese struggle. What apparently happened was that Americans easily generalized from the European situation and linked Japanese imperialism in Asia with the aggressions of Germany and Italy. The Tripartite Pact looked like the final proof that the "Axis" powers had formed a conspiracy to dominate the world.[3] Neither the great mass of Americans nor the Roosevelt administration seems to have realized that the Japanese "militarists" were not the same as the Nazis, that Japan was not the same sort of totalitarian society Germany and Italy had become, and that, to a great extent, Japanese expansionism was motivated by the kind of sincere, if mistaken, notion of civilizing "mission" and "destiny" which had powered the American imperial thrust a generation and a half earlier.

An equally distorted view of China formed in American minds in the late thirties. If Americans tended to see Japan in the image of Nazi Germany, they also tried to superimpose their conception of their own country on China. Over the years the glowing reports of Christian missionaries, the popular novels of Pearl S. Buck, and the activities of a few influential citizens who had been born in China, like Henry Luce, helped convince Americans that China was an authentic, unified nation-state whose huge population, animated by intense national pride and dedication, gave its unflagging allegiance to the great democratic leader of the East, Chiang Kai-shek. China was the awakening giant, a nation whose march toward major-power status and democratic stability had been thwarted by the demonic Japanese. With the help of the United States, the demons could be exorcised and China could fulfill its destiny. That was the American image and dream of China. The reality was a country in chaos, plagued by internal strife and official corruption, really governed by no one—by neither Chiang's military dictatorship, which was the nominal national government, nor by the fanatical Communist revolutionaries of Mao Tse-tung.

Imagery and abstractionism, not such substantive considerations as investments and trade in China or the vulnerability of the Philippines to Japanese attack, dominated the discussion and formulation of United States policy toward Japan. The term "Fascism," in its original, capitalized usage, referred to the particular political and economic system instituted by Mussolini in Italy during the 1920s. After 1933 in the United States, "fascism," written with a little "f," came to be inclusive of and synonymous with the Nazi system in Germany. Still later, American writers lifted the term out of its Western context, where it had its only real meaning, and began applying it carelessly to Japan. To people like Mumford, MacLeish, and Becker, "fascism" first called to mind Germany, then Italy, and finally Japan. In the vast amount of interventionist literature published between 1939 and 1941, specific references to Japanese aggression and American obligations to aid China came almost as afterthoughts, if they appeared at all. Few writers made any serious effort to go beyond the abstractions and to analyze Japanese "fascism" and Chinese "democracy." While isolationists eschewed all collective security proposals and denied that the United States had any responsibilities outside the Western Hemisphere, interventionists conceived of the need for worldwide cooperation on the part of the "free nations" to combat a worldwide totalitarian menace. They implied, if they seldom said explicitly, that the security of the United States was directly threatened by Japanese expansion on the mainland of Asia. Neither isolationists nor interventionists tried to arrive at a systematic policy which recognized the critical differences between American interests and responsibilities in Europe, the Atlantic, and the Pacific, on one hand, and in Asia on the other.

Indifference and indecision regarding the American course in Asia remained widespread up until the Pearl Harbor attack. But what happened that Sunday morning, December 7, obliterated all qualms and solidified the American determination to destroy the Japanese Empire. In the wave of anti-Japanese hysteria that swept the nation after Pearl Harbor, Japan became even more the symbol of fundamental evil than Hitler's Germany, which became America's formal enemy on December 11.[4] Henceforth no more than a handful of people would deny that the American Cause was worldwide, that the national welfare was tied to Asia no less than to Europe. The immediate goal was simply to survive. Beyond that, goals were uncertain. Carl Becker wrote early in 1942 that America should be content to insure that its democratic institutions were safe in the world. But as they girded for total war, the people of the United States understandably looked forward to a time when, with their enemies smashed, American notions of right conduct would be the guiding principles of world order.

Notes: Chapter VII

1. Roosevelt, despite his original enthusiasm for Wilsonian internationalism and the League of Nations, did not reopen the question of American membership in the League after he became president. It seems that, as Selig Adler has written, "Roosevelt . . . came to the White House after having reached a proper understanding with the isolationists in his own party." Roosevelt did, however, propose early in 1935 that the United States enter the World Court. Inundated by isolationist protests, the Senate refused to approve the proposal.
2. In November 1939 Congress rescinded the embargo on sales of armaments and munitions to belligerent countries, although stipulating that all war goods must be purchased on a "cash and carry" basis.
3. For a thoroughgoing refutation of the view that the Tripartite Pact formed a closely knit alliance aimed at worldwide conquest, see Frank W. Ikle, *German-Japanese Relations, 1936–1940* (1950) and Paul W. Schroeder, *The Axis Alliance and Japanese-American Relations, 1941* (1958).
4. Italy also declared war on the United States on December 11.

Chapter VIII

For a Better World?

Future historians may write that the period from the Pearl Harbor attack to the Japanese surrender was one in which the American people felt the greatest sense of national unity and collective purpose in their history. Whereas the Great Depression had sharpened class divisions and ideological differences among Americans, the experience of the Second World War gave them common cause and direction. The economic woes which had persistently frustrated the New Deal all but disappeared under the impact of the war production program instituted by the Roosevelt administration in 1940 and enormously expanded after Pearl Harbor. Buoyed by full employment, record high wages and profits, and massive savings, Americans endured rapid price inflation, scarcities, and unprecedented economic regimentation with a minimum of grumbling. Temporarily forgetting their historic dispute over foreign policy, they prepared to fight until their enemies were totally vanquished.

By providing mutual goals and commanding mutual sacrifices, the war undoubtedly heightened the American sense of nationhood. In other ways, however, the war demonstrated the limits of nationalism. The United States was, after all, but one member of a global concert of nations battling totalitarian aggression, and as the war progressed a preponderance of Americans came to feel an obligation to work with other peoples for a just and peaceful postwar world. At the same time the war underscored the fact that the nation had not yet resolved the conflict between its own cultural diversities and its majoritarian prejudices. As in previous national crises, Americans quickly reached the limits of their tolerance. Finally, the war seemingly proved the irrelevance of what Americans had always believed about the proper conduct of warfare. They learned that they, too, could accept the most horrible military expedients in the name of gaining victory and saving American lives. Thus in the years 1942–1945, as they discovered international bonds of brotherhood and hope, perhaps the people of the United States also came to understand better their own flaws and failings, both as Americans and as human beings.

Moods of a Nation at War

Nearly every writer who tried to analyze national attitudes during the war years discerned fundamental differences between the responses of Americans to the present conflict and the way they had reacted to the First World War. In the first place, there was marked variation in the way people viewed the three enemies. World War II saw no repetition of the anti-German hysteria that had convulsed the nation in 1917–1918; German-Americans and German influences in American culture remained generally secure and respected. The common tendency was to distinguish between the German people, who still seemed redeemable, however misguided and militaristic, and their Nazi rulers, for whom unlimited obloquy was reserved. Benito Mussolini, though a less sinister figure than Adolf Hitler, nevertheless qualified as an archfiend in American thinking. Yet American attitudes toward the Italian people remained generally benign, and hostility toward American citizens of Italian ancestry was virtually non-existent. By contrast, the Japanese people, Japanese-Americans, and all things Japanese became targets for violent, almost uncontrollable animosity. American suppositions regarding the innate depravity and treachery of the Japanese seemed confirmed by Pearl Harbor, by reports of the harsh treatment of American troops captured in the Philippines, and by the suicidal resistance put up by Japan's soldiers in the Pacific fighting. The vast majority of Americans, easily assuming that race and ancestry were more powerful behavioral influences than nationality, applauded when early in

1942 the Roosevelt administration authorized the forced removal of Japanese-Americans to barbed-wire enclosures scattered over the interior of the country. Hatred of the Japanese was probably more intense than feeling against any previous American foe. By the summer of 1945 the public was amply prepared for the use of atomic bombs against Japan, America's one remaining enemy.

The second major contrast between American responses to the First and Second World Wars had to do with popular conceptions of the war's purposes. In 1917–1918 there had been a great deal of bluster and rhetoric about saving civilization, spreading democracy over the world, and fighting a war to end wars. Apparently many people believed that victory over Imperial Germany would usher in some kind of golden age of peace and security. But in 1942–1945, beyond the obvious negative goal of destroying the military power of the Axis countries, few citizens seemed to have any real conception of why the war was being fought. "The American people do not question the necessity of fighting this war through to the bitter end," wrote one public opinion analyst early in 1943. "Nevertheless only two-thirds of the people claim to have a clear idea of what we are fighting for." Archibald MacLeish saw many "who are willing, if need be, to die to help their people win it; but who are nevertheless unable to understand clearly, or to imagine precisely, what our victory in this war will be. . . ." Nothing in the way of official pronouncements stirred the popular imagination as had Woodrow Wilson's Fourteen Points in 1918—neither the "Four Freedoms" posited by President Roosevelt in January 1941, nor the generalities embodied in the Atlantic Charter issued by Roosevelt and Winston Churchill the following August, nor the Unconditional Surrender doctrine the two Allied leaders enunciated a little more than a year after Pearl Harbor.

In place of the crusading idealism of the First World War, Americans seemed "grimly sober" as they entered the greatest conflict in their history. The contrast in moods, according to Allan Nevins, resulted from the almost universal realization that the war would be long and victory would be hard won, from the fresh memory of the letdown following the earlier war, and from a widespread feeling that the United States, through its disdain for collective security measures, had contributed to the disintegration of international order in the late thirties. It may have been, as Nevins contended, that this "troubled conscience" gave many Americans a sense of moral obligation. At any rate, there appeared to be little taste for high-sounding phrases. American morale during the Second World War, reported the sociologist Herbert Blumer, was clearly of the "practical" type. Americans were scarcely susceptible to "the beating of tom-toms, the resort to strategems, the reliance on emotional appeals, and the evocation of religious sanctions. . . ." The typical attitude toward the war, Blumer said, was simply "Let's get it over with."

Social scientists who tried to determine what members of the armed services thought about the war found that confusion, ignorance, fatalism, and cynicism were common responses, but seldom idealism. Few servicemen seemed to have any real purpose beyond crushing the enemy quickly, doing the job with as little bloodshed as possible, and going home. Samuel Stouffer and his co-workers, in a massive study of the psychology of Americans under arms, revealed a composite soldier who had little personal commitment to the war, seldom thought about its meaning, and tended to agree with whatever interpretation of the conflict his interviewer suggested. His main motivation and loyalties seemed to belong to his own immediate comrades, especially under combat conditions. Apparently patriotism had little if any relevance to soldierly performance. After the war one sociologist, referring to the Stouffer findings, expressed wonder that the nation's armed forces fought as well as they did. If the United States had lost the war, he added, the psychological studies of the war years would doubtless have been offered in explanation of the defeat.

Two wartime fictional creations—a cartoon series and a novel—paralleled and helped confirm what the various social science studies indicated about the feelings of American servicemen. "Willie" and "Joe," the grimy, laconic soldiers in Bill Mauldin's cartoons for Army newspapers, provided a brilliantly, sometimes brutally satirical commentary on the aimless routine and ignobility of military life. Harry Brown's *A Walk in the Sun* (1944), probably the best novel set in a military context to appear during the war years, depicted a group of American infantrymen who were neither moved by high ideals nor outraged by the inhumanity of war. Resigned to doing a dirty job that had to be done, they used sparse, ironic humor to mask their fears. There was scarcely a hint of any higher purpose than survival and completing the immediate task.

The fact remains that American forces did fight well on all fronts. One can question whether devotion to common ideals has ever animated more than a small portion of any army, whether military motivation has not always been primarily a matter of group ties and the drive simply to stay alive. One might also ask whether such a definable condition as "national morale," "mood," or "temper" actually exists, and whether there need be any common purpose in war besides a determination to make the sacrifices necessary to win. Yet many American intellectuals did assume that the war against the Axis should have some nobler goal than national survival, and they worried about the difficulty of convincing the American masses that more was involved. They made frequent efforts to supply the missing elan, to spark Americans into realizing the enduring international responsibilities that victory would bring.

For most of the time before his death in April 1945, President Roosevelt declined to discuss the United States's long-range goals for the postwar world. The chief spokesman for the administration on postwar issues was Vice President Henry Wallace. In May 1942 Wallace provided an eloquent cue for American idealists when he proclaimed that "the century on which we are entering—the century which will come out of this war—can be and must be the century of the common man." In succeeding speeches, articles, and books Wallace urged his countrymen to extend the principles of New Deal democracy throughout the world.

Even more articulate, if less influential, was Archibald MacLeish, who had written and spoken tirelessly in the cause of interventionism before Pearl Harbor. "We who win this war," he announced in the summer of 1942, "will win the right and power to impose upon the opening age the free man's image of the earth we live in. We who win this war will win the future." Two years later he argued that American thinking about the war was too tough-minded, too realistic. While there had been a great deal of talk about making realities and facts the basis for the postwar settlements, what was needed was devout adherence to the great American abstractions of democracy and human freedom. Margaret Mead was another who wished to relate American ideals to the problem of postwar reconstruction. For Mead, in fact, the only way to win the war was to "fight it in terms that do make sense—to Americans." The nation was fighting for a chance to make a better world, to "harness American shrewdness, that mixture of mysticism and a knowledge of machinery which has been so falsely dubbed 'practicality,' to the problem of making social inventions. . . ." The anti-Stalinist radical Dwight Macdonald agreed that the war presented an opportunity to achieve lasting changes both at home and abroad. Macdonald thought the war could do much for the cause of democratic socialism in the United States and for the abolition of economic rivalries and colonial empires—if Americans recaptured their revolutionary idealism.

Against such calls for idealism, dedication, and hope, Carl Becker cautioned Americans not to expect too much from the war. His countrymen had rightly set their hopes on making a better world. Nevertheless, they should continually ask themselves, "How new will the better world be?" Victory over the Axis, however smashing, would not obliterate the historical forces that had produced the war—nationalism, the sovereign state, power politics, imperialism. Idealists tended to think of such forces as evil abstractions, Becker noted, when in fact the presence of any or all could be desirable or undesirable, depending on who benefited from them. For example, it happened to be to the advantage of the United States to ally with British imperialism, which many Americans detested. But to save itself the United States would have to save the British Empire as well. And that Empire was one of the realities this country would have to deal with in the postwar years. In short, America, recognizing that it was not unique, that it had responsibilities to world civilization as well as to itself, could and must work for a better world. But it could never create a perfect one.

The sober counsel of Becker—and of others such as Reinhold Niebuhr, Charles Beard, and Mortimer Adler—provided a useful counterweight to the grand abstractionism of people like Wallace and MacLeish. Yet Becker at least left room for ideals in the conduct of the war and in the rebuilding of the international structure. For Nicholas J. Spykman and Walter Lippmann, however, the goals of democracy and human freedom seemed to be mostly irrelevant to the task of establishing peace and security in the postwar period. Both scolded Americans for their self-righteous, millennialist approach to foreign affairs and for their traditional unwillingness to understand the realities of geography and power politics. Both set for themselves the task of educating the nation in those realities in order to provide the basis for a rational postwar foreign policy. For both, the critical consideration was the relationship between the United States and the world balance of power.

In 1942 Spykman, Sterling Professor of International Relations at Yale University, published a thick volume entitled *America's Strat-*

egy in World Politics, in which he tried to relate the special problems of the United States to "the basic power aspect of international relations." His blunt, even brash phraseology was one of the main reasons his book attracted wide attention. Since there was no such thing as international order, he argued, the sole object of the nation-state in its foreign relations was to acquire and preserve a "power position." Nations withdrawing from the incessant struggle for advantage, as the United States had tried to do before the war, risked absorption by stronger states. Americans had often been afraid of war, or at least unwillingly to accept the fact that war was a legitimate means of pursuing national ends. Now they refused to understand that war in the twentieth century had become total war, requiring the complete integration of military, economic, political, and ideological resources. The distinction between wartime and peacetime no longer had any real meaning. "The struggle is waged continuously," Spykman declared. "Total war is permanent war."

Spykman had no confidence in the creation of a postwar international organization to succeed the defunct League of Nations, nor in the concept of an "Anglo-American community" based on the perpetuation of the close working relationship with Great Britain. America had one set of national interests, Britain another; the two countries might, in fact, become rivals in various parts of the world. Spykman put his faith in regional organization. The United States should weld itself and the nations of Latin America into a single hemispheric economic unit. At the same time, the United States should maintain its military power to determine the course of events in the Atlantic and Pacific. Above all, the American people must realize that "the national domain is a military base from which the state fights and prepares for war during the temporary armistice called peace."

Spykman's argument contained readily discernible elements of Karl von Clausewitz, Alfred Thayer Mahan, and other military and naval determinists. His treatment was also replete with geopolitical allusions, which he developed more explicitly in the posthumously published *The Geography of the Peace* (1944).[1] His icily logical conclusions and his harsh, amoral tone probably offended a good portion of his readers. But others were doubtless persuaded by his vigorous efforts to divest Americans of their illusions, to fix their attention on international power relationships, and to convince them that they could not escape the consequences of their own power.

Lippmann's *United States Foreign Policy: Shield of the Republic*, which appeared in the spring of 1943, was shorter and less scholarly than Spykman's books, yet also less abrasive and more widely read. Lippmann's premise was hardly debatable: A nation had to be able to balance its commitments with its resources and capabilities. From 1823 to 1899, in the form of the Monroe Doctrine, the United States had followed a firm policy which squared with its commitments. But since 1899, when it acquired an overseas empire after defeating Spain, the nation had steadily extended its commitments throughout the world without formulating a policy based on its farflung interests. Instead, Americans had chased mirages like "peace," "disarmament," and "no entangling alliances." Isolationism or its euphemism, "continentalism," was a policy of insolvency; to be isolated, said Lippmann, "is for any state the worst of all predicaments." The United States had to have a foreign policy that was, like the Monroe Doctrine, "a commonplace," derived from valid, definable considerations. Lippmann advocated a species of collective security, founded not in some world association of nations but in the Old World concept of spheres of interest and influence. The starting point was the recognition that "the Atlantic Ocean is not the frontier between Europe and the Americas," but "an inland sea of a community of nations allied with one another by geography, history, and vital necessity." The United States and Great Britain must come together in an "Atlantic Community." That would be one sphere of interest. There were others, over which Great Britain, China, and the Soviet Union would hold sway. These four great powers should form a "nuclear alliance" whose combined strength should be adequate to maintain the peace of the world.[2]

Lippmann's idea for a postwar nuclear alliance was essentially the same as the "Four Policemen" concept then central to the Roosevelt administration's thinking about postwar relationships. Lippmann understood the absolute necessity of achieving stability and accord in Soviet-American relations and the dreadful consequences of a breakdown in the wartime alliance. So did Roosevelt, who by the time of his death had apparently come to realize the fundamental divergence between the aims of his country and those of the U.S.S.R., and thus had abandoned the Four Policemen scheme in favor of reliance on Anglo-American cooperation and the influence of the nascent United Nations organization. But Lippmann, like nearly every other analyst during the war years, failed to comprehend the nature of the China imbroglio. For Americans, Chiang Kai-shek remained the heroic symbol of a heroic people, a sort of Far Eastern George Washington (or maybe Andrew Jackson). The incorrigible corruption of the Chiang regime, the feudalistic nature of popular loyalties in China, the irreconcilable conflict between Chinese Nationalists and Communists—these were realities that writers like Lippmann and Spykman overlooked, despite their insistence on 'realistic' assessments of postwar prospects. Neither they nor anyone else foresaw the postwar collapse of the Nationalists, the Communization of the vast country, and the fateful involvement of the United States on the mainland of Asia.

Despite their supposed sobriety and tough-mindedness, the American people were optimistic enough to expect that they would gain more from the war than the substitution of one set of totalitarian enemies for another. After Pearl Harbor most Americans enthusiastically approved of their country's alliance with the Soviet Union. The Moscow purge trials, the Nazi-Soviet Pact, the Russian aggression against Finland—these and other Stalinist sins were obscured as Americans joined in admiration of the Russian people's tenacious defense of their homeland. Imbibing such effusive Hollywood productions as *Mission to Moscow* (1943), *North Star* (1943), and *Song of Russia* (1944), they became convinced not only that the Russian war effort was saving American lives (which was true), but that the Soviet Union was one of the "democracies" fighting to hold back the fascist barbarians. There seemed little doubt that the wartime marriage of convenience between the United States and the U.S.S.R. would form the basis for postwar amity.

At the same time that they opened their arms to the Russian autocracy, the people of America began to put their faith in postwar international organization. Millions of them bought and read Wendell Willkie's exhortatory *One World* when it appeared in the fall of 1942. The argument of the most recent Republican presidential candidate, that modern science and technology had shrunk the globe and that henceforth "our thinking must be world-wide," seemed incontrovertible. But Willkie's book was only one factor in a strenuous campaign carried on by such internationalist groups as the Council on Foreign Relations, the Foreign Policy Association, and the Woodrow Wilson Foundation, and by a host of individual champions of what Vice President Wallace called "a second chance to erect a lasting structure of peace. . . ." After Pearl Harbor, as Robert A. Divine has pointed out, the truly meaningful foreign policy debate was not between isolationists and interventionists. Rather, it was between people who agreed on the necessity for the United States to assume a role of world leadership, but who argued the merits of particular forms of internationalism—world government, regional associations, dominance by big-power "policemen," a revived League of Nations, or a much strengthened organization which nevertheless retained national sovereignty.

To be sure, there remained a sizable number of unrepentant isolationists—such as Charles Beard, Oswald Garrison Villard, the sociologist Harry Elmer Barnes, and the journalist John T. Flynn—who refused to have anything to do with the increasingly powerful movement for international organization. They accepted unhesitatingly the harsh task of defending the homeland, but they refused to abandon their conviction that America was a place apart, uniquely endowed with a mission to provide an example in liberty and democracy for the rest of mankind. This mission, they felt, could be fulfilled only if the nation kept free of long-term overseas commitments. At the same time, however, others who had earlier opposed non-hemispheric involvement—men like the journalists Walter Millis and C. Harley Grattan and the jurist Jerome Frank—became converts to internationalist thinking. Millis worked for the Office of War Information, and after the war he would write a strong defense of Roosevelt's Asian policy in the year before Pearl Harbor. Grattan discovered the cultural ties and, by implication, the mutual obligations of Americans and faraway Australians. Frank, an arch proponent of legal relativism and an extreme economic nationalist in the thirties, showed during the war years that he understood the dangers of relativist thinking when confronted with Nazi barbarism. He began to emphasize the transcendent moral and ethical values that should influence the exercise of authority.

The campaign to win over Americans to internationalism was brilliantly—and speedily—successful. By mid-1944 the public opinion polls indicated that 70 per cent of the people favored world organization, and both houses of Congress and both political parties had overwhelmingly endorsed United States' participation in a new multinational body. It is probably true that for most Americans internationalism had meaning only in terms of America's own national interests, of which the foremost were security and the avoidance of future wars. Yet Americans were willing to give the new policy a chance. The United Nations organization, when it formally came into existence in April 1945, carried their hopes for a lasting peace.

American opinion in the years 1942–1945 was thus a compound of grim determination and confident expectation, of realism and naiveté, of maturity and youthful yearning. Somehow, Americans hoped, the ideals of their Declaration of Independence would be accepted by the rest of the world. Of course many of their own principles violently contradicted those ideals. Racism remained a characteristic element in American thinking. Many wartime observers, both Negro and white, pointed out that the United States was fighting—and asking other countries to fight—for human freedom and dignity while it continued to deny "the dream of democracy" to its black citizens. Perhaps the most glaring manifestation of this denial was the treatment of Negroes in the armed services, where they were rigidly segregated and, for the most part, relegated to menial functions. Despite manpower shortages, the military authorities remained reluctant to train and use Negro combat units and to commission Negro officers. At home hundreds of thousands of Negroes sought jobs in the burgeoning centers of war industry. Plagued by discriminatory hiring and pay practices, crowded into the least desirable residential areas, constantly haunted by the gulf between their nation's ideals and its actions, restive urban Negroes often clashed with resentful whites. A major race riot hit Detroit in June 1943; lesser disturbances occurred in Los Angeles, New York City, and Beaumont, Texas. The war bred a sense of impatience and expectation throughout the Negro population. By 1945, black Americans were about to enter a new and more militant phase in their quest for political, economic, and social justice.

Indian Americans, Mexican-Americans, and the swelling number of immigrants from Puerto Rico also suffered from a great variety of insults and indignities, while public opinion polls uncovered a remarkable amount of latent anti-Semitism in the country that called itself "the land of the free." For Japanese-Americans, total war meant the outright suspension of citizenship, an act of expediency that became all the more ominous when the United States Supreme Court sanctioned the government's relocation policy. The constitutional scholar Edwin S. Corwin hardly exaggerated when he referred to the treatment of Japanese-Americans as "the most drastic invasion of the rights of citizens of the United States by their own government that has . . . occurred in the history of our nation."

Total war severely strained American democracy and laid bare the actual limits of the national polity. But if the war years brought the enthronement of conformity and the proscription of liberty, Americans were still among the freest people in the world in 1945. There was not as much public dissent during World War II as in 1917–1918, but this was attributable less to official repression than to the fact that, since the nation had been attacked, argument about American participation in the war was virtually non-existent. Moreover, Roosevelt, the consummate politician, was brilliantly successful in holding public confidence in his wartime leadership.

Even more than the Great Depression, the war became the central, catalytic factor in American life. Thus the years 1942–1945 have an even greater historical unity than the 1930s. Scarcely any facet of the national existence went untouched by the spirit and sacrifices engendered by the global struggle. Although American culture remained a vast kaleidoscope, a swirl of many different and diverse ideas and influences, the experience of war was the most powerful force affecting the nation's art, learning, and religious life.

The Arts in Wartime

The significance of the war for the literary art in America can be gauged more in terms of its indirect effect on the mood and outlook of writers than in the amount of worthwhile composition it directly inspired. The acute concern with social issues, especially the economic crisis in America and the spread of native and international fascism, had begun to fade rapidly even before Pearl Harbor. As Granville Hicks noted, "the decline of the social protest novel began on August 22, 1939"—the date of the Nazi-Soviet Pact. Of the novelists who had contributed to the vociferous literature of protest and criticism in the thirties, only John Steinbeck addressed himself directly to the moral issues involved in the war. The result was *The Moon Is Down* (1942), set in an unnamed land, presumably occupied Norway. Although this short novel was a sincere effort to portray the struggle against Nazi tyranny and thus to inspire all lovers of freedom, it fell far short of the pinnacle Steinbeck had reached in *The Grapes of Wrath*. Soundly criticized on esthetic grounds, the book also provoked hyper-nationalistic censure from the *New Republic* and some other readers, who felt Steinbeck had muddled his message by showing the human qualities of his Germans.

The leading exponents of the angry literary naturalism of the Depression years, like Erskine Caldwell, John O'Hara, Richard Wright, and James T. Farrell, failed to equal what they had achieved in fiction before Pearl Harbor. Wright did publish in 1945 a bitterly moving autobiography. Farrell completed his "Jimmy O'Neill" tetralogy with *My Days of Anger* (1943), but by this time the deterministic milieu of his working-class Chicago Irish had lost most of its appeal. Whereas *Studs Lonigan* had been a stern social document in the Depression era, Farrell's fiction during the war years and after began to seem badly dated. In his essays, however, he continued to demonstrate his considerable talents as esthetic and social critic.

The war period was not an especially fruitful time for three of the literary giants of the thirties—William Faulkner, Ernest Hemingway, and John Dos Passos. A volume of Faulkner's collected stories, appearing in 1942, evoked the customary critical response—a mixture of effusive admiration, restrained approval, confusion, and disgust. Hemingway wrote even less, which was perhaps surprising in view of his great descriptive powers when dealing with physical combat or the reactions of men in war. Dos Passos, who had become completely disenchanted with Marxism by the end of the thirties, continued to move backward and rightward, philosophically and politically. Probably the best of several anti-dictatorship novels published in the thirties and forties was Dos Passos's *Number One* (1943), which became the middle volume in the *District of Columbia* trilogy. Here Dos Passos made the most explicit statement to date of his own peculiar brand of American nationalism, which was really a form of early-nineteenth-century liberalism—severely distrustful of authority, wedded to the agrarian life, worshipful of Jefferson. But while Dos Passos's fiction became more philosophically coherent, it no longer had the force and sweep that distinguished *U.S.A.* Dos Passos, like a number of his contemporaries, had lost the critical yet vital and hopeful vision of the thirties. In short, he had lost the Great Depression.

The literary mood of the early forties was characterized by an intellectual rejection of the possibility of finding one solution to the problems of men, and by an increasing awareness of the difficulties and dangers in trying to find any solutions. Distrustful of ideology and causes, skeptical about any rational basis for politics, the new writing was highly introspective, centering on personal experience, inner thoughts and feelings, and the pervasive ambiguities of human existence. The writers who first came to prominence after 1940 frequently took the theme of man's search for himself. They were also much concerned with the omnipresent factor of evil in human affairs. Not surprisingly, the literary reputations of Faulkner and Thomas Wolfe began to acquire new luster, while such relatively obscure writers of the thirties as Nathanael West and the expatriate Henry Miller began to receive close critical attention. More than ever, critics hailed Henry James as America's finest novelist.

While it may be that few among the new generation of writers were familiar with recent trends in theology, there were certain clear parallels between their conceptions and the ideas of the neo-orthodox movement, particularly the Christian Existentialism of the emigre German theologian Paul Tillich. For many American writers, as for many religious thinkers, the events of the years 1939–1945—the collapse of the Popular Front dream, the outbreak of fighting in Europe, America's involvement—exerted a crucial influence, but an essentially negative one. The dark cloud of the cruelest of wars obscured—perhaps permanently—the faiths and strivings of the thirties.

One of the earliest examples of the changing literary disposition was Robert Penn Warren's *Night Rider* (1939). Warren gained considerable notoriety as a poet and essayist in the thirties, being usually identified with the reactionary social philosophy of Southern Agrarianism. By the end of the decade, however, he had abandoned the battle against urban, industrial civilization and, turning to the novel form, had begun to deal subtly and profoundly with problems of motives, identity, and meaning. Warren continued to build his stature as a novelist with *At Heaven's Gate* (1943); at the close of the war he was writing *All the King's Men* (1946), one of the most powerful works of the forties.

Other writers who, despite their pronounced differences, shared the apolitical, introspective disposition of the early forties were Walter Van Tilburg Clark, Carson McCullers, Eudora Welty, Saul Bellow, and Katherine Anne Porter. All seemed far removed from the mood of national rediscovery and protest in which so many writers had worked in the thirties. The major novels of the war years, so strikingly devoid of either collective idealism or collective anger, established the philosophical and psychological contours within which American fiction would develop over the next two decades.

The war was a time of relative quiescence for the American theater, partly because of the passing of the issues of the thirties, partly because of shortages of personnel and building materials and restrictions on travel. The exigencies of the war served to tighten New York's near-monopoly of theatrical money and talent, a condition Hallie Flanagan and other crusaders for decentralized, popularized drama had attacked with such vigor in the Depression years. After Pearl Harbor there were still many who, like the designer and director Norris Houghton, wanted a "theater for the common man," one that could get closer to the real life of Americans and exploit native themes. The Camp Shows staged by the United Service Organizations had brought legitimate theater to millions of servicemen for the first time. Perhaps, Houghton suggested in the summer of 1943, they could act as the same kind of democratizing agent the Federal Theatre Project had been in the late thirties. At the end of the war, however, the hope for truly national theater in America seemed as far from realization as ever.

The years 1942–1945 probably saw an increase in the number of short-run Broadway farces designed to "take people's minds off their troubles." Most of the more serious efforts, including Paul Green's off-Broadway adaptation of Richard Wright's *Native Son* and Steinbeck's stage version of *The Moon Is Down,* were not memorable. In general, the prominent dramatists of the thirties seemed to have little to say during the war years, while significant new playwriting talent failed to appear. The left-wing theater movement was dead; Clifford Odets, its finest discovery, was in Hollywood. Meanwhile Robert E. Sherwood, the much-praised portraitist of Lincoln, wrote speeches for President Roosevelt and worked with the Office of War Information. Eugene O'Neill remained silent, as he had since 1934.

Two notable exceptions in an otherwise drab four years of theater were plays by Thornton Wilder and Maxwell Anderson. In *The Skin of Our Teeth* (1942), Wilder broadened what he had said in *Our Town* into a testimony to mankind's genius for survival. Featuring many unusual stage devices and much moving backward and forward in time, the play carried the Antrobus family, representative of all mankind, through a long chronicle of natural and man-made calamities. Man always emerged chin-up, ready to rebuild his institutions and values and try to overcome his failings. *The Skin of Our Teeth* well-suited the American wartime mood of restrained optimism. Anderson in *Joan of Lorraine* (1945) handled a familiar subject in ingenious fashion, presenting the play in the form of a rehearsal in which the "director" and the "leading lady" discuss whether

Joan should compromise with evil. Although Anderson had been preoccupied with this theme for many years, his new treatment was clearly relevant to the war era.

For American poetry the main importance of the early forties was the appearance of several fine young poets who were each deeply affected by the convulsions of another world war. Most of the outstanding figures of the thirties continued to write verse in the next decade, although only Wallace Stevens, steadily enlarging his circle of critical admirers, seemed to have improved with age. But it was the younger group that really fired the poetic imagination. Perhaps the three most promising new poets of the war years were Randall Jarrell, Karl Shapiro, and Robert Lowell. All three experienced what Louis Untermeyer described as "a recoil from horror and a revulsion from a society so inept as to permit, within twenty-five years, two universal catastrophes aimed not against nations but against civilization." Inspired by a combination of moral outrage and deep compassion for the victims of the war, Jarrell's poetry featured a remarkable economy of words. Shapiro's *V-Letter* (1943) and *Troop Train* (1945) were probably the finest poems of their kind to appear during the war years. Lowell, an adamant pacifist who served several months in federal prison for resisting conscription, was not yet thirty when the war ended. His early work showed an intense concern with the influence of the past on the present, with violent death, and with religious experience. All these elements appear in *The Quaker Graveyard in Nantucket* (1945), still one of his best-known poems.

Poetry, not fiction or the drama, continued to be the favorite concern of the practitioners of the New Criticism, the mode of intensive, asocial literary analysis which had developed in the 1930s. By the end of the war the New Criticism, no longer new or very controversial, was well on its way to becoming the strongest ingredient in American literary scholarship. Marxist-inspired criticism, which had flourished during the thirties, was, like the novel of protest, a scarce commodity by the early forties. Yet arguments persisted regarding the social utility of literature—whether it should have an immediate relevance to American life and an immediate ideological function.

The controversy swirled around the pre-Pearl Harbor charges made by Archibald MacLeish and others that American writers of the twenties, because of their cynicism, amorality, and pacifism, had weakened the people's resolve to resist fascist tyranny in the thirties. Bernard De Voto continued in this vein in a confused little book, *The*

Literary Fallacy (1944). De Voto maintained that the writers of the interwar decades had lost touch with "American realities." Their fiction, rife with despair instead of hope, had been a "trivial literature." Thus it was not America that was "tawdry, cheap, empty, and base," but "the half-bushel of writers who presumed to find [it] so." A scorching rebuttal came from James T. Farrell. To Farrell, the whole effort to explain the country's recalcitrance before Pearl Harbor in terms of the allegedly demoralizing effect of some of its fiction was as absurd as the earlier Marxist effort to develop a proletarian esthetic, which he, as a political radical, had reproached in the thirties. Literature, Farrell wrote, "must solve its own problems and . . . it cannot be turned into the mere handmaiden of politics and into a mere looking-glass of ideologies." Those who worried about the lack of moral, spiritual, or religious qualities in literature, who wished to narrow the writer's vision to fit preconceived values, were nothing more than "frightened Philistines."

While Farrell and many of his fellow writers were properly offended by the idea of putting literature into the conscious service of society, suggestions from other quarters that the visual arts could aid the war effort seemed more plausible. For architecture, in fact, there was never any doubt that wartime necessity would completely dominate taste and expression. Private building for commercial and residential purposes halted for the duration of the war. Professional architects, plagued throughout the thirties by the economic slump, now were expected to apply their imaginations to the urgent problems created by industry's need for rapid plant expansion and by the federal government's need for numerous housing projects for both military and civilian personnel.

The results of this period of frenzied construction, carried on across the nation as well as overseas, were highly dubious with regard to both esthetics and utility. Albert Kahn, one of the country's busiest industrial architects, claimed early in the war that the production crisis since 1940 had taught designers much about planning for future expansion, consolidating functions under one roof, eliminating space-wasting interior walls, and making construction uniform. But others criticized the lack of foresight in America's wartime industrial architecture, which usually just revised old building plans to meet new and sometimes radically different needs. Housing projects for war workers were commonly located some distance from plants; apparently little thought was given to the creation of well-planned industrial communities. The war housing itself, with a few exceptions, was accurately characterized by two architectural historians as "a dreary array of two-story houses and apartment buildings, crowding too many people on small sites. . . ." In general, the large individual public structures erected during the war years, usually as part of military installations, were undistinguished. War construction defaced a good portion of what remained of the American landscape and left a multitude of ugly "temporary" structures. An amazing number was still in use twenty years after the war.

By carrying millions of Americans into all parts of the world and exposing them to many new esthetic influences, the war enriched the architectural taste of the nation. Moreover, the war accelerated the development and use of new materials and techniques such as reinforced concrete, structural aluminum, bonded plywood, and prefabrication. Still another beneficial effect was the huge backlog of wealth which the wartime prosperity brought to firms and individuals. This, coupled with the hiatus in private commercial and residential construction, would produce an unprecedented peacetime building boom in which functionalism, inspired by the "International Style" of Le Courbusier and Walter Gropius, would be ascendant. At the end of the war, however, American architectural design was still an eclectic wonderland, a hodge podge of concepts and styles. A uniquely American style—the goal sought by many architects and architectural critics in the thirties—remained unreachable, but perhaps not the more modest goal of a land of attractive, comfortable places to live and work. "This is the country of tomorrow," wrote the critic G. E. Kidder Smith in the fall of 1945, "the land of progress and promise; the land, too, of miserable, hideous, unplanned cities, and miserly, confined and very poor buildings." That verdict could hardly be challenged a generation later.

It seemed that painters and sculptors, more rèadily than other kinds of artists, could use their talents to inspire Americans in the defense of democracy. The federal government did make a rather concerted effort to give painters a role in the war effort. Three days after Pearl Harbor the Office of Emergency Management initiated a campaign to secure works of art that could be used in war displays and advertisements. The OEM also hired painters to provide a steady stream of posters on a great variety of themes. Finally, the OEM engaged eight established artists, of whom the best known was Reginald Marsh, to sketch the progress being made on various classified military and industrial projects. The War Department went even further when, in 1942, it chose forty-two artists to travel overseas and describe actual combat scenes. This project was hardly underway when Congress cut its funds from the War Department's budget. All in all, the direct contribution of American artists to the war effort was not great; their work during the war, as Oliver H. Larkin has written, "reflected their own sense of responsibility rather than wide official recognition of their usefulness."

The people and artifacts of wartime America naturally provided many new subjects for American painters and sculptors; thus the war years, despite the continuation of the abstractionist revival which had begun in the late thirties, brought an increase in the number of strict realist, romantic realist, and expressionist works depicting the "real America." As early as February 1942 the National Art Gallery organized a traveling exhibition of paintings on subjects related to the war, collected from more than a thousand American artists. However patriotic the spirit of the exhibit may have been, the paintings themselves were mostly sober and often grim portrayals of a nation marshaling its energies for a protracted struggle. The exhibition, according to one critic, accurately reflected the mood of America, where "old-fashioned Fourth-of-July histrionics are absent. The theme is action today." About a year later the Metropolitan Museum of Art staged the largest and most ambitious of several "Artists for Victory" shows. The Metropolitan displayed the works of some 1,400 native-born painters and sculptors, whose thematically heterogeneous pieces, when taken together, were supposed to convey some sense of "what we are fighting for." The collection revealed much about the impact of the war on the artist's changing choice of subject—the increased attention to American Negro life, for example. Yet it was probably impossible to offer or to receive one overall conception in such an exhibition. The outstanding paintings were Ivan Le Lorraine Albright's morbidly suggestive *That Which I Should Have Done I Did Not Do,* which simply showed a wreath-laden door, and Jack Levine's heavily satirical *String Quartet.* Although these two pictures represented some of the best work of the war period, it was hard for most viewers to imagine what either had to do with the "good life" the nation was trying to preserve or the "better world" it hoped to achieve.

Music was probably the least affected of the traditional arts by the coming of war. Happily, there was no recurrence of the ridiculous bans on German music imposed by a xenophobic public during the First World War. One music critic, noting that the works of Italians like Verdi and Puccini and Germans like Beethoven, Wagner, and Richard Strauss were performed as frequently as ever, concluded in 1944 that, "in terms of the hysteria of the last war, the musical scene appears remarkably sober." One of the positive effects of the war on American musical taste was a wave of enthusiasm for the works of the best-known Russian composers, especially the contemporaries Sergei Prokofiev and Dimitri Shostakovich. The American composers Roy Harris and Morton Gould even wrote pieces to celebrate the heroism of Russia's army and people. The upsurge of patriotism which accompanied the war also made audiences and conductors more receptive to music by Americans. Whereas in 1939–1940 only eight per cent of the works performed by major orchestras in the United States were written by native-born composers, in 1942–1943 more than eleven per cent were American pieces and in 1943–1944 more than ten per cent. By the second season after the war, however, less American-written symphonic music was being played than before Pearl Harbor.

The fact that such statistics were kept pointed up the continuing preoccupation of composers and some critics with the disadvantages under which Americans worked and the obstacles to creating a truly American music. Native musical expression was still being frustrated, the music critic Alfred Frankenstein wrote late in 1943. While American works were played more frequently, conductors usually only offered short pieces or snips from longer ones. For the most part, audiences remained hostile to experimentation and to works by anyone except well-known Europeans. Frankenstein's complaint was a familiar one: "The American musical scene . . . is so cluttered up with masterpieces that the American composer with a new score under his arm is lucky if he makes his way into the concert hall by the tightest of squeezes."

Yet the years in which the nation was at war did see substantial progress toward the achievement of an independent, if not a definably national, music expression. Musical nationalists continued to be of two kinds: 'neutralists,' who simply wanted recognition for American-born composers, and 'Americanists,' who insisted that American composers should use native themes and try to incorporate native idioms. Probably the most successful of the Americanists in the early forties were Harris, who continued to rail against European domination of American music; Gould, who treated several Stephen Foster songs symphonically in *Foster Gallery* (1941), then the next year offered his stirring *An American Salute;* and Ernst Bacon, who dealt with various kinds of Americana in the suites *Ford's Theatre* and *From These States,* both completed in 1943, as well as an opera, *A Tree on the Plains* (1942).

Two musical forms in which American accomplishments had never been especially impressive were opera and ballet. For both the war period was a time of growing maturity and promise. Italian-born Gian-Carlo Menotti emerged as one of America's finest musical dramatists with his one-act tragedy *The Island God* (1942), although Menotti's best work was still to come. In general, American audiences seemed more willing than ever to listen to opera, with English libretti, written by their countrymen. The climate for American ballet also seemed more favorable by the early forties. For more than a decade the preeminent figure in American dance had been Martha Graham, whose highly innovative productions often used musical scores by outstanding composers. In 1944 Graham did the choreography and Paul Hindemith composed the score for *Herodiade;* that same year Graham collaborated with Aaron Copland on the much better-known *Appalachian Spring.* Copland, intensely aware of the need for giving theater and the films a meaningful musical orientation, also wrote the score for *Rodeo* (1942), an exuberant effort to depict a bit of Americana for which Agnes De Mille did the choreography.

Ballet soon became an important feature of musical comedy, the one form of traditional music in which, by the end of war, the United States was the unquestioned leader. In musical comedy—popularly designated "Broadway musicals"—the most prominent figures were Lorenz Hart, Richard Rodgers, and Oscar Hammerstein II. Far and away the foremost musical comedy of the early forties was Rodgers's and Hammerstein's *Oklahoma!* (1943), which had a six-year run on Broadway, several successful national tours, and numerous local revivals over the next two decades. Some critics denied that *Oklahoma!* was true Americana; it was, they said, only lively escapism, filled with equal portions of tartness and sentimentality. All reviewers, however, praised the choreography of Agnes De Mille, whose vigorous ballet sequences were so effectively integrated that they actually became an essential part of the story. In this sense *Oklahoma!* marked the beginning of a new era in musical productions.

For jazz, America's indigenous musical form, the war was also a period of innovation and transition, as more and more jazz musicians became restless under the dominance of swing. Eventually such men as the trumpeter Dizzy Gillespie, the saxophonist Charlie Parker, and the band leaders Earl Hines and Coleman Hawkins broke completely with the big-band arrangements, the smooth rhythms, and the vertical harmonies of swing. Seeking to combine individuality with a new complexity, they developed a style called "bebop" jazz, or simply "bop." At the end of the war the eclipse of swing was already underway, while Negro musicians had regained their central role in the evolution of the jazz form.

Popular Culture's Response

The forms of American popular culture—especially motion pictures—absorbed and diffused the experience of war, but received little inspiration from it. Just as Hollywood had eluded most of the realities of Depression America, so it refused to deal honestly with the realities of America at war. Hollywood producers and directors seemed to feel that they had done enough if they had the Americans utter school-boy platitudes and if they showed the Nazis as beastly, the Japanese as demonic, and the Russians and Chinese as valiant. "They did not perceive," Bosley Crowther commented, "that the thing was to give audiences a sense of the immense and impersonal conflict into which all peoples [had] been collectively drawn." About one-third of the films produced by Hollywood between 1942 and 1945 could be classed as "war movies." Almost all were romantic-adventure yarns, offering much patriotic bombast but little development of either characters or issues. A good example was Robert Rossen's and Lewis Milestone's version of *A Walk in the Sun* (1945), which turned out to be the usual stylized "action" film.

In their technical aspects the war pictures did improve rapidly, although for meaningful and comprehensive coverage of the war itself Hollywood drama could never equal the numerous newsreels and documentary films. Stimulated by the cataclysmic events at home and abroad, film journalism had already reached a high level of development before Pearl Harbor. But America's involvement in war rapidly accelerated the use of the motion picture camera as a reportorial device. Several Hollywood directors, notably John Huston, William Wyler, and Frank Capra, entered military service and arranged to make documentaries for their studios. The most impressive such undertaking was Capra's trilogy—*Prelude to War, The Battle of Russia,* and *War Comes to America*—put together from a huge amount of footage, mostly foreign-made, including the technically brilliant Nazi propaganda films. Of course the American government, especially the Office of War Information and the Office of Price Administration, also used propaganda films to great effect. For this purpose the Hollywood studios willingly made available their facilities.

Probably the most ambitious and certainly the most ballyhooed motion picture of the war years was Darryl F. Zanuck's *Wilson* (1944). A sprawling, confused venture, this film portrayed one of the most difficult figures of the twentieth century as an ordinary middle-class American and reduced the complex struggle over ratification of the League of Nations to the level of a personal quarrel between Wilson, the hero, and Henry Cabot Lodge, the villain. Yet *Wilson,* first appearing at most theaters early in 1945, not only helped solidify support among Americans for the inaugural session of the United Nations in San Francisco that April, but completed the wartime process by which Wilson's unfavorable historical image was reversed. It was an interesting example of Hollywood's power to destroy one set of myths, only to replace them with another.

For radio and printed journalism in America, the major consequences of the war lay in the successful handling of the prodigious reportorial problems it posed. On the whole, the reporting of the war by airwave and printed page was superlative and was made all the more remarkable by the global scope of military operations, communications difficulties, the personal hazards endured by war correspondents, and unprecedentedly systematic and severe government censorship. The radio and newspaper treatment of the mammoth amphibious invasion of France in June 1944 was especially thorough.

In other respects, however, the character of the American press and radio changed little during the early forties. No bright new magazines successfully challenged the established popular, semi-popular, and political weeklies and monthlies. The diminishing number of daily newspapers continued to offer a potpourri of news, editorials, sports, comics, features, and advertising. Syndicated newspaper columnists continued to reach tens of millions of faithful readers, but now even more people listened to the growing number of network news commentators and analysts. The radio networks also still carried most of the regular symphonic and operatic broadcasts initiated in the thirties. But radio theater, which had inspired such high hopes in the previous decade, lapsed into a dreary cycle of trite romances, adventures, and detective stories, broken by an occasional glimmer of promise like "The American Story," NBC's series of impressionistic historical dramas written by Archibald MacLeish. The bulk of the broadcast time of local stations consisted of evanescent popular ballads and insipid singing commercials, between which it was hard to make a qualitative judgment. At the end of the war radio's original promise seemed far—perhaps impossibly far—from fulfillment. "Radio is certainly getting no better," editorialized the *New Republic* early in 1945, "and many people believe it is getting worse. . . . The radio has become increasingly a device to sell goods by any means, fair or foul, while the question of usefulness to the public is more or less neglected."

Putting Science and Scholarship to Work

While there had been considerable discussion in the Depression years about how the natural and social sciences could serve the needs of the ailing nation, the material contributions that actually resulted were almost insignificant alongside the subsequent massive involvement of American professional scholars in the war effort. It would be hard to exaggerate the extent to which the military success of the United States and its allies came to depend on the rapid accumulation of applicable knowledge in the federal government's vast wartime research establishment. "The federal capital became the intellectual center of the nation," Merle Curti has written. The war "accelerated investigations in many fields, demonstrated new uses of existing knowledge, and proved that research and scholarship were as necessary to war as to peace." When in 1938 the National Resources Committee termed scientific research "a national resource," it was describing a hopeful potential more than a present reality. Up to that time, except for the brief period of the First World War, the federal government had done relatively little to marshal America's scientific and scholarly capabilities to promote the national welfare. Within eight years, however, nearly every American had come to realize how vital was organized and coordinated research to the nation's survival.

The year 1940 was a turning point in the history of American science, and especially in the history of the relationship between the natural sciences and the federal government. In that year of incipient rearmament and boom, the Roosevelt administration, by creating the National Defense Research Committee, began mobilizing the nation's scientific establishment for military purposes. Some seven months before Pearl Harbor, Roosevelt approved the creation of the Office of Scientific Research and Development as an operational agency alongside NDRC, which retained its advisory function. Headed by Vannevar Bush, president of the Carnegie Institution, OSRD was to organize and coordinate both militarily applicable research and engineering development. It was empowered to assess what the armed services needed, to override military opinion when it saw fit, and to do whatever was necessary to achieve weapons development as well as advances in military medicine.

Enlisting a substantial portion of the country's scientific personnel and supporting research at a large number of academic institutions, OSRD proceeded according to NDRC's original policy decision—to concentrate on work that would bear immediate fruits in weapons development. Thus while OSRD's triumphs were numerous and spectacular, they belonged properly to the area of applied science and invention and not to basic science, which seeks knowledge of the physical world for its own sake, without regard to actual or potential practical uses. Wartime scientific activity did almost nothing to advance the state of knowledge at the theoretical level. The brilliant progress in aeronautics, electronics, medicine, development of substitute materials, and weaponry overshadowed the fact that in such fields as genetics and astrophysics the war, by drawing off personnel and money, may actually have retarded the growth of information. For the first time, moreover, problems of government-imposed secrecy annoyed and sometimes hampered a large portion of the American scientific community.

The foremost accomplishment of American science during the war years was, of course, the development of the atomic bomb. The decision in 1941 to build an atomic fission weapon whose nuclear chain reaction would be derived from the uranium isotope U-235; the organization of United States, British, and Canadian scientists into the ultra-secret "Manhattan Engineer District," under OSRD; the attainment of the first controlled chain reaction at the University of Chicago late in 1942; the race to produce a bomb ahead of Nazi Germany; the successful testing of an atomic device in the New Mexico desert on July 16, 1945; and the deliberate decision to use the bomb against Japanese cities—these and other events make up a highly suspenseful story, one that has been well told several times and is familiar enough.

These are, however, a few points that should be emphasized. One is that the bomb was preeminently an achievement in administration, applied science, and technology, not basic science. From the time the Manhattan project was organized in 1942, through the frantic work of the next two years, to the assembly of the explosive device at Los Alamos, New Mexico, the principal tasks involved creating and coordinating a sprawling research apparatus, applying previously discovered principles and processes, and contriving detonation mechanisms. Secondly, despite the popular image of the atomic bomb as America's greatest feat in science, the truth is that a large percentage—perhaps a majority—of the scientists working at the core of the project were Europeans who had found refuge in this country before Pearl Harbor. It was ironic that such people should have escaped the most vicious regime in modern history, only to end up helping devise history's most frightful weapon for the United States, supposedly the last bulwark of civilization. Thirdly, the bomb project made Americans more aware than ever before of the inextricable relationship between scientific prowess and modern military might. As a consequence, scientists, especially physicists, emerged from the war as mystically heroic figures, beneficiaries of a popular adulation that would mount steadily in the postwar decades. Finally, this war-inspired adulation would be a vital factor in winning postwar support for the long-term, generous federal subsidy for research in the natural sciences which Bush advocated in his 1945 report to Roosevelt, *Science—the Endless Frontier.*

During the war the nation's men of science worked willingly for the federal government, motivated by the kind of devotion to the welfare of the nation and to human betterment that Karl T. Compton had talked about in the Depression period. In the postwar years tens of thousands of them would remain in the service of the government —and thus presumably of American society—either as outright employees of federal agencies and the armed forces or as recipients of federal grants and contracts. For them secrecy, traditionally thought of as the mortal enemy of true science, would become the normal condition, while intellectual independence, science's traditional imperative, would become a steadily diminishing quality.

The contributions of the social sciences to the war effort were less glittering than those of the natural sciences, but perhaps no less important. More than ten thousand specialists in the social science disciplines—economists, political scientists, psychologists, sociologists, anthropologists, even some historians—left behind their academic and professional employments to work with a multiplicity of government agencies. The number of economists and administrative experts in the Roosevelt administration was already large at the time of Pearl Harbor; the war brought many more into the councils of government. Political scientists studied and made recommendations for administering the welter of new wartime agencies and providing effective military governments in occupied countries. Economists influenced decisions on a wide variety of matters, such as allocations of materials and labor, wage and price controls, rationing, taxation, export and import restrictions, and investment practices. "This was positive economics on a grand scale," one economist has written, "and the whole complex afforded a magnificent model for the testing of economic hypotheses across the board. . . . You can learn quite a lot about . . . an economy—by trying to run one."

By 1945 about four-fifths of all the psychologists in the United States were involved in one way or another with the federal government; some 1,700 were employed by the military services. Psychologists and sociologists developed aptitude tests and placement procedures for the War Manpower Commission, analyzed Axis propaganda, improved government and military techniques of mass persuasion, and trained prospective administrators for occupied areas. Never before had there been such attention to problems of motivation and morale, for both civilian and military personnel. Meanwhile scholars in the relatively new field of cultural anthropology adapted the "national character" approach to improve America's understanding of itself, its allies, and its enemies. The broad aim of this "therapeutic" anthropology of wartime was the same as that of the "pure research" of peacetime—to achieve, in Margaret Mead's words, "an integrating system of values as almost an abstract synonym for the culture as a whole"—but the foremost consideration was the immediate applicability of anthropological findings for military and diplomatic purposes. Cultural anthropologists, working for the State and War Departments as well as independently, tried to define and analyze the "cultural constellations" of the Japanese, the Germans, and the British, and also studied factors of cultural diversity in relation to the problems of postwar international organization. Scholars even compiled thick treatises on the Burmese and Thais, although, surprisingly, almost no attention was given to Russian national traits.

At the end of the war there remained little doubt that social science could aid mightily in solving concrete, vital problems of concern to all Americans. For people like Stuart Chase, the war provided a graphic demonstration of what the organized, purposeful investigation of man's social conduct could accomplish. The war experience seemed to make more plausible the bright dream of a "science of society," one of the principal intellectual legacies of the nineteenth century. Despite the imponderables of human behavior, despite the lack of agreement on how men were supposed to behave, despite a seeming infinitude of obstacles to creating a scientifically ordered world, Chase and others continued to believe that through "the proper study of mankind" the dream could be realized.

Education and Religion: The Search Continues

During the 1930s both educational theory and theology in America had been subjected to stringent criticism by scholars dissatisfied with the set of optimistic, positivistic assumptions that underlay prevalent patterns of belief. By 1941 the generalist movement in education and the neo-orthodox movement in theology, both embodying a search for fundamental values in an era of chaotic change, had established themselves as powerful influences in the American consciousness. Four years later, at war's end, neo-orthodoxy was ascendant in Protestant thought. By contrast, the general education movement, hampered by a host of difficulties spawned by the war emergency, seemed to have lost some of its momentum. But then so had its antithesis, progressive education.

Like the thirties, the Second World War was a time of great material privation for education in the United States. In 1946 Benjamin Fine summarized the war's deleterious effects: "The war damaged our teaching staff; it depleted the ranks of our best teachers. Men and women left the classroom and were replaced by those less competent. It permitted the school plant to deteriorate; it cut supplies and equipment necessary for educational progress." The shortage of teachers in public schools, colleges, and universities was the gravest problem created by the war. Within a matter of three years or so, the dismal surplus of the Depression decade became a desperate scarcity as masses of male teachers entered the armed services and as both men and women found better-paying jobs in goverment agencies or war industries. The war boom demonstrated, as had nothing before, the essentially unstable and transient nature of the teaching profession in America.

The war also disclosed some rather startling facts about the shortcomings of the nation's multifarious educational system. At the end of the war the Selective Service System reported that some 676,000 men were rejected for the draft as "functional illiterates," which meant that they had less than four years of schooling. But it was also apparent that eleven or twelve years of formal education still left much to be desired as far as military fitness and intelligent citizenship were concerned. Shortly before Pearl Harbor, Admiral Chester W. Nimitz reported that on the standard examination given by the Naval Reserve Officers Training Corps to 4,200 freshmen at 27 well-known universities, 62 per cent failed all sections. The next year the *New York Times* found a dismaying ignorance of elementary United States history among some 7,000 students in 36 colleges and universities. A study committee formed by the American Historical Association, the Mississippi Valley Historical Association, and the National Council for the Social Studies blamed the widespread lack of knowledge of the nation's past on teachers and methods in the public schools, a conclusion that, as Isaac L. Kandel has remarked, "would have been reached if any other subject had been investigated." The underlying trouble was not so much the inadequacy of elementary and secondary school history teachers, or even the 'pragmatic' merger of history with other subjects into an amorphism called "social studies," but rather the anti-historical attitudes of the American people, who, for all their worship of national heroes and traditions, really refused to understand the indissoluble unity of past and present.

During the war the federal government did make a heavy—if mostly temporary—contribution to American education. The Army and Navy took up some of the slack caused by an almost 50 per cent drop in total civilian college enrollment by organizing specialized military training programs at nearly 500 insititutions of higher learning. At the end of 1944 about 380,000 service trainees were enrolled in such studies. Much broader was the program of the Armed Forces Institute, which, working with the Extension Division of the University of Wisconsin, set up correspondence courses for servicemen at home and overseas, and on-site instruction for those in isolated areas. Altogether, the Armed Forces Institute and its 83 contracting institutions offered 275 courses to about 1,800,000 servicemen. By

1944 the federal government's expenditures on educational projects equaled the total outlays of all colleges and universities, state governments, and local communities. That year Congress, in offering cash subsidies to returning veterans who wished to further their educations (the so-called "G.I. Bill of Rights"), administered a powerful tonic to postwar college enrollments.

This government-financed expansion of technically oriented instruction in American colleges and universities was the main reason for the mounting vehemence of the controversy over the purposes and composition of America's higher learning. After Pearl Harbor those who, in the thirties, had bemoaned the excess of materialism and the absence of a guiding philosophy in the nation's educational system became alarmed and indignant when hundreds of institutions eagerly affiliated with the various military training programs, accepted large infusions of federal money, and began offering a flock of courses in such fields as radar electronics, explosive chemistry, and military government. The general education movement now enlisted the backing of a sizable number of educators and scholars who earlier had watched with interest, but not wholly approved, the efforts of Robert M. Hutchins and his associates at the University of Chicago and elsewhere to establish a "common learning" derived from medieval scholasticism.

Although Hutchins, Mortimer Adler, Mark Van Doren, and others continued to push for curricular reorganization around the "intellectual verities" of Western Civilization, the main problem seemed to be the danger that such disciplines as classical languages, literature, history, and philosophy—collectively known as the "humanities"—would be overwhelmed in the rush to enthrone the sciences, engineering, and other 'practical' areas of study. Would not the traditional liberal education, already proscribed by more than two generations of increasing atomization and commercialization in the bachelor of arts curriculum, be driven permanently into exile? How could the small liberal arts college, historically the backbone of the humanities, survive the conscription of students and teachers and the diversion of money and energy to fields that would supposedly yield an immediate dividend for the war effort? How, in fact, could American democracy survive if it abandoned its intellectual foundations, if it allowed to fall into decay the substance of what Hutchins called "education for freedom"? If that happened, wrote the philosopher Irwin Edman, "We should then have a generation that would have no use for political freedom because it had lost a care for and a discipline in those arts and interests which constitute a free mind."

The war undoubtedly put the humanities at a severe disadvantage. Several liberal arts colleges closed down; many others averted disaster only because they maintained fairly large enrollments of women. The longstanding American apotheosis of the useful and practical—of whatever served the material interests of society—probably reached a peak between 1942 and 1945. Howard Mumford Jones described what had happened by the fall of 1943: "In the colleges and universities . . . the liberal arts were adjourned for the duration, English teachers were a dime a dozen, and the demand for physicists, chemists, mathematicians, economists, and 'Government experts' [could] not be filled." Some scholars in the humanities nevertheless came to the defense of the wartime reorientation of American higher education. Early in the war, for example, Horace M. Kallen of the New School for Social Research argued that since a democracy must sometimes defend itself, academicians should accept wars as an element in the maintenance of human freedom. "Might it not be . . . true," asked Kallen, "that to cut off and isolate the military virtues and the arts of war is . . . mistaken and self-defeating?" The philosopher George Boas bluntly summed up what most people felt about education's wartime role: "If training men in trigonometry and physics and chemistry, to the detriment of the humanities, will win the war, then for God's sake and our own, let us forget our Greek, our Latin, our art, our literature, our history, and get to business learning trigonometry and physics and chemistry."

Although somewhat overshadowed by the debate over the place of the humanities in the war, the attacks on progressive educational theory commenced during the preceding decade gathered force in the early forties. In 1944, as the exchange between friends and foes of progressivism became more intense, the educator Wilbur A. Yauch remarked wryly that "World War II is in grave danger of being relegated to second-page publicity if the present battle in education continues to rage and mount in fury." The complaints against progressivism continued to pile up: The wartime increase in juvenile delinquency, for example, supposedly resulted from the failure of progressive-dominated schools to instill the proper amount of discipline in the nation's youth, while the poor performance of inductees on intelligence and aptitude tests was blamed on progressivism's alleged disdain for subjects with intellectual backbone.

The war itself hurt the progressive education movement, both materially and philosophically. In the first place, the shortage of teachers and other privations imposed on the public schools diminished the opportunity for experimentation with progressive theory. It was probably true that, as Yauch said, no more than three per cent of all the public schools had "effectively" applied progressive principles. Secondly, progressive education had always consisted of two partially contradictory integrants: an emphasis on the practical consequences of learning and a concern that the individual be free to discover his own interests and aptitudes. The war not only pushed scientific and technical instruction to the forefront in higher education, but it imparted an urgent sense of direction to the entire educational system of the country. The times were highly unpropitious for broad-ranging interests and free discovery. In other words, the war exalted social-service progressivism, expounded so forcefully by George S. Counts in the thirties, while it further constricted individualistic progressivism, which had dominated theory in the twenties and still had many followers among administrators and teachers in the forties. No wonder that the membership of the Progessive Education Association dwindled steadily after Pearl Harbor, until in 1944 the remaining members, trying to broaden the appeal of their organization, changed the name to American Education Fellowship.

Amidst the steady wartime clamor over education, Harvard University tried nobly to achieve some kind of synthesis. In 1943 President James Bryant Conant of Harvard chose a committee from his faculty to take "a total view of the total American educational scene" and to draw up recommendations which could serve as a basis for revitalizing learning at all levels. After two years of work, the Committee published its findings under the title *General Education in a Free Society*. Noting the obvious absence of a cohesive educational philosophy in America, the Committee offered "the sense of heritage" as the key to such a philosophy. The Committee's conception of heritage embodied not only the humanities but the other two "great divisions" of knowledge, the natural and social sciences. By reconciling the "pattern and direction" of the humanities with the "sense of experiment and innovation" of the sciences, American education would be able to fulfill its true task: to give both the three-fourths of the youths who stopped with a high school diploma and the one-fourth who went on to college "some common and binding understanding of the society which they will possess in common."

Beyond its hardly arguable generalities, the Harvard report contributed few fresh ideas and often contradicted itself. The report said very little about elementary education, which had traditionally been of greatest concern to progressivists. With regard to higher education, the report attacked both the pure elective system, which (except at a few small colleges) had been on the wane for decades, and the system of early and intensive specialization in "major" fields. The pursuit of strictly utilitarian knowledge, at any level, came in for criticism, but the Harvard Committee also recognized the need for technical training, especially for those who had no plans for college. On one hand, the Committee deplored the plethora of methods courses required of prospective teachers; on the other, the inadequacy of teacher-training. The Committee recommended more attention in high school to the natural sciences and languages, but apparently thought enough time was given to the study of history and government. At the college level, there should be a common core of "general" subjects required of all students in addition to subsequent specialized study. This last recommendation actually described curricular development in most of the nation's colleges and universities over the previous generation.

Not surprisingly, the Harvard report provoked much commentary, pleased scarcely anyone, and settled nothing. In the postwar period armies of theories would continue to fight what Conant called the "academic civil war," with hardly a lull for the reconversion to peacetime operations. Professors of pedagogy in teachers colleges and public-school administrators would continue to blame rigid college entrance requirements for preventing the schools from implementing progressive principles. Scholars in the humanities and natural sciences would continue to regard progressivists with suspicion and hostility while they virtually ignored what was actually happening in the secondary schools. Ten years after the end of the war, still another White House Conference on Education began by asking "What should our schools accomplish?" The question indicated that, as Kandel said, "after nearly fifty years of extensive discussion and the growth of a vast educational literature, the issue . . . remained unsettled."

The effect of the war on American religion and religious thought was primarily to accelerate trends that were already in motion at the time of Pearl Harbor. The war shattered what was left of Christian pacifism in the United States. Protestant ministers, many of whom only a few years earlier had vowed never again to "bless a war," now wedded themselves to the national cause and, at least for the time being, accepted the necessity of force to defend the homeland. The leaders of American Judaism enthusiastically supported what was for them literally a holy war, a struggle to prevent the obliteration of the Jewish people and religion. The war received the full backing of the Roman Catholic hierarchy and laity in America, despite the fact that Mussolini had made Catholicism the official state religion in Italy. Memories of the Church's equivocal attitude toward the Spanish Civil War partly explained the continuation of widespread anti-Catholic feeling in America (although during the war the Roosevelt administration, striving to insure Spain's neutrality, frowned on open criticism of the Franco government).[3] Another reason for the persistent abrasiveness of Protestant-Catholic and Jewish-Catholic relations was the reluctance of the Vatican to issue a forthright condemnation of the mounting atrocities perpetrated by the Nazis against Jews throughout Europe. Anti-Catholicism had always been a fact of religious, social, and political life in America, and not even the surging national unity inspired by the war could wipe out three centuries and more of distrust. For both servicemen and civilians, however, the viscissitudes of war enlarged contacts and undoubtedly helped improve relations between the nation's Protestants, Catholics, and Jews.

In fact, it seems that the war, the climax to a long succession of twentieth-century social disasters, considerably enhanced the appeal of Catholic theology in America. A growing number of intellectuals heard, read, and accepted the teachings of the French neo-Thomist philosopher Jacques Maritain, who remained in the United States after his country fell to the Nazis, held wartime professorships at Princeton and Columbia universities, and after the war became a member of Princeton's Institute for Advanced Study. Maritain's writings made no lasting impact on American technical philosophy and apparently had little direct relationship to the growth of the generalist movement in educational theory. Yet the favorable reception accorded him and the continuing popularity of his works did impart new freshness and vigor to Roman Catholic thought in this country. Contending that materialism and self-glorification had sapped European society and led to its downfall, Maritain called upon the democratic West to lead a spiritual revival based on the unchanging principles of natural law. By the end of 1945 some sort of revival appeared to be already underway. Not only had the number of Catholic converts increased, but the membership of almost all religious bodies in America had begun to rise dramatically.

The war also speeded the triumph of the neo-orthodox movement in American Protestant theology. In 1943 Reinhold Niebuhr published the second volume of *The Nature and Destiny of Man,* a ponderously written but persuasive analysis of original sin, the inevitable tragedy of human existence, and the necessity for seeking God's redemptive grace. The war seemed to demonstrate conclusively that Niebuhr and his American and Continental counterparts were right: Basic evil did exist and was everywhere present; man's reliance on reason, love, and faith in progress was futile. The end of the war found liberal theology clearly on the defensive, struggling to find intellectually and spiritually acceptable answers in a world in turmoil.

The End in Sight

There was, of course, no necessary connection between the new, 'realistic' theology and political conservatism. Niebuhr's political writings and activities demonstrated that. Yet the period of the Second World War, in which theological liberalism began to yield ground to neo-orthodoxy, also saw the inception of a vigorous assault on the ideological framework of political liberalism. Since four or five years before Pearl Harbor, a rightwing element, made up of most northern Republicans and most southern Democrats, had held the balance of power in Congress. The strength of this "conservative coalition" after the 1938 congressional elections was probably the main reason why Roosevelt, at the beginning of 1939, gave up trying to extend the New Deal and focused his attention on the approaching war in Europe and the actual war in Asia. Hopes that the nation, if it became involved, would fight a "New Deal war," with the management of the war economy in the hands of economic and social reformers, were dashed when Roosevelt turned to conservative industrialists, financiers, and merchandisers for advice and administrative expertise in gearing the nation for defense production. Roosevelt may have maintained ultimate control over his sprawling wartime administrative empire, but the nation's business elite—its "dollar-a-year men"—actually managed the production effort.

The resurgence of conservative influence in Washington in the early forties was accompanied by the appearance of a body of systematic, forceful rightist political literature. In the vanguard of American conservatism's ideological offensive were two European-born thinkers, Peter Drucker and Frederick A. von Hayek. Drucker, a native of Germany, had immigrated to England to escape Naziism, then come to the United States as a resident newspaper correspondent. In his first book, *The End of Economic Man* (1939), he explained the rise of fascism as a result of the breakdown of the rationalistic nineteenth-century belief in the supremacy of economic over social values. Three years later, in *The Future of Industrial Man,* he sought an organizing substitute for the long-lost pursuit of personal interest in the free market-place, and thus a way to counteract the destruction of individual function and status, the shift of controlling power from property-holding to management, and the growth of suffusive corporate and government bureaucracies. Rejecting both centralized economic planning, which he thought led to unlimited governmental power, and business dominance, which would only enthrone the corporate managers, he called for "the development of the [industrial] plant into a self-governing community," featuring "neither total planning nor the restoration of nineteenth-century laissez-faire, but the organization of industry on the basis of local and decentralized self-government." Thus could the conservative principles of personal freedom and collective order be accomodated to modern industrialism. Although Drucker's proposal for a kind of capitalist syndicalism held little appeal for rightist critics of the New Deal, who thought mainly of turning the clock back to the 1920s, he did offer a sophisticated analysis of industrial society and a strong argument against the further centralization of economic planning.

Less sagacious, but much more effective as a conservative call to arms, was Hayek's *The Road to Serfdom* (1944). Hayek, an Austrian economist living in England, dedicated his book to "the socialists of all parties," especially the members of the British Labor party. Yet, significantly, the book had its largest readership in the United States, where it was condensed in the *Reader's Digest* and sold through the Book-of-the-Month Club.[4] Hayek's message was that totalitarian political systems inevitably sprang from the centralization of economic planning in the national government. This was what had happened in Germany, Italy, and Russia; and, if the trend toward planning continued, the peoples of the remaining democracies would find themselves reduced to the same condition of twentieth-century serfdom. Although Hayek added nothing new to the planning debate of the Depression years, the enthusiastic audiences he drew on a whirlwind lecture tour of the United States in the spring of 1945 furnished a harsh reminder that the issues raised by the New Deal were by no means dead, but only awaiting noisy revival in the postwar years.

Uncertainty regarding postwar economic conditions—and the extent to which the government would have to continue to shore up the economy—was one problem on the minds of Americans in midsummer 1945, with Germany conquered and the end of the war in sight. The sociologist Eli Ginzberg reported a strong undercurrent of anxiety among servicemen: ". . . when they talk of peace, they are uneasy. These soldiers recall that the country fumbled badly in coming to grips with the scourge of peace—unemployment. . . . they wonder what will happen when they have won the victory on the battlefield." But even if the country managed to avoid a postwar depression, would the final defeat of the Axis bring the peace and security Americans longed for? There were already indications from the new Truman administration that the alliance with the Soviets was breaking up; the Potsdam Conference of July and August, despite its facade of Big Three unity, only raised further doubts. China, even before the expulsion of the Japanese, was about to renew a civil war which had never really ended, and which would blast America's dream for a strong, democratic nation developing under its tutelage.

The postwar world would be different; there was no doubt of that. But would it be better? Would America be any better? What most people wanted, after all, was the kind of country Irwin Shaw's soldiers imagined in *The Young Lions* (1948): ". . . an America of friends and neighbors, an America in which a man could finally put away his overcivilized doubts, his book-soured cynicism, his realistic despair, and humbly and gratefully lose himself." It was not a matter of trying to withdraw from the rest of the world. America had responsibilities—global ones—that it could not shirk. But surely there would be peace. Surely the Americans, the British, and the Russians, having formed the mightiest military combination in history and having won the most terrible of wars, could find some way to cooperate in achieving the kind of "world community" the United Nations promised but had not yet made a reality.

There remained one enemy to destroy. Japan still would not surrender, even though its naval and air forces were wiped out, most of its cities were reduced to wasteland, and it faced full-scale invasion. The extent to which the Japanese government was seeking a negotiated peace in the summer of 1945, the nature of Japanese peace overtures in relation to the American insistence on "unconditional surrender," the problem of getting Japan's military leaders to accept any agreement to stop the fighting—these and other matters, despite considerable investigation by historians, have never been wholly cleared up. In retrospect, it seems proper to say that before August 1945 the United States government, which almost unilaterally determined Anglo-American policy toward Japan, could have tried at least as hard to end the war, even if it had to hedge on the unconditional surrender doctrine, as it tried to get the Soviet Union to enter the conflict. It is also probably true that the United States, even if it refused to negotiate, could have eventually brought Japan to its knees through a total blockade combined with continued aerial and naval bombardment. Instead, President Truman endorsed the views of those military experts who were convinced of the necessity for an all-out assault on the Japanese home islands. The whole point of bringing the Russians into the war against Japan was to avoid the estimated one million casualties American forces would otherwise suffer in the final subjugation of the islands.

After July 16, when an atomic device was successfully detonated in New Mexico, there was a fourth alternative, and President Truman speedily chose it. At Potsdam later that month the United States and its allies warned the Japanese to submit or face "prompt and utter destruction." On August 6, having received no explicit response to its cryptic warning, the United States destroyed the city of Hiroshima with a single atomic bomb. Eight days later, after another bomb had laid waste to Nagasaki, Japan surrendered.

Eighty-five per cent of those polled by the American Institute of Public Opinion shortly after the Hiroshima blast approved of the use of the bomb; the percentage of college-educated interviewees who approved was even higher. The emotional steam roller of total war had carried American thinking a long way since the late thirties. The people of the United States had begun with certain assumptions about the way wars should and should not be fought. Women, children, and old men, they felt, should be kept out of the fighting as much as possible; schools, hospitals, and places of worship should not be damaged. Consequently Americans reacted with feelings of horror and indignation when German, Italian, and Japanese aircraft indiscriminately bombed civilian populations. Pearl Harbor did a lot to change American minds. Late in March 1942 an AIPO poll indicated that more than two-thirds of the people favored "an all-out war including bombing of Japanese cities." By 1943 Americans had accepted fully the logic of the advocates of "strategic bombing," who argued that, through unrestricted, "saturation" bombardment of cities, the enemy's will to fight could be broken, the war significantly shortened, and American lives saved. They came to regard the killing of hundreds of thousands of German and Japanese civilians (more than 80,000 in the incendiary raid on Tokyo, May 9 and 10, 1945, alone) as a necessary, even morally defensible, part of modern warfare. In August 1945, therefore, there were no remaining moral impediments to the use of the atomic bomb, whose destructive potential, though measured in tons of TNT, was a vastly different order from what would soon be labeled "conventional" weaponry.

But even if Truman and his military advisers had had the same scruples that troubled some of those who made the bomb, it seems unlikely the United States could have refrained indefinitely from using it. In view of the fact that thousands of people, including members of both parties in Congress, knew about the bomb project and at least partially understood its nature, it is doubtful that the "best-kept secret of the war" could have remained a secret. As the war dragged on and as huge sums of national treasure—if not American lives—continued to be expended, there would probably have developed some sort of public awareness that the United States had a new weapon which, if used, would quickly end the war and bring American boys home. When that happened, the people of America, consumed by violent hatred for the Japanese, would almost certainly have demanded that the bomb be dispatched—and immediately. The momentum of the steam roller had become irresistible.

At war's end Americans stood blinking in the glare of the atomic era. They felt an overriding uneasiness. The war not only left them with the burdens of world power and leadership, but it stripped them of a great deal of their claim to moral primacy and historical uniqueness. They were about to enter a time of terror, the terror of the weapon they had first made and alone used. After Hiroshima more and more American intellectuals, while they continued to view the relativist approach as a useful adjunct to the scientific method, would begin to seek universal standards that could become the basis for understanding and peaceful exchange between diverse peoples.

There could be no quarreling with the declaration of Norman Cousins, editor of the *Saturday Review of Literature*, that "Modern man is obsolete." But how could mankind—how could America—remake itself? In the postwar decades some Americans would come to understand the dichotomy Reinhold Niebuhr had drawn in 1944 between "the children of light," the naive devotees of humane reason and collective betterment, and the "children of darkness," the moral cynics for whom self-interest and power were the sole determinants. In the conduct of their public affairs they would actually achieve something like the synthesis Niebuhr urged. They would perhaps come to realize that the search for a stable international order was, as Niebuhr said, "the perpetual problem as well as the constant fulfillment of human hopes."

Yet, for all their increased maturity and realism, their frequent frustrations and anguish, Americans would keep the vision of a nation living in peace, enjoying material abundance, and offering opportunity for full achievement to all its citizens. Abroad they would often try to remold distant and strange cultures in their own image. Nearly a generation after Hiroshima, with America locked in Vietnam in its fourth major war of the twentieth century, some of them would find new meaning in what Thomas Wolfe had written about his country and his countrymen:

> All we know is that having everything we yet hold nothing, that feeling the wild song of this great earth upwelling in us we have no word to give it utterance. All we know is that here the passionate enigma of our lives is so bitterly expressed, the furious hunger that so haunts and hurts Americans so desperately felt—that being rich, we all are yet poor, that having an incalculable wealth we have no way of spending it, that feeling illimitable power we yet have found no way of using it.

Notes

1. In this book Spykman disagreed with the famous British geopolitician Halford J. Mackinder, who had contended for forty years that the critical factor in world power was control of the Eurasian "heartland." Spykman thought con-

trol of the "Rimland" of Europe and Asia determined which nation would dominate the world. Presumably the United States, through its naval might, would be in a position to control the Rimland region.

2. It should be kept in mind that Lippmann used the term "nuclear alliance" in the sense of organizational "nucleus," not nuclear armaments.
3. In line with the circumspect official policy toward Spain, Hollywood, always sensitive to State Department wishes, omitted all references to places and sides in the film version of Hemingway's *For Whom the Bell Tolls* (1943).
4. Hayek was not completely unknown in the United States before the war; Walter Lippmann, in his preface to *The Good Society* in 1937, had acknowledged the influence of Hayek's writings.

Bibliography

What follows is by no means an exhaustive list of publications relating to the intellectual and cultural history of the United States for the years 1930–1945. Such a compilation would include most of the editorials, articles, and reviews appearing in such periodicals as the *Nation, New Republic, Saturday Review of Literature, School and Society, Radical Religion,* and *Partisan Review,* as well as a good portion of the books written during the period. This is a topically arranged commentary which deals mostly with the secondary works that have been of greatest utility for understanding the ideational context of recent American history and the developments in attitudes, ideas, and art described in this book.

General Works

Nearly every bibliography in American intellectual history begins by mentioning four surveys: Merle Curti, *The Growth of American Thought* (3rd ed., New York: Harper and Row, Publishers, 1964); Ralph H. Gabriel, *The Course of American Democratic Thought: An Intellectual History since 1815* (2nd ed., New York: The Ronald Press Company, 1956); Henry Steele Commager, *The American*

Mind: An Interpretation of American Thought and Character since the 1880's (New Haven: Yale University Press, 1950); and Stow Persons, *American Minds: A History of Ideas* (New York: Holt, Rinehart and Winston, Inc., 1958). My own approach has probably been influenced most by Curti, who describes his work as "a social history of American thought" which emphasizes "the functional or instrumental nature of intellectual activities within changing social climates and shifting situations. . . ." Other broad treatments include Nelson M. Blake, *A History of American Life and Thought* (New York: McGraw-Hill, Inc., 1963) and Harvey Wish, *Society and Thought in Modern America* (2nd ed., 2 vols., New York: David McKay Co., Inc., 1962), vol. II, both of which are a great deal more "life" than "thought." Russell B. Nye's *This Almost Chosen People: Essays in the History of American Ideas* (East Lansing: Michigan State University Press, 1966) is insightful and interesting, as is Richard Hofstadter's *Anti-intellectualism in American Life* (New York: Alfred A. Knopf, Inc., 1963), which has much to say about America's "practical culture." In *American Nationalism: An Interpretive Essay* (New York: The Macmillan Company, 1957), Hans Kohn is not as perceptive as he should be for the twentieth century. Four useful symposia, consisting of essays by scholars from various disciplines, are: Robert E. Spiller and Eric Larrabee, eds., *American Perspectives: The National Self-Image in the Twentieth Century* (Cambridge: Harvard University Press, 1961); Elting Morrison, ed., *The American Style: Essays in Value and Performance* (New York: Harper & Row, Publishers, 1958); Michael McGiffert, ed., *The Character of Americans* (Homewood: Dorsey Press, 1964); and Arthur M. Schlesinger, Jr., and Morton White, eds., *Paths of American Thought* (Boston: Houghton Mifflin Company, 1963). Interesting slants on American attitudes and ideals can be gained from the widely different books of two Englishmen: Denis W. Brogan, *The American Character* (New York: Alfred A. Knopf, Inc., 1944) and Harold J. Laski, *The American Democracy* (New York: The Viking Press, 1948). David D. Van Tassel, ed., *American Thought in the Twentieth Century* (New York: Thomas Y. Crowell Company, 1967) and Gerald N. Grob and Robert N. Beck, eds., *American Ideas* (2 vols., New York: Free Press of Glencoe, 1963), vol. II: *Dilemmas of Maturity (1850–1962)* present helpful selections of source material.

The study of American ideas and art in the 1930s and 1940s can be approached through a number of general accounts. Frederick Lewis

Allen's *Since Yesterday: The Nineteen Thirties in America* (New York: Harper & Row, Publishers, 1940) is neither as spritely nor as cogent as his *Only Yesterday* (New York: Harper & Row, Publishers, 1931) on the twenties. Dixon Wecter's *Age of the Great Depression, 1929–1941* (New York: The Macmillan Company, 1948) is a valuable survey, especially good on popular culture, but it lacks perspective. George E. Mowry, *The Urban Nation, 1920–1960* (New York: Hill and Wang, Inc., 1965) and David A. Shannon, *Between the Wars: America, 1919–1941* (Boston: Houghton Mifflin Company, 1965) touch on political and social thought, the arts, religion, education, and the growth of a mass culture; while Leo Gurko, *The Angry Decade* (New York: Dodd, Mead & Company, 1947) emphasizes social consciousness in literature. Fred J. Ringel, ed., *America as Americans See It* (New York: Literary Guild, 1932) and Harold E. Stearns, ed., *America Now: An Inquiry into Civilization in the United States* (New York: Literary Guild, 1938) present contemporary essays on numerous aspects of American culture in the thirties. The serious, subdued tone of the latter volume should be contrasted with the sardonic *Civilization in the United States* (New York: Harcourt, Brace & World, Inc., 1922), edited by Stearns at the height of intellectual disillusionment after the First World War. Charles and Mary Beard's *America in Midpassage* (2 vols., New York: The Macmillan Company, 1939) is an excellent digest of what was happening throughout American life in the thirties. Its vintage and pronounced leftism should not cause this work to fall into disuse. Murray Kempton helps to illumine various figures and facets of the decade in *Part of Our Time: Some Ruins and Monuments of the Thirties* (New York: Simon and Schuster, Inc., 1955), as does the symposium edited by Rita J. Simon, *As We Saw the Thirties* (Urbana: University of Illinois Press, 1967). Two of the best of several anthologies on the Depression decade are edited by Don Congdon—*The Thirties: A Time to Remember* (New York: Simon and Schuster, Inc., 1962)—and by Milton Crane—*The Roosevelt Era* (New York: Boni and Gaer, 1947).

Chapter I
Depression Years: New Era, New Nationalisms

For moving impressions of the social impact of the Great Depression, see Edmund Wilson, *The American Jitters: A Year of the Slump* (New York: Charles Scribner's Sons, 1932); Gilbert Seldes, *The Years of the Locust* (Boston: Little Brown and Company, 1933); Louis Adamic, *My America, 1928–1938* (New York: Harper & Row, Publishers, 1938); and David A. Shannon, ed., *The Great Depression* (Englewood Cliffs: Prentice-Hall, Inc., 1960). The economic history of the thirties is meticulously treated in Broadus Mitchell, *Depression Decade: From New Era Through New Deal, 1929–1941* (New York: Holt, Rinehart and Winston, Inc., 1947). The intellectual origins of the New Deal and the critical responses it evoked from many American leftists are analyzed in Arthur M. Schlesinger, Jr., *The Age of Roosevelt* (3 vols. to date, Boston: Houghton Mifflin Company, 1957–1960); Schlesinger, "Sources of the New Deal," in Schlesinger and White, eds., *Paths of American Thought;* William E. Leuchtenberg, "The New Deal and the Analogue of War," in John Braeman *et al.*, eds., *Change and Continuity in Twentieth Century America* (Columbus: Ohio State University Press, 1964); Leuchtenberg, *Franklin D. Roosevelt and the New Deal, 1932–1940* (New York: Harper & Row, Publishers, 1963), far and away the best single volume on the New Deal era; Paul K. Conkin, *The New Deal* (New York: Thomas Y. Crowell Company, 1967), a lively and provocative extended essay; Otis L. Graham, *An Encore for Reform: The Old Progressives and the New Deal* (New York: Oxford University Press, 1967); Eric F. Goldman, *Rendezvous with Destiny: A History of Modern American Reform* (New York: Alfred A. Knopf, Inc., 1952); and Bernard Sternsher, *Rexford G. Tugwell and the New Deal* (New Brunswick: Rutgers University Press, 1964). Two excellent monographs which trace the development of New Deal thinking on particular problems are Ellis W. Hawley, *The New Deal and the Problem of Monopoly* (Princeton: Princeton University Press, 1966) and Richard S. Kirkendall, *Social Scientists and Farm Politics in the Age of Roosevelt* (Columbia: University of Missouri Press, 1966). On the role of the closed frontier idea in the economic and social thought of the thirties, see Steven Kesselman, "The Frontier Thesis and the Depression," *Journal of the History of Ideas,* XXIX (April–June 1968), 253–268.

Roosevelt's economic and social ideas are discussed in Daniel Fusfeld, *The Economic Thought of Franklin D. Roosevelt and the Origins of the New Deal* (New York: Columbia University Press, 1956), and in less systematic fashion in Frank Freidel, *Franklin D. Roosevelt* (3 vols. to date, Boston: Little, Brown and Company, 1952–1956), which when completed will undoubtedly stand as the preeminent biography for many years. James M. Burns, *Roosevelt: The Lion and the Fox* (New York: Harcourt, Brace & World, Inc., 1956) and Rexford G. Tugwell, *The Democratic Roosevelt* (Garden City: Doubleday & Company, Inc., 1957) should also be consulted. The ideas of John Maynard Keynes, which aroused much excitement during the thirties but never gained official acceptance within the Roosevelt administration, are delineated in Seymour E. Harris, *John Maynard Keynes* (New York: Charles Scribner's Sons, 1955) and Robert Lekachman, *The Age of Keynes* (New York: Random House, Inc., 1966), and repudiated in Henry Hazlitt, *The Failure of the "New Economics"* (Princeton: D. Van Nostrand Company, Inc., 1959).

On the appeal of the Soviet Union for American political radicals during the Depression years, see Frank A. Warren, *Liberals and Communism: The "Red Decade" Revisited* (Bloomington: Indiana University Press, 1966); Peter G. Filene, *Americans and the Soviet Experiment, 1917–1933* (Cambridge: Harvard University Press, 1967); and Paul M. Sweezy, "The Influence of Marxian Economics on American Thought and Practice,' 'in Donald D. Egbert and Stow Persons, eds., *Socialism and American Life* (2 vols., Princeton: Princeton University Press, 1952). Henry Elsner, Jr., *The Technocrats: Prophets of Automation* (Syracuse: Syracuse University Press, 1967) is disappointing.

There is an extensive literature on rural preservation, regional planning, and the Tennessee Valley Authority. Some of the best items are Clifford B. Anderson, "The Metamorphosis of American Agrarian Idealism in the 1920's and 1930's," *Agricultural History,* XXXV (October 1961), 182–188; Paul K. Conkin, *Tomorrow a New World: The New Deal Community Program* (Ithaca: Cornell University Press, 1959); Thomas A. Krueger, *And Promises to Keep: The Southern Conference for Human Welfare, 1938–1948* (Nashville: Vanderbilt University Press, 1967); and Merrill Jensen, ed., *Regionalism in America* (Madison: University of Wisconsin Press, 1951). Examples of the efforts of southern scholars to develop a regional concept relevant to planning schemes are Rupert P. Vance's *Human Geography of the South* (Chapel Hill: University of North Carolina Press, 1932); Howard W. Odum's *Southern Regions of the United States* (Chapel Hill: University of North Carolina Press, 1936); and the Odum and Harry E. Moore *American Regionalism* (New York: Holt, Rinehart and Winston, Inc., 1938). That David Lilienthal's lyrical generalizations in *TVA: Democracy on the March* (New York: Harper & Row, Publishers, 1944) often have little relation to TVA reality is evident from Philip Selznick, *TVA and the Grass Roots* (Berkeley: University of California Press, 1949); Roscoe E. Martin, ed., *TVA: The First Twenty Years* (University, Ala.: University of Alabama Press, 1956); and Norman Wengert, "TVA—Symbol and Reality," *Journal of Politics,* XIII (1951), 369–392. The anti-New Deal, anti-urban, and anti-industrial regionalism of the Southern Agrarians is given full exposure in Alexander Karanikas, *Tillers of a Myth: Southern Agrarians as Social and Literary Critics* (Madison: University of Wisconsin Press, 1966); see also Thomas J. Pressly, "Agrarianism: An Autopsy," *Sewanee Review,* XLIV (April–June 1941), 145–163; and Albert E. Stone, "Seward Collins and the *American Review:* Experiment in Pro-Fascism, 1933–1937," *American Quarterly,* XII (Spring 1960), 3–19.

On the conservative reaction to the New Deal, see George Wolfskill, *The Revolt of the Conservatives: A History of the American Liberty League, 1934–1940* (Boston: Houghton Mifflin Company, 1962) and Richard Polenberg, "The National Committee to Uphold Constitutional Government, 1937–1941," *Journal of American History,* LII (December 1965), 582–598. For Walter Lippmann's evolution into conservatism, see David E. Weingast, *Walter Lippmann: A Study in Personal Journalism* (New Brunswick: Rutgers University Press, 1949) and Clinton Rossiter and James Lare, eds., *The Essential Lippmann* (New York: Random House, Inc., 1963).

Chapter II
America Rediscovered: Literature in the Thirties

For general treatments of American literary developments in the 1930s, see Robert E. Spiller *et al, Literary History of the United States* (3rd ed., 2 vols., New York: The Macmillan Company, 1963); Spiller, ed., *A Time of Harvest: American Literature, 1910–1960* (New York: Hill and Wang, Inc., 1962); Willard Thorp, *American Writing in the Twentieth Century* (Cambridge: Harvard University Press, 1960); Heinrich Straumann, *American Literature in the Twentieth Century* (3rd ed., New York: Harper & Row, Publishers, 1965); and Walter F. Taylor, *The Story of American Letters* (Chicago: Henry Regnery Company, 1956). Alfred Kazin's classic *On Native Grounds: An Interpretation of Modern American Prose Literature* (New York: Harcourt, Brace & World, Inc., 1942) is historically based literary criticism at its very best. More specialized studies relevant to the thirties include Frederick J. Hoffman, *The Modern Novel in America, 1900–1951* (Chicago: Henry Regnery Company, 1951); Maxwell Geismar, *Writers in Crisis: The American Novel, 1925–1940* (Boston: Houghton Mifflin Company, 1942); Wilbur M. Frohock, *The Novel of Violence in America, 1920–1950* (Dallas: Southern Methodist University Press, 1950); and Robert A. Bone, *The Negro Novel in America* (New Haven: Yale University Press, 1958). Louis D. Rubin and Robert D. Jacobs, eds., *Southern Renascence: The Literature of the Modern South* (Baltimore: Johns Hopkins University Press, 1953) is useful for Faulkner, Wolfe, Caldwell, the Agrarians, and others.

Every prominent writer of the thirties and a number of minor ones have been subjected to thoroughgoing textual analyses. Such critical studies, however, are not of great usefulness to the general student of American literary history. By contrast, there is only a handful of good biographies; the best ones are probably Arthur Mizener, *The Far Side of Paradise: A Biography of F. Scott Fitzgerald* (Boston: Houghton Mifflin Company, 1951); Mark Shorer, *Sinclair Lewis* (New York: McGraw-Hill, Inc., 1961); and Andrew Turnbull, *Thomas Wolfe* (New York: Charles Scribner's Sons, 1968). Kazin's memoir, *Starting Out in the Thirties* (Boston: Little, Brown and Company, 1965), provides many insights into the intellectual climate of the thirties, as does the *Partisan Review* symposium, "The Situation in American Writing," VI (Summer 1939).

Much has been written about the "red romance" of the Depression decade, the Popular Front honeymoon, and the subsidence of literary Marxism. Good starting points are Daniel Aaron, *Writers on the Left: Episodes in American Literary Communism* (New York: Harcourt, Brace & World, Inc., 1961) and Willard Thorp, "American Writers on the Left," in Egbert and Persons, eds., *Socialism and American Life.* Granville Hicks, "The Fighting Decade," *Saturday Review of Literature,* XXII (July 6, 1940), 3–5ff; Hicks, *Where We Came Out* (New York: The Viking Press, Inc., 1954); and Malcolm Cowley, "Farewell to the 1930's," *New Republic,* CI (November 8, 1939), 42–44, are illuminating partial memoirs. The novelist Richard Wright and the journalist Louis Fischer, among others, explain their attraction to Communism and their ultimate disenchantment with it in Richard Crossman, ed., *The God That Failed* (New York: Harper & Row, Publishers, 1949); another apologia is James Wechsler's *The Age of Suspicion* (New York: Random House, Inc., 1953). Norman H. Pearson's "The Nazi-Soviet Pact and the End of a Dream," in Daniel Aaron, ed., *America in Crisis* (New York: Alfred A. Knopf, Inc., 1952) is the best single item for the impact of the Russo-German rapprochment on American thinking. Walter B. Rideout's *The Radical Novel in the United States, 1900–1954* (Cambridge: Harvard University Press, 1956) is an excellent critical study which highlights the thirties. Robert Rosenstone, in "The Men of the Abraham Lincoln Battalion," *Journal of American History,* LIV (September 1967), 327–338, demonstrates that a smaller number of writers actually fought in the Spanish Civil War than has traditionally been supposed. Two handy collections of leftist writings are edited by Granville Hicks *et al, Proletarian Literature* (New York: International Publishers, 1935) and by Harvey Swados, *The American Writer and the Great Depression* (Indianapolis: The Bobbs-Merrill Company, Inc., 1966).

In addition to a large number of contemporary articles on the Federal Writers' Project, the best retrospective items are Ray Allen Billington, "Government and the Arts: The W.P.A. Experience," *American Quarterly,* XIII (Winter 1961), 466–479, and Daniel M. Fox, "The Achievement of the Federal Writers' Project," *American Quarterly,* XIII (Spring 1961), 3–19. Surveys of the American theater in the period 1920–1930 include Alan S. Downer, *Fifty Years of American Drama, 1900–1950* (Chicago: Henry Regnery Company, 1951); Joseph Wood Krutch, *The American Drama since 1918* (Rev. ed., New York: George Braziller, Inc., 1957); Edmond M. Gagey, *Revolution in American Drama* (New York: Columbia University Press, 1947); and the *Theatre Arts* symposium, "Theatre in the Thirties," XLIV (September 1960). The biography of Eugene O'Neill by Crosswell Bowen and Shane O'Neill, *The Curse of the Misbegotten: A Tale of the House of O'Neill* (New York: McGraw-Hill, Inc., 1959), is of more interest to the historian than the large number of critical analyses his work has inspired. For the Federal Theatre Project, see Jane DeHart Mathews, *The Federal Theatre, 1935–1939: Plays, Politics, and Relief* (Princeton: Princeton University Press, 1967), a model monograph in American cultural history, and Hallie Flanagan Davis's *Arena* (New York: Duell, Sloan, and Pearce, 1940), the personal account of the director of the Theatre Project. The achievement of Federal Theatre can be appreciated first hand in the compendium *Federal Theatre Plays* (2 vols., New York: Random House, Inc., 1938). The leftist theater movement of the thirties is well covered in Morgan Y. Himelstein, *Drama Was a Weapon: The Left-Wing*

Theater in New York, 1929–1941 (New Brunswick: Rutgers University Press, 1963) and in the reminiscences of Group Theatre's director, Harold Clurman, *The Fervent Years* (New York: Alfred A. Knopf, Inc., 1950).

On the poetry of the thirties, see Horace Gregory and Marya Zaturenska, *A History of American Poetry, 1900–1940* (New York: Harcourt, Brace & World, Inc., 1946); Louis Untermeyer, ed., *Modern American Poetry* (8th ed., New York: Harcourt, Brace & World, Inc., 1962), especially Untermeyer's long introduction; Louise Bogan, *Achievement in American Poetry, 1900–1950* (Chicago: Henry Regnery, Company, 1951); and F. O. Matthiessen, "American Poetry, 1920–1940," *Sewanee Review*, LV (January–March, 1947), 24–55. Philip Horton's *Hart Crane: The Life of an American Poet* (2nd ed., New York: The Viking Press, Inc., 1957) is a satisfactory biography; Charles Norman's *The Magic-Maker: E. E. Cummings* (New York: The Macmillan, Company, 1958) is chatty and superficial. Langston Hughes's autobiography is *The Big Sea* (New York: Alfred A. Knopf, Inc., 1940). There are, of course, numerous critical studies of individual poets for the period.

The flowering of American literary criticism in the thirties is covered in William Van O'Connor, *An Age of Criticism, 1900–1950* (Chicago: Henry Regnery Company, 1952) and Robert E. Spiller, "Literature and the Critics," in Spiller and Larrabee, eds., *American Perspectives.* Morton D. Zabel, ed., *Literary Opinion in America* (3rd ed., New York: Harper & Row, Publishers, 1962) is the largest collection of critical writings; Charles I. Glicksberg, ed., *American Literary Criticism, 1900–1950* (New York: Hendricks House, 1952) is also useful. Edmund Wilson's *The Shores of Light: A Literary Chronicle of the Twenties and Thirties* (New York: Farrar, Straus, and Young, 1952) presents many selections from the Depression years by America's foremost literary critic. The most significant new development in criticism during the decade is the subject of a monograph by Richard Foster, *The New Romantics: A Reappraisal of the New Criticism* (Bloomington: Indiana University Press, 1962).

Chapter III
Toward a National Culture: Visual Arts and Music

Unquestionably the best history of American architectural development is John Burchard and Albert Bush-Brown, *The Architecture of America: A Social and Cultural History* (Boston: Little, Brown and Company, 1961). Wayne Andrews, *Architecture, Ambition, and Americans* (New York: Harper & Row, Publishers, 1955) is strongest on the nineteenth century, while James Marston Fitch, *American Building: The Forces That Shape It* (Boston: Houghton Mifflin, Company, 1948) emphasizes technology rather than esthetics. Elizabeth Mock, ed., *Built in USA: 1932–1944* (New York: The Museum of Modern Art, 1944) and Frederick A. Gutheim, *One Hundred Years of Architecture in America, 1857–1957* (New York: Reinhold Publishing Corporation, 1957) are good pictorial collections. Oliver Larkin's *Art and Life in America* (2nd ed., New York: Holt, Rinehart and Winston, Inc., 1960), although emphasizing painting and sculpture throughout, has some good material on architecture in the thirties. Carl W. Condit, *The Chicago School of Architecture* (Chicago: University of Chicago Press, 1964) is helpful for the origins of twentieth-century American design, as are several of Lewis Mumford's books, especially *The Roots of Contemporary American Architecture* (New York: Reinhold Publishing Corporation, 1952), *From the Ground Up* (New York: Harcourt, Brace & World, Inc., 1956), and *The City in History: Its Origins, Its Transformations and Its Prospects* (New York: Harcourt, Brace & World, Inc., 1961). Roy Lubove gives a good introduction to the city planning movement in which Mumford was so active in "New Cities for Old: The Urban Reconstruction Program of the 1930's," *Social Studies*, LIII (November 1962), 203–212. On the architectural and social theories of Frank Lloyd Wright, see Grant C. Manson, *Frank Lloyd Wright* (New York: Reinhold Publishing Corporation, 1958); the pertinent portions of Morton and Lucia White, *The Intellectual versus the City: From Thomas Jefferson to Frank Lloyd Wright* (Cambridge: Harvard University Press, 1962); and Wright's *Autobiography* (New York: Longmans, Green & Company, 1932).

For painting and sculpture in the thirties, Larkin's *Art and Life in America* is indispensable. The epilogue to Milton W. Brown, *American Painting, from the Armory Show to the Depression* (Princeton: Princeton University Press, 1955) points up the rapid change of mood in art wrought by the economic collapse. Among the general treatments, Edgar P. Richardson, *Painting in America: From 1502 to the Present* (2nd ed., New York: Thomas Y. Crowell Company, 1965) and the abridged version, *A Short History of Painting in America* (New York: Thomas Y. Crowell Company, 1963) are sober and judicious;

John I. H. Baur, *Revolution and Tradition in Modern American Art* (Cambridge: Harvard University Press, 1951) is brief but enlightening; Lloyd Goodrich, "Painting and Sculpture," in Spiller and Larrabee, eds., *American Perspectives,* is still briefer, yet insightful; and Rudi Blesh, *Modern Art U.S.A.: Men, Rebellion, Conquest, 1900–1956* (New York: Alfred A. Knopf, Inc., 1956) is breezy. John A. Kouwenhoven, *Made in America: The Arts in Modern Civilization* (Garden City: Doubleday and Company, Inc., 1948) advances a brilliant thesis regarding America's development of a vernacular art in the design of its tools and machines. Constance Rourke argues for an even broader conception of indigenous art in *The Roots of American Culture* (New York: Harcourt, Brace & World, Inc., 1943). Frederick P. Keppel and Robert L. Duffus, *The Arts in American Life* (New York: McGraw-Hill, Inc., 1933) is a pessimistic contemporary survey of the status of American art forms. On the American Scene regionalists of the thirties, see Virgil Barker, "Americanism in Painting," *Yale Review,* XXV (June 1936), 778–793; Thomas Hart Benton's autobiography, *An Artist in America* (New York: Robert M. McBride & Company, 1937); and Darrell Garwood, *Artist in Iowa: A Life of Grant Wood* (New York: W. W. Norton & Company, Inc., 1944).

Gilbert Chase, *America's Music, from the Pilgrims to the Present Day* (New York: McGraw-Hill, Inc., 1955) and John T. Howard and George K. Bellows, *A Short History of Music in America* (New York: Thomas Y. Crowell Company, 1957) are adequate surveys. Howard's *Our American Music: A Comprehensive History from 1620 to the Present* (4th ed., New York: Thomas Y. Crowell Company, 1965) is encyclopedic. Examples of musical nationalist writing in the thirties are Aaron Copland, *Our New Music* (New York: McGraw-Hill, Inc., 1941); Roy Harris, "Does Music Have to Be European?" *Scribner's Magazine,* XCI (April 1932), 204–209, and "American Music Enters a New Phase," *Scribner's Magazine,* XCVI (October 1934), 218–221; and Howard Hanson, "Conditions Affecting the Development of an American Music," *Etude,* L (April 1932), 247–248. On the WPA Music Project, see "Unemployed Arts: WPA's Four Arts Projects: Their Origins, Their Operation," *Fortune,* XV (May 1937), 108–117ff, and "The Federal Music Project," *Current History,* XLIX (September 1938), 42–44. The best surveys in a large body of writing on jazz are Barry Ulanov, *A History of Jazz* (New York: the Viking Press, Inc., 1952) and Marshall W. Stearns, *The Story of Jazz* (New York: Oxford University Press, 1956), both of which clearly establish the relationship between the hot jazz of the twenties and the swing craze of the thirties and early forties. Neil Leonard, *Jazz and the White American: The Acceptance of a New Art Form* (Chicago: University of Chicago Press, 1962) is a fascinating study which treats the same problem in greater detail. On Benny Goodman, see Irving Kolodin, "No. 1 Swing Man," *Harper's Magazine*, CLXXIX (September 1939), 431–440.

Chapter IV
Varieties of Cultural Experience: Films, Radio, Journalism

The whole field of popular culture in twentieth-century America is wide open to historical scholars, although social scientists have amassed a vast literature on films, radio, and the press, particularly since the Second World War. Some of the possibilities for historical study are suggested in Reuel Denney, "The Discovery of Popular Culture," in Spiller and Larrabee, eds., *American Perspectives*. There is quite a bit on motion-picture and radio history in Barry Ulanov's *The Two Worlds of American Art: The Private and the Popular* (New York: The Macmillan Company, 1965). Lewis Jacobs's *The Rise of the American Film* (New York: Harcourt, Brace & World, Inc., 1939), though badly dated, is still the best history of American motion pictures. Arthur Knight's *The Liveliest Art: A Panoramic History of the Movies* (New York: The Macmillan Company, 1957) is sketchy but valuable, not only for the United States but for Europe and Japan as well. Margaret F. Thorp, *America at the Movies* (New Haven: Yale University Press, 1939) is a lively contemporary survey which emphasizes the dominant factor of mass audience. For the thirties the best of many illustrated volumes is Deems Taylor *et al.*, *A Pictorial History of the Movies* (New York: Simon and Schuster, Inc., 1943). Leo C. Rosten, *Hollywood: The Movie Colony, the Movie Makers* (New York: Harcourt, Brace & World, Inc., 1941) describes the values and social structure of the film capital at the end of the thirties. Gilbert Seldes, the most prolific analyst of American popular culture, treats both films and radio in *The Great Audience* (New York: The Viking Press, 1951) and *The Public Arts* (New York: Simon and Schuster, Inc., 1956), the latter being a revision and updating of his seminal *The Seven Lively Arts* (New York: Harper & Row, Publishers, 1924). James Rorty, "Dream Factory," *Forum*, XCIV (Septemper 1935), 162–165, is a slashing contemporary critique, while

Kurt Pinthus looks at the effect of social change on films in "History Directs the Movies," *American Scholar,* X (October 1941), 483–497. On problems of film censorship and suppression, see Ruth A. Inglis, *Freedom of the Movies* (Chicago: University of Chicago Press, 1947); "The Hays Office," *Fortune,* XVIII (December 1938), 68–72ff; and James Rorty, "It Ain't No Sin!" *Nation,* CXXXIX (August 1, 1934), 124–127.

The closest thing we have to a history of radio is Francis Chase, *Sound and Fury: An Informal History of Broadcasting* (New York: Harper & Row, Publishers, 1942). On the commercialization of radio in the thirties, see John T. Flynn, "Radio: The Medicine Show," *American Scholar,* VII (October 1938), 430–437; on popular adulation, "Fortune Survey: Radio Favorites," *Fortune,* XVII (January 1938), 88ff; and on the radio theater movement, William H. and Kathryn C. Cordell, "The Future Theater of the Air," *Sewanee Review,* XLIV (October-December 1936), 405–419. A variety of radio's problems receive attention in the symposium "New Horizons in Radio," edited by Herman S. Hettinger, *Annals* of the American Academy of Political and Social Science, CCXIII (January 1941). The scope and nature of radio's appeal are analyzed in Hadley Cantril and Gordon W. Allport, *The Psychology of Radio* (New York: Peter Smith, Publisher, 1941); Paul F. Lazarsfeld, *Radio and the Printed Page* (New York: Duell, Sloan, and Pearce, 1940); and Lazarsfeld, *The People Look at Radio* (Chapel Hill: University of North Carolina Press, 1946). On censorship see Llewellyn White, *The American Radio* (Chicago: University of Chicago Press, 1947) and Zechariah Chafee, *Government and Mass Communications* (Chicago: University of Chicago Press, 1947).

Frank L. Mott's *American Journalism: A History, 1690–1960* (3rd. ed., New York: The Macmillian Company, 1962) is a superb overview which relates social, economic, and technological factors in the evolution of newspapers and magazines. Mott's *The News in America* (Cambridge: Harvard University Press, 1952) is cross-sectional rather than historical. Two of the best of numerous writings on the problem of news censorship and control are by the Commission on Freedom of the Press—*A Free and Responsible Press* (Chicago: University of Chicago Press, 1947)—and by Morris Ernst—*The First Freedom* (New York: The Macmillan Company, 1946). Simon Bessie, *Jazz Journalism: The Story of the Tabloid Newspapers* (New York: E. P.

Dutton & Co., Inc., 1938) is a competent study. Good studies of American magazines in the twentieth century, in addition to the pertinent chapters in Mott's *American Journalism,* are James P. Wood's *Magazines in the United States: Their Social and Economic Influence* (2nd ed., New York: The Ronald Press Company, 1956) and Theodore Peterson's *Magazines in the Twentieth Century* (2nd ed., Urbana: University of Illinois Press, 1964). John Bainbridge's *Little Wonder; or The Reader's Digest and How It Grew* (New York: Reynal and Hitchcock, 1946), though done with tongue-in-cheek, is highly perceptive. Frederick J. Hoffman *et al., The Little Magazine* (Princeton: Princeton University Press, 1946) is authoritative. The best biography of H. L. Mencken, whose *American Mercury* lost its influence with young intellectuals during the Depression years, is William Manchester's *Disturber of the Peace* (New York: Harper & Row, Publishers, 1951). See also Cedric Cowing, "H. L. Mencken: The Case of the 'Curdled' Progressive," *Ethics,* LXIX (July 1959), 255–267.

Chapter V
Science and Scholarship in an Age of Depression

The need for a general history of American science is fast becoming desperate. For the thirties, one of the best discussions of scientific progress and scientific thought is in Curti, *Growth of American Thought.* Everett Mendelsohn, "Science in America: The Twentieth Century," in Schlesinger and White, eds., *Paths of American Thought,* is moderately helpful; so are Bernard Jaffe's *Men of Science in America: The Role of Science in the Growth of Our Country* (New York: Simon and Schuster, Inc., 1944) and *Fortune* editors, *Great American Scientists* (Englewood Cliffs: Prentice-Hall, Inc., 1961). David D. Van Tassel and Michael G. Hall, eds., *Science and Society in the United States* (Homewood: Dorsey Press, Inc., 1966) consists of nine well-done topical essays, but hardly suffices for the kind of survey that is needed. Courtney R. Hall, *History of American Industrial Science* (New York: Science Library, 1954) is good on applied science and invention, while A. Hunter Dupree, *Science in the Federal Government: A History of Policies and Activities to 1940* (Cambridge: Harvard University Press, 1957) is a splendid study which has much material on the thirties.

Technical philosophy, the social sciences, and history are all treated in Merle Curti, ed., *American Scholarship in the Twentieth Century*

(Cambridge: Harvard University Press, 1953). On technical philosophy, William H. Werkmeister, *A History of Philosophical Ideas in America* (New York: The Ronald Press Company, 1949) is pedestrian but informative; the same is true of Herbert W. Schneider, *A History of American Philosophy* (2nd ed., New York: Columbia University Press, 1963), although this book is weak on the twentieth century and, except for the bibliography, was not revised for the second edition. Morris R. Cohen's essays in *American Thought: A Critical Sketch,* ed. Felix S. Cohen (Glencoe: Free Press, 1954) are often brilliant. Brand Blandshard, "The Changing Climate of Philosophy," *Liberal Education,* XLVII (May 1961), 229–254, is a highly perceptive survey of recent developments; see also William C. DeVane's comments on philosophy in *Higher Education in Twentieth Century America* (Cambridge: Harvard University Press, 1965). For John Dewey's thought, consult, among many analytical works, Richard J. Bernstein, *John Dewey* (New York: Washington Square Press, 1968); Edward C. Moore, *American Pragmatism: Peirce, James, and Dewey* (New York: Columbia University Press, 1961); and Sidney Hook, ed., *John Dewey, Philosopher of Science and Freedom: A Symposium* (New York: The Dial Press, Inc., 1950). Ernest Nagel, "The Fight for Clarity: Logical Empiricism," *American Scholar,* VIII (January 1939), 45–59, is a lucid exposition of the most important new development of the decade in philosophy.

A good summary of the situation in the social sciences in the 1930s is L. L. Bernard, "The Social Sciences as Disciplines: The United States," in E. R. A. Seligman and Alvin Johnson, eds., *Encyclopedia of the Social Sciences* (15 vols., New York: The Macmillan Company, 1938), I. The state of legal thought is sketched in Zechariah Chafee, "The Law," in Stearns, ed., *America Now.* The career of one of the foremost academic exponents of legal realism is covered in Helen S. Thomas, *Felix Frankfurter: Scholar on the Bench* (Baltimore: Johns Hopkins University Press, 1960), and the relativist movement in law is given considerable attention by Cohen in *American Thought.* Loren Baritz, *The Servants of Power: A History of the Use of Social Science in American Industry* (Middletown: Wesleyan University Press, 1960) demonstrates the growing application of social science expertise in business during the thirties; while Kirkendall, *Social Scientists and Farm Politics in the Age of Roosevelt* describes the role of social scientists, especially agricultural economists, in one portion of the New Deal. Volume five of Joseph Dorfman's magistral *The*

Economic Mind in American Civilization, 1606–1933 (5 vols., New York: The Viking Press, Inc., 1946–1959) treats the impact of the Great Depression on American economic thought. For the New Deal and World War II years, see Ben W. Lewis, "Recent Developments in Economics," *Liberal Education,* XLVII (May 1961), 255–279.

Bernard Crick, *The American Science of Politics: Its Origins and Conditions* (Berkeley: University of California Press, 1959) is a fairly good history of the growth of the political science discipline. George Gallup, *A Guide to Public Opinion Polls* (Princeton: Princeton University Press, 1944) and Hadley Cantril, *Gauging Public Opinion* (Princeton: Princeton University Press 1944) are useful on opinion studies. Edward Shils, "The Contemplation of Society in America," in Schlesinger and White, eds., *Paths of American Thought,* and Louis Wirth, "The Social Sciences," in Curti, ed., *American Scholarship in the Twentieth Century,* are good brief surveys of the development of American sociology. For the rise of urban sociology in the twenties and thirties, see the first six chapters of Maurice R. Stein, *The Eclipse of Community: An Interpretation of American Studies* (Princeton: Princeton University Press, 1960). George B. Tindall, *The Emergence of the New South, 1913–1945* (Baton Rouge: Louisiana State University Press, 1967) and Dewey W. Grantham, "The Regional Imagination: Social Scientists and the American South," *Journal of Southern History,* XXXIV (February 1968), 3–32, both describe the expansion of southern-based regional sociology in the thirties. The metamorphosis of cultural anthropology and the national character approach are treated in Margaret Mead, "The Study of National Character," in Daniel Lerner and Harold D. Lasswell, eds., *Policy Sciences* (Stanford: Stanford University Press, 1951). For trends in historical writing in the thirties, see John Higham *et al, History* (Englewood Cliffs: Prentice-Hall, Inc., 1965); Higham, "The Schism in American Historical Scholarship," *American Historical Review,* LXXII (October 1966), 1–21; and W. Stull Holt, "Historical Scholarship," in Curti, ed., *American Scholarship in the Twentieth Century.* On Carl Becker and Charles Beard, the leading formulators of historical relativist thinking, see Harvey Wish, *The American Historian* (New York: Oxford University Press, 1960); Cushing Strout, *The Pragmatic Revolt in American History* (New Haven: Yale University Press, 1958); Burleigh T. Wilkins, *Carl Becker,* (Cambridge: M.I.T. Press, 1961); and David W. Noble, *Historians Against History:*

The Turner Thesis and the National Covenant in Historical Writing Since 1830 (Minneapolis: University of Minnesota Press, 1965).

Chapter VI
Storm and Stress in Education and Religion

The best overview of recent educational history is Isaac L. Kandel, *American Education in the Twentieth Century* (Cambridge: Harvard University Press, 1957). Edgar W. Knight, *Fifty Years of American Education* (New York: The Ronald Press Company, 1962) is more detailed but less interesting. One aspect of the Depression's impact on American education is treated in Robert L. Duffus, *Our Starving Libraries* (Boston, Houghton Mifflin, 1933), while Howard K. Beale, *Are American Teachers Free? An Analysis of the Restraints upon the Freedom of Teaching in American Schools* (New York: Charles Scribner's Sons, 1936) catalogs the growth of proscriptive actions in the thirties. Unfortunately Richard Hofstadter and Walter Metzger, *The Development of Academic Freedom in the United States* (New York: Columbia University Press, 1955) is very sketchy for the period after the First World War. Lawrence A. Cremin, *The Transformation of the School: Progressivism in American Education, 1876–1957* (New York: Alfred A. Knopf, Inc., 1961) is a fine history which ties educational progressivism to general reform impulses in twentieth-century America. John L. Childs, *American Pragmatism and Education* (New York: Holt, Rinehart and Winston, Inc., 1956) should not be overlooked. Alfred L. Hall-Quest gives a handy summary of "Three Educational Theories: Traditionalism, Progressivism, Essentialism," in *School and Society*, LVI (November 14, 1942), 452–459. Merle Curti, *The Social Ideas of American Educators* (Rev. ed., Paterson: Pageant Books, 1963) is also of use for the conflict in education ideologies.

There are several good surveys of the history of college and university education, including Frederick Rudolph, *History of Higher Education in the United States* (New York: Alfred A. Knopf, Inc., 1962); Richard Hofstadter and C. DeWitt Hardy, *The Development and Scope of Higher Education in the United States* (New York: Columbia University Press, 1952); Hofstadter and Wilson Smith, eds., *American Higher Education: A Documentary History* (2 vols., Chicago: University of Chicago Press, 1961); and DeVane, *Higher Education in Twentieth Century America.* The plight of institutions of higher learning in the Depression is described in Malcolm M. Willey, ed., *Depression, Recovery, and Higher Education* (New York: McGraw-Hill, Inc., 1937). Robert L. Duffus, *Democracy Enters College: A Study of the Rise and Decline of the Academic Lockstep* (New York: Charles Scribner's Sons, 1936) is an admiring look at efforts to apply progressive principles in higher education, while Abraham Flexner, *Universities: American, German, English* (New York: Oxford University Press, 1930) is critical of prevalent practices for entirely different reasons. On the nature and goals of the general education movement, see Brand Blanshard, "Speculative Thinkers," in Spiller *et al*, eds., *Literary History of the United States,* I; Patricia Beesley, *The Revival of the Humanities in American Education* (New York: Columbia University Press, 1940); Russell Thomas, *The Search for a Common Learning: General Education, 1800–1960* (New York: McGraw-Hill Inc., 1962), which, despite its sweeping title, is much more a contemporary view than a history; and Edgar W. Knight, "Some Recent Changes in the College Curriculum," *South Atlantic Quarterly,* XXXIV (July 1935), 314–332. Stringfellow Barr, "A College in Secession," *Atlantic Monthly,* CLXVIII (July 1941), 41–49, tells of the "Great Books" course of study at St. Johns College.

On religion and religious thought, the most comprehensive work is one edited by James W. Smith and Albert L. Jamison, *Religion in American Life* (4 vols., Princeton: Princeton University Press, 1961). Clifton E. Olmstead, *Religion in America, Past and Present* (Englewood Cliffs: Prentice-Hall, Inc., 1961), though thin, and Willard L. Sperry, *Religion in America* (New York: The Macmillan Company, 1946), though badly dated, are of some use. Herbert W. Schneider *Religion in Twentieth Century America* (Cambridge: Harvard University Press, 1952) is brief but wise. Will Herberg, *Protestant, Catholic, Jew: An Essay in Religious Sociology* (Garden City: Doubleday & Company, Inc., 1955) is enlightening on recent developments. Three short but highly informative general accounts are John Tracy Ellis, *American Catholicism* (Chicago: University of Chicago Press, 1956); Nathan Glazer, *American Judaism* (Chicago: University of Chicago Press, 1957); and Winthrop S. Hudson, *American Protestantism* (Chicago: University of Chicago Press, 1961).

Of more particular value for the thirties are Lyman Bryson *et al.*, eds., *Perspectives on a Troubled Decade: Science, Philosophy, and Religion, 1939–1949* (New York: Harper & Row, Publishers, 1950) and Hornell Hart, "Religion: Changes During the Past Decade,"

American Journal of Sociology," XLVII (May 1942), 888–897. For the decline of organized Fundamentalism, see Norman F. Furniss, *The Fundamentalist Controversy, 1918–1931* (New Haven: Yale University Press, 1954). Aaron I. Abell, *American Catholicism and Social Action: A Search for Social Justice, 1865–1950* (Garden City: Hanover House, 1960) is a trenchant monograph, especially good on the issues of the thirties symbolized by John A. Ryan and Charles Coughlin. For Protestant social activism in the Depression period, three thorough studies should be consulted: Daniel B. Myer, *The Protestant Search for Political Realism, 1919–1941* (Berkeley: University of California Press, 1960); Paul A. Carter, *The Decline and Revival of the Social Gospel . . . in American Protestant Churches, 1920–1940* (Ithaca: Cornell University Press, 1956); and Robert M. Miller, *American Protestantism and Social Issues, 1919–1939* (Chapel Hill: University of North Carolina Press, 1958). For the rise and development of neo-orthodox theology, see John A. Hutchison, ed., *Christian Faith and Social Action* (New York: Charles Scribner's Sons, 1953); Mary F. Thelen, *Man as Sinner in Contemporary American Realistic Theology* (New York: King's Crown Press, 1947); Arnold S. Nash, ed., *Protestant Thought in the Twentieth Century* (New York: The Macmillan Company, 1951); Charles W. Kegley and Robert W. Bretall, eds., *Reinhold Niebuhr, His Religious, Social, and Political Thought* (New York: The Macmillan Company, 1956); and Kegley and Bretall, eds., *The Theology of Paul Tillich* (New York: The Macmillan Company, 1952). On the political ramifications of neo-orthodoxy, see especially Reinhold Niebuhr, "Religion as a Source of Radicalism," *Christian Century,* LI (April 11, 1934), 491–494; Myer, *Protestant Search for Political Realism;* and Arthur M. Schlesinger, Jr., "The Role of Reinhold Niebuhr in Political Thought," in Nash, ed., *Protestant Thought in the Twentieth Century.* Representative critiques of neo-orthodoxy are Julius S. Bixler, "Must Religion Be Unreasonable?" *American Scholar,* VII (July 1939), 358–371, and the *Partisan Review* symposium "The New Failure of Nerve," X (January-February, March-April 1943).

Chapter VII
Defining the American Cause

While the history of United States foreign relations has traditionally been a crowded area of scholarship, relatively little has been done to explain the complex sets of attitudes, assumptions, and ideas that have conditioned the formulation of foreign policy. Thomas A. Bailey, *The Man in the Street: The Impact of American Public Opinion on Foreign Policy* (New York: The Macmillan Company, 1948) is a pioneering study which has considerable use for the decade before Pearl Harbor. Selig Adler, *The Isolationist Impulse: Its Twentieth Century Reaction* (New York: Abelard-Schuman, 1957) is an almost equally original venture which emphasizes the interactive development of ideas and positions on the part of political leaders, journalists, intellectuals, and the mass of Americans. Adler continues in much the same vein in *The Uncertain Giant, 1921–1941: American Foreign Policy Between the Wars* (New York: The Macmillan Company, 1965). Robert E. Osgood, *Ideals and Self-Interest in American Foreign Relations: The Great Transformation of the Twentieth Century* (Chicago: University of Chicago Press, 1953) describes American entry into the Second World War in terms of the growing "realism" of national opinion. Arthur Ekirch, *Ideas, Ideals, and American Diplomacy: A History of Their Growth and Interaction* (New York: Appleton-Century-Crofts, 1966) is, despite its imposing title, little more than a brief resume of diplomatic history, while Norman A. Graebner, ed., *Ideas and Diplomacy: Readings in the Intellectual Tradition of American Foreign Policy* (New York: Oxford University Press, 1964) is generally disappointing. Manfred Jonas, *Isolationism in America, 1935–1941* (Ithaca: Cornell University Press, 1966) is a thoughtful analysis which, while reaching no startling new conclusions, does represent a significant achievement in the ideational approach to foreign policy. On a much larger scale, Edward M. Burns, *The American Idea of Mission: Concepts of National Purpose and Destiny* (New Brunswick: Rutgers University Press, 1957); Charles L. Sanford, *The Quest for Paradise: Europe and the American Moral Imagination* (Urbana: University of Illinois Press, 1961); Cushing Strout, *The American Image of the Old World* (New York: Harper and Row Publishers, 1963); and Ernest L. Tuveson, *Redeemer Nation: The Idea of America's Millennial Role* (Chicago: University of Chicago Press, 1968) all help explain why Americans felt as they did in the 1930s. So do Curti, *Growth of American Thought,* and Gabriel, *The Course of American Democratic Thought.* A highly valuable compendium on public opinion polls is Hadley Cantril, ed., *Public Opinion, 1935–1946* (Princeton: Princeton University Press, 1951).

On specific conditioners of American thinking in the thirties, see Warren I. Cohen, *The American Revisionists: The Lessons of Intervention in World War I* (Chicago: University of Chicago Press, 1967) and John E. Wiltz, *In Search of Peace: The Senate Munitions Inquiry, 1934–1936* (Baton Rouge: Louisiana State University Press, 1963). Harold Lavine and James Wechsler, *War Propaganda and the United States* (New Haven: Yale University Press, 1940) reveals the persistent fear of being duped into another war by foreign experts in mass persuasion, while Merle Curti, *Peace or War: The American Dilemma, 1636–1936* (2nd ed., Boston: J. S. Canner, 1959) shows the variety and strength of organized pacifism. The best treatment of Christian pacifism before Pearl Harbor is in Myer, *Protestant Search for Political Realism.* On two of the leading leftist isolationists see Michael Wreszin, *Oswald Garrison Villard: Pacifist at War* (Bloomington: Indiana University Press, 1965) and Bernard C. Borning, *The Political and Social Thought of Charles A. Beard* (Seattle: University of Washington Press, 1962). F. Jay Taylor, *The United States and the Spanish Civil War, 1936–1939* (New York: Bookman Associates-Twayne, 1956) and Allen Guttmann, *The Wound in the Heart: America and the Spanish Civil War* (New York: Free Press of Glencoe, 1962) both probe deeply into American reactions. See also Warren, *Liberals and Communism* and Aaron, *Writers on the Left.* Donald P. Kent, *The Refugee Intellectual: The Americanization of the Immigrants of 1933–1941* (New York: Columbia University Press, 1953) is a sociological study, but the cultural and intellectual significance of the migration is discussed in Alvin S. Johnson's autobiography, *Pioneer's Progress* (New York: The Viking Press, Inc., 1952); in Charles I. Glicksberg, "The Culture of the Refugees in the United States," *South Atlantic Quarterly*, XL (January 1941), 73–83; and especially in Laura Fermi, *Illustrious Immigrants: The Intellectual Migration from Europe, 1930–1941* (Chicago: University of Chicago Press, 1968). The standard organizational histories of the two main groups in the foreign policy debate of 1939–1941 are Walter Johnson, *The Battle Against Isolation* (Chicago: University of Chicago Press, 1944) and Wayne S. Cole, *America First: The Battle Against Intervention, 1940–1941* (Madison: University of Wisconsin Press, 1953).

On the fatal miscalculations that pervaded American thinking about Asian affairs up to Pearl Harbor, see William L. Neumann's excellent *America Encounters Japan: From Perry to McArthur* (Baltimore: Johns Hopkins University Press, 1963); Edwin O. Reischauer, *The United States and Japan* (2nd ed., Cambridge: Harvard University Press, 1957); John Masland, "American Attitudes Toward Japan," *Annals* of the American Academy of Political and Social Science, CCXV (May 1941), 160–165; and John K. Fairbank, *The United States and China* (2nd ed., Cambridge: Harvard University Press, 1959). Eleanor Tupper and George C. McReynolds, *Japan in American Opinion* (New York: The Macmillan Company, 1937) is still of some value.

Chapter VIII
For a Better World?

Apart from diplomatic and military studies, there is very little in the way of solid historical scholarship for the period of American participation in the Second World War. For the social, cultural, and intellectual developments of the years 1942–1945, one must rely heavily on the writings of contemporary observers and social scientists. On wartime moods and attitudes, Curti's *Growth of American Thought* and Gabriel's *Course of American Democratic Thought* are suggestive, as are the essays in Jack Goodman, ed., *While You Were Gone: A Report on Wartime Life in the United States* (New York: Simon and Schuster, 1946), especially Allan Nevins, "How We Felt about the War." Other helpful items are Herbert Blumer's "Morale," in William F. Ogburn, ed., *American Society in Wartime* (Chicago: University of Chicago Press, 1943) and portions of Eli Ginzberg *et al.*, *The Unemployed* (New York: Harper & Row, Publishers, 1943) and Margaret Mead, *And Keep Your Powder Dry* (New York: William Morrow and Company, Inc., 1942). For the treatment of Japanese-Americans and the general problem of persistent racism in America, see Carey McWilliams, *Brothers under the Skin* (2nd ed., Boston: Little, Brown and Company, 1951). On the war's effects on civil liberties, see Edwin S. Corwin, *Total War and the Constitution* (New York: Alfred A. Knopf, Inc., 1947). Samuel A. Stouffer *et al.*, *The American Soldier* (2 vols., Princeton: Princeton University Press, 1949) is an exhaustive analysis of attitudes and actions among military personnel. The growth of the concept of American world leadership and the movement for international organization are admirably described in Robert A. Divine's *Second Chance: The Triumph of Internationalism in America During World War II* (New York:

Atheneum Publishers, 1967); see also Ellsworth Barnard's *Wendell Willkie: Fighter for Freedom* (Marquette: Northern Michigan University Press, 1966) and Adler's *Isolationist Impulse*. Kenneth Davis, *Experience of War: The United States in World War II* (Garden City: Doubleday & Company, Inc., 1965) and A. Russell Buchanan, *The United States and World War II* (2 vols., New York: Harper & Row, Publishers, 1964) both give minimal attention to domestic developments.

For the effect of the war on literature, the visual arts, and music, many of the general works previously mentioned in regard to the thirties should be consulted. See, in addition, Chester E. Eisinger's thorough and perceptive *Fiction of the Forties* (Chicago: University of Chicago Press, 1963); Granville Hicks, "Fiction and Social Criticism," *English Journal*, XLI (April 1952), 173–179; Edmund Wilson, *Classics and Commercials: A Literary Chronicle of the Forties* (New York: Farrar, Straus & Company, 1950); John Gassner, "War and the Theatre," *Current History*, III (December 1942), 360–363; Percival and Paul Goodman, "Architecture in Wartime," *New Republic*, CIX (December 20, 1943), 878–882; James W. Lane, "Art at War," *Commonweal*, XXXVII (February 12, 1943), 424–425; Arthur Berger, "Music in Wartime," *New Republic*, CX (February 7, 1944), 175–178; and Alfred Frankenstein, "The Plight of the American Composer," *American Scholar*, XII (October 1943), 482–489. On the musical team of Rodgers and Hammerstein, see Deems Taylor, *Some Enchanted Evenings* (New York: Harper & Row, Publishers, 1953). Aspects of wartime film-making are discussed in Bosley Crowther, "The Movies," in Goodman, ed., *While You Were Gone;* Manny Farber, "Movies in Wartime," *New Republic*, CX (January 3, 1944), 16–20; and Dorothy B. Jones, "Hollywood Goes to War," *Nation*, CLX (January 27, 1945), 93–95.

On the role of science in the Second World War, see "Fundamental Knowledge but Little Advanced by War-necessitated Research," *Scientific American*, CLXX (April 1944), 179–180; Clarence G. Lasby, "Science and the Military" and Carroll W. Pursell, "Science and Government Agencies," in Van Tassel and Hall, eds., *Science and Society in the United States;* and James P. Baxter, *Scientists Against Time* (Boston: Little, Brown and Company, 1946). Richard G. Hewlett and Oscar E. Anderson, *A History of the Atomic Energy Commission*, vol. I: *The New World, 1939–1946* (University Park: Penn State University Press, 1963) is an extraordinarily good official history of the atomic bomb project. The uses of scholarship in the war are indicated in Merle Curti, "The Setting and Its Problems," in Curti, ed., *American Scholarship in the Twentieth Century;* Thomas C. Cochran, "The Social Sciences," in Spiller and Larrabee, eds., *American Perspectives;* Margaret Mead, "The Comparative Study of Cultures and the Purposive Cultivation of Democratic Values, 1941–1949," in Bryson *et al.*, eds., *Perspectives on a Troubled Decade;* and Mead, "The Study of National Character," in Lerner and Lasswell, eds., *Policy Sciences.*

Isaac L. Kandel, *The Impact of the War upon American Education* (Chapel Hill: University of North Carolina Press, 1949) is a dryly written but adequate survey. Benjamin Fine briefly describes the war's deleterious effects in *Our Children Are Cheated: The Crisis in American Education* (New York: Holt, Rinehart and Winston, Inc., 1946). A fairly good contemporary view of the wartime educational situation can be gained from the *Saturday Review of Literature* symposium "Education in the United States," XXVI (September 18, 1943). Cremin, *Transformation of the School;* Theodore Brameld, "Progressive Education on the Defensive," *Current History, VII (August 1944),* 95–100; and Howard Mumford Jones *et al.*, "On the Conflict Between the 'Liberal Arts' and the 'Schools of Education,' " *ACLS Newsletter,* V (1954), 17–58, highlight the doctrinal debates of the war years. Jacques Barzun, "Harvard Takes Stock," *Atlantic Monthly,* CLXXVI (October 1945), 52–56, is a good critique of the Harvard Committee report, *General Education in a Free Society* (Cambridge: Harvard University Press, 1945). For religious developments during the war years, see, besides the general works mentioned earlier, "The Christian Churches in the War," *Fortune,* XXVII (March 1943), 118–121ff.

There are many books and articles on American diplomacy during the Second World War. Here it seems necessary to mention only two quite different items, perhaps the most thoughtful general treatments: William Appleman Williams, *The Tragedy of American Diplomacy* (Cleveland: World Publishing Company, 1959) and Gaddis Smith, *American Diplomacy During the Second World War, 1941–1945* (New York: John Wiley & Sons, Inc., 1965). Nearly all of the diplomatic and military histories and a number of other works—like those of Hewlett and Anderson and Baxter—discuss the use of the atomic bomb, and nearly all conclude that Truman's decision was justified. This is true of the fullest account, Herbert Feis's *Japan Subdued: The Atomic Bomb and the End of the War in the Pacific*

(Princeton: Princeton University Press, 1961), which, though critical of the Truman administration for not publicizing the nature of the new weapon, makes little effort to deal with the ethical and moral questions it raised. On the other hand, Robert C. Batchelder's *The Irreversible Decision—1939–1950* (Boston: Houghton Mifflin Company, 1961) not only loosely chronicles the development of the bomb and places it within its military context, but also makes a strenuous effort to deal with the ethics of its use. The changing nature of American opinion regarding the bombing of civilian populations is treated in George E. Hopkins, "Bombing and the American Conscience During World War II," *Historian,* XXVIII (May 1966), 451–473.

Index

Aaron, Daniel, 31
Abe Lincoln in Illinois (Sherwood), 49, 92
Abrams, Ray, 171
Absalom! Absalom! (Faulkner), 42
Adagio for Strings (Barber), 80
Adamic, Louis, 40
Adler, Luther, 48
Adler, Mortimer, 150, 152, 177, 184–85, 195, 219
Adler, Selig, 166
Adventures of a Young Man (Dos Passos), 39
Afro-American Symphony (Still), 81
Agar, Herbert, 19
Agee, James, 44, 90, 106–07
Agrarianism, 15, 18–20
  (*See also* Regionalism, Southern Agrarians)
Agricultural Adjustment Administration, 11–12, 15, 126
Ah, Wilderness (O'Neill), 50
Aldington, Richard, 176
Algren, Nelson, 39
Albright, Ivan Le Lorraine, 208
Allen, Frederick Lewis, 1
Allen, Hervey, 36
All the King's Men (Warren), 203
Allport, Gordon, 95
Alsberg, Henry, 44
American First Committee, 176
America Goes to War (Tansill), 166
American Association for Adult Education, 182
American Council on Education, 111
Americans for Democratic Action, 163
American Dilemma, An (Myrdal *et al.*), 131
American Education Fellowship, 221
American Gothic (Wood), 71
American Guide Series (*see* Works Progress Administration, Federal Writers' Project)
American Guild for German Cultural Freedom, 175
American Historical Association, 134, 145, 218
American Historical Association—*cont.*
  Commission on the Social Studies, 145
American Institute of Public Opinion, 129, 154, 166, 168, 176, 186–87, 227
American League against War and Fascism, 32, 173
American Legion Magazine, 153
American Liberty League, 17–18
American Mercury, 2, 103
American Public Mind, The (Odegard), 129
American Reformed Church, 155
American Review, 19
American Salute, An (Gould), 210
"American Story, The," 213
American Student Union, 142, 170
American Stuff, 45
American Writers' Congress (*see* Congress of American Writers)
American Youth Congress, 142
America's Coming-of-Age (Brooks), 25
America's Strategy in World Politics (Spykman), 195–96
America Was Promises (MacLeish), 181
"Amos 'n Andy," 86, 95
Anderson, Maxwell, 49, 204–05
Anderson, Sherwood, 25
And Keep Your Powder Dry (Mead), 132
Annals of the American Academy of Political and Social Science, 12
Anthony Adverse (Allen), 36
Anthropology (*see* Science, social)
Anti-Catholicism (*see* Religion, Roman Catholic)
Anti-Semitism (*see* Religion, Jewish)
Appalachian Spring (Graham and Copland), 211
Aquinas, Thomas, 119, 150
Architectural Forum, 67
Architecture, 60–67, 206–07
  commercial, 61, 64
  governmental, 65–67
  and Great Depression, 61

Architecture—*cont.*
Greek Revival, 66
modern, 62–63, 66–67, 179
and Second World War, 206–07
"Arch Obeler's Plays," 97
Are American Teachers Free? (Beale), 141
Armed Forces Institute, 218
Armory Show, 68
Arnold, Thurman, 18, 124–25
Art and Experience (Dewey), 69
Associated Press, 101
Astronomy (*see* Science, natural)
At Heaven's Gate (Warren), 203
Atlantic Charter, 192
Atlantic Monthly, 103
Atomic bomb(s), 192, 214–15, 227–28
Attack on Leviathan, The (Davidson), 20
Austria, 115, 167, 175
Awake and Sing (Odets), 48

Babbitt (Lewis), 35
Babbitt, Irving, 27, 55
Bacon, Ernst, 80–81, 210
Bagley, William C., 147
Bainbridge, John, 104
Ballet (*see* Music, ballet)
Baptist Church, 155
Barber, Samuel, 80
Bard College, 148
Barker, Virgil, 72
Barnes, Harry Elmer, 199
Barr, Stringfellow, 150–51
Barry, Philip, 50
Barth, Karl, 160
Battle of Russia, The, 212
Bauhaus, 62, 75
Beale, Howard K., 141
Beard, Charles A., 7, 17, 90, 102, 122, 133–36, 145, 151, 168–69, 172–74, 177–79, 183, 195, 199
Beard, Mary, 17, 90, 102, 151
Becker, Carl, 18, 23, 133–34, 169, 177, 180–81, 188–89, 195
Beethoven, Ludwig von, 209
Behrman, S.N., 49–50
Belgium, 177
Belloc, Hillaire, 19
Bellow, Saul, 203
Benedict, Ruth, 132, 163
Benét, Stephen Vincent, 51–52, 81
Bennington College, 148
Benny, Jack, 95
Benton, Thomas Hart, 70–71, 73–74
Berkshire Music Festival, 175
Berle, Adolph A., 10, 127
Bessie, Simon, 106
Beyond Tragedy (Niebuhr), 162
Bierce, Ambrose, 42
Big Money, The (Dos Passos)
Bingham, Alfred, 7, 173
Biology (*see* Science, natural)
Birth of a Nation, The, 87, 93
Black Legion, 173
Black Mountain College, 148
Blackmur, R.P., 56
Blitzstein, Marc, 47
Bliven, Bruce, 174
Blockade, 92
Blue Guitar, The (Stevens), 51
Blumer, Herbert, 193
Boas, Franz, 132
Boas, George, 220
Bode, Boyd H., 144–45, 148
Bohr, Neils, 114
Book of the Month Club, 225
Boston Symphony, 80
Both Your Houses (Anderson), 49
Bourke-White, Margaret, 106
Bowes, Major, 95
Brandeis, Louis, 123
Bridge, The (Crane), 53
British Broadcasting Company, 82
Broadacre City (Wright), 64
Brookings Institution, 10–11
Brooks, Cleanth, 56
Brooks, Van Wyck, 25, 53, 57–58
Broun, Heywood, 103
Browder, Earl, 32, 99, 145
Brown, Harry, 193
Brown, John, 71, 74
Brown University, 113
Brunner, Emil, 160
Bryan, William Jennings, 154
Bryn Mawr College, 154
Bryson, Lyman, 99
Buchanan, Scott, 150–51
Buck, Pearl S., 187
Buell, Raymond L., 177
Burchfield, Charles, 70
Burke, Kenneth, 27, 56, 122
Burroughs, Edward Arthur, 112
Bury the Dead (Shaw), 48, 171
Bush, Vannevar, 214–15

Cagney, James, 89
Cahill, Holger, 68, 72–73
Cain, James M., 39
Calder, Alexander, 75
Caldwell, Erskine, 39–40, 106, 202
California Institute of Technology, 115–16
Calhoun, John C., 20
Calverton, V.F., 54, 56
Cantril, Hadley, 95
Cantwell, Robert, 39
Capra, Frank, 211
Carnegie, Dale, 23
Carnegie Foundation, 149, 214
Carter, Boake, 102
Cash, W.J., 15
Caste and Class in a Southern Town (Dollard), 131
Cather, Willa, 34–35
Catholicism (*see* Religion, Catholic; Theology, Catholic)
Catholic University, 156
Catholic World, 151
Central Conference of American Rabbis, 156
Century, 103
Chamberlain, John, 2, 5, 28, 31, 56
Chamberlain, Neville, 98, 168
Chaplin, Charles, 87, 91–92
Chase, Stuart, 7–8, 14, 22, 122, 168, 217
Chemical bond, 116
Chemistry (*see* Science, natural)
Chenery, William L., 104
Cheney, Shelton, 76
Chesterton, G.K., 19
Chiang Kai-shek, 187–88, 198
Chicago exposition (1933), 62
Chicago Tribune, 102
Children's Hour, The (Hellman), 50
Children's Theatre (*see* Works Progress Administration, Federal Theatre Project)
China, 167, 186–88, 197–98, 226
Christian Century, 88, 170
Christian Church, 155
Christian Existentialism, 162, 203
Church of England, 112
Churchill, Winston, 192
Citadel, The, 91
Citizen Kane, 93
City planning (*see* Planning, urban)
Civilian Conservation Corps, 140
Clark, John Maurice, 127
Clark, Walter Van Tilburg, 203
Clausewitz, Karl von, 196
Cleveland Symphony, 79
Clurman, Harold, 48
Coffee bill, 17
Collectivism, 5–14, 21, 118, 126, 144–46, 148, 151
  (*See also* Planning)
Collier's, 103–04
Colonial Williamsburg, 67
Columbia Broadcasting System, 94, 96–97, 99
Columbia University, 9–10, 99, 115, 119, 132, 175, 223
  Department of Industrial Engineering, 9
  Department of Philosophy, 118–19, 142
  New School for Social Research, 9, 175, 220
  Teachers College, 142, 144–45, 147
"Columbia Workshop," 97
Comic strips, 86
Commager, Henry Steele, 118
Commerce Building, 66
Committee on the Costs of Medical Care, 116
Committee to Defend America by Aiding the Allies, 176–77
Common Sense, 7
Commonweal, 78
Communism, 12, 32–33, 57, 99, 162, 175
  (*See also* Communist party)
Communist party, 13, 30–33, 49, 54
  (*See also* Communism)
Compton, Arthur H., 114–15
Compton, Karl T., 110–11, 215
Conant, James Bryant, 221–22
Congregational Church, 155
Congress of American Writers, 30–31, 181–82
Conquistador (MacLeish), 52
Conroy, Jack, 30
Conservative coalition, 224
Conversation at Midnight (Millay), 52
Copland, Aaron, 78–79, 97, 210
Cornell University, 133
Corwin, Edwin S., 200
Corwin, Norman, 97
Coughlin, Charles, 12, 157, 173
Council on Foreign Relations, 198

Country Roads, Unpaved (Bacon), 81
Counts, George S., 144–46, 148, 221
Course of American Democratic Thought, The (Gabriel), 137
Cousins, Norman, 228
Cowles, John, 101
Cowley, Malcolm, 6, 27–28, 36, 43, 56,
Coyle, David Cushman, 19
Cradle Will Rock, The (Blitzstein), 47
Cram, Ralph Adams, 63
Crane, Hart, 53
Craven, Thomas, 70–71
Cremin, Lawrence, 143
Croce, Benedetto, 134
Cronbach, Robert, 75
Crowther, Bosley, 211
Cuban Overture (Gershwin), 81
Cultural pluralism, 154–55
Culture of Cities, The (Mumford), 63
Cummings, E.E., 51
Curry, John Steuart, 70–71
Curti, Merle, 170, 213
Czechoslovakia, 98, 168

Daladier, Eduard, 168
Dantzig, Tobias, 114
"Daring Young Man on the Flying Trapeze, The" (Saroyan), 49
Darwinism, 26, 154
Daughters of Revolution (Wood), 71
Davidson, Donald, 19–20, 71
Davis, Bette, 97
Davis, Stuart, 73, 75
Days without End (O'Neill), 50
Death in the Afternoon (Hemingway), 37
Debs, Eugene V., 34, 38
Declaration of Independence, 200
De Kooning, Willem, 75
De Mille, Agnes, 210
Dempster, Arthur, 115
Denmark, 114–15, 117
Dennis, Lawrence, 12–13, 18, 145
Denny, George V., Jr., 98–99
Deoxyribonucleic acid (DNA), 116
Depression, 23, 27–28, 30, 39, 45–46, 57, 69, 74, 76, 82, 92, 95, 118, 155, 163, 170, 190, 201–02, 204, 215
  and arts, 16–17, 46, 54, 60–61, 68, 76
  attitudes toward, 1–5
  and education, 139–42, 146
Depression—*cont.*
  and films, 87–88
  and journalism, 99, 103
  and planning, 6–14
  and science and scholarship, 108–10, 126–28, 130–31, 136, 213
Detroit Symphony, 77, 96
Devil and Daniel Webster, The (Moore), 81
De Voto, Bernard, 15, 205–06
Dewey, John, 7, 12, 69, 118–19, 121–22, 134, 142–45, 147–48, 151, 159, 163, 168
Dictionary of American Biography, 135
Dionne quintuplets, 101
Disney, Walt, 92–93
Distributism, 19–20
District of Columbia (Dos Passos), 39, 202
Divine, Robert A., 198
Dollard, John, 131
Dorsey brothers, 83
Dos Passos, John, 32, 36–39, 182, 202
Drama (*see* Literature, theater; Radio, theater)
Dreiser, Theodore, 25–26, 32, 40
Drucker, Peter, 225
Duffus, R.L., 68

Eastman, Max, 54, 56
Eccles, Marriner, 13, 127
Economic planning (*see* Planning; Regionalism)
Economics (*see* Science, social)
Edinburgh University, 162
Edison, Thomas A., 111
Edman, Irwin, 5, 219
Education, 139–53, 217–22
  college and university, 108–09, 147–52, 221
  general, 147–52, 163, 217, 219–20, 223
  and Great Depression, 140–46, 217
  progressive, 142–48, 153, 217, 220, 222
  public, 140, 148, 221–22
  and Second World War, 217–22
Edward VIII, 101
Einstein, Albert, 114–15, 154, 175
Elias, Hans, 153
Eliot, T.S., 27, 51, 53, 55–56
Ellington, Edward "Duke," 83
Emerson, Ralph Waldo, 57

Emile Zola, 92
Empire State Building, 61
Encyclopedia of the Social Sciences, 133
End of Economic Man, The (Drucker), 225
Engineers and the Price System, The (Veblen), 9
Englebrecht, Helmuth C., 165
Episcopal Church, 155
Essay for Orchestra (Barber), 80
Essentialist Committee, 147
Estheticism, 58
ETC., 123
Ethiopia, 167
Evangelical Synod of North America, 155
Evans, Walker, 106–07
Everest, Wesley, 38
Existentialism (*see* Christian Existentialism)

Fall of the City, The (MacLeish), 97
"Falling Water" (Wright), 64
Farm Security Administration, 91, 106, 116
Farrell, James T., 32, 39–40, 52, 55–56, 202, 206
Fascism, 4, 23, 32, 49, 52, 92, 99, 156, 173, 178, 180–81, 185, 188
(*See also* Naziism)
Faulkner, William, 41–42, 202–03
Fearing, Kenneth, 51
Federal Arts Project (*see* Works Progress Administration, Federal Arts Project)
Federal Bureau of Investigation, 89
Federal Council of Churches, 157–58
Federal Emergency Relief Administration, 72, 140
Federal Music Project (*see* Works Progress Administration, Federal Music Project)
Federal Radio Commission, 94
Federal Reserve Board, 13, 127
Federal Theatre Project (*see* Works Progress Administration, Federal Theatre Project)
Federal Writers' Project (*see* Works Progress Administration, Federal Writers' Project)
Fellowship of Socialist Christians, 158, 160, 170
Fermi, Enrico, 115
Fiction (*see* Literature, fiction)
Films, 85–94, 107, 198, 211–13
block-booking and, 88, 90
censorship and, 88–90
documentary, 91, 211–12
and Second World War, 211–13
silent, 87
social censciousness in, 91–92
social effects of, 88–90
talking, 87
Fine, Benjamin, 217
Finland, 174, 198
First Symphony (Harris), 80
Fischer, Louis, 173
Fitch, John Marston, 67
Fitzgerald, F. Scott, 1–2, 25, 34
Five-Year Plan, 8, 29
Flanagan, Hallie, 17, 45–46, 204
Flexner, Abraham, 149
Florida Southern University, 64
Flowering of New England, The (Brooks), 57
Flynn, John T., 199
Foerster, Norman, 27
Folklore of Capitalism, The (Arnold), 124–25
Ford, Henry, 38
Ford, John, 91–92
"Ford Sunday Evening Hour," 96
Ford's Theatre (Bacon), 210
Foreign Policy for America, A (Beard), 178
Foreign Policy Association, 177, 198
Fortune, 105, 129, 154, 165
42nd Parallel, The (Dos Passos), 38
For Whom the Bell Tolls (Hemingway), 37, 39
Fosdick, Harry Emerson, 158
Foster, Stephen, 210
Foster Gallery (Gould), 210
Four Freedoms, 192
"Four Policemen," 197
Fourteen Points, 192
Fox, Dixon Ryan, 136
France, 33, 68, 165, 167–68, 172, 176–77, 182, 212
Franco, Francisco, 32, 52, 167, 171, 223
Frank, Jerome, 124, 199
Frank, Leo, 92
Frankenstein, Alfred, 209
Frankfurter, Felix, 124

Freeman, Douglas Southall, 135
Freeman, Joseph, 54
Frescoes for Mr. Rockefeller's City (MacLeish), 52
Freudianism, 26, 58, 184
From These States (Bacon), 210
Frontiers of Democracy, 145
Frost, Robert, 25, 51
"Fugitives," 18
Functional architecture (*see* Architecture, modern)
Fundamentalism (*see* Religion, Protestant)
Furniss, Norman F., 154
Fusfeld, Daniel R., 11
Future of Industrial Man, The (Drucker), 225

Gable, Clark, 86
Gabriel, Ralph H., 137, 169
Gallup, George, 129
Garfield, Jules (John), 48
General education (*see* Education, general)
General Education Board, 149
General Education in a Free Society (Harvard Committee), 221–22
General Theory of Relativity, 113–14
Gentle People, The (Shaw), 48
Geography of the Peace, The (Spykman), 196
German-American Bund, 173
German-Americans, 191
Germany, 12, 32, 43, 92, 95, 114–15, 164–65, 167, 170, 174–75, 177, 179, 185–88, 192, 214, 225–26
Gershwin, George, 80–81
G. I. Bill of Rights, 219
Gideonese, Harry D., 152
Gillespie, Dizzy, 211
Gilson, Étienne, 119
Ginzburg, Benjamin, 117
Ginzburg, Eli, 226
Girl Washing Her Hair (Robus), 75
Glasgow, Ellen, 34–35
Glazer, Nathan, 156
God's Little Acre (Caldwell), 40
Gold, Michael, 54
Golden Boy (Odets), 48
Gone with the Wind (Mitchell), 36, 92
Goodman, Benny, 83
Good Society, The (Lippmann), 21–22
Gould, Morton, 209–10
Graham, Martha, 210
Grand Canyon Suite, (Grofé), 81
Grapes of Wrath, The (Steinbeck), 40–41, 91, 201
Grattan, C. Hartley, 165–66, 168–69, 199
Gray, George W., 114
Great Britain, 33, 101, 114, 165, 167–68, 172, 176, 178–79, 182, 196–97
Great Dictator, The, 92
Great Plains, The (Webb), 136
Great Plains drouth, 101
Great Tradition, The (Hicks), 54
Green, Paul, 204
Green Hills of Africa (Hemingway), 37
Gregory, Horace, 51
Griffith, D.W., 87
Grofé, Ferde, 80–81
Gropius, Walter, 62–63, 175, 207
Gropper, William, 70, 73
Gross, Chaim, 75
Grosz, George, 175
Group Theatre, 48
Grover Cleveland (Nevins), 135
Guggenheim Foundation, 75
Gutheim, Frederick A., 65
Guthrie, Woody, 79
Guttmann, Allen, 173

Hadden, Briton, 104–05
Hall, G. Stanley, 147
Hammerstein, Oscar, II, 210
Hanson, Howard, 78–79
Harlow, Jean, 86
Harper's, 103
Harris, Roy, 80, 209
Hart, Hornell, 154
Hart, Lorenz, 210
Hartley, Marsden, 74–75
Harvard Committee, 221–22
Harvard University, 20, 27, 43, 80, 117, 124, 181, 183, 221
law school, 123
Hawkins, Coleman, 211
Hayakawa, S. I., 122–23
Hayek, Frederick A. von, 225–26
Hays, Will, 88
Hearst, William Randolph, 93, 101–02
Hegel, Georg Wilhelm Friedrich, 119
Heinsenberg, Werner, 114
Hellman, Lillian, 49

Hemingway, Ernest, 25, 32, 36–37, 39, 182, 202
Herberg, Will, 156
Here Come the Clowns (Barry), 50
Herodiade (Graham and Hindemith), 210
Herskovits, Melville J., 132
Heussi, Karl, 134
Hicks, Granville, 28–29, 33, 54, 57, 201
Higham, John, 133, 135
Higher Learning in America, The (Hutchins), 149
Higher Learning in a Democracy, The (Gideonese), 152
High Tor (Anderson), 49
Himelstein, Morgan Y., 49
Hindemith, Paul, 77, 175, 210
Hines, Earl "Fatha," 83, 211
Hirsch, Joseph, 70
History, 133–37, 219, 222
  "progressive," 135–36
  relativism in, 133–35
  and social sciences, 133, 136
Hitler, Adolf, 20, 98, 167, 172, 180, 188, 191
Hoffman, Frederick J., 36
Holland, 177
Hollywood Suite (Grofé), 81
Holmes, John Haynes, 158
Holmes, Oliver Wendell, 123
Hook, Sidney, 117, 119, 163
Hoover, Herbert, 9, 11, 23, 29, 116, 131
Hopkins, Harry, 17, 72
Hopper, Edward, 68–70
Hot Still-Scape for Six Colors (Davis), 75
Houghton, Norris, 204
Houseman, John, 97
How to Win Friends and Influence People (Carnegie), 23
Hubble, Edwin, 115–16
Hughes, Langston, 51
Hull, Cordell, 186
Human geography (*see* Science, social)
Humanism and America (ed. Foerster), 27
Huston, John, 211
Huston, Walter, 97
Hutchins, Robert Maynard, 148–52, 163, 184, 219

I Am a Fugitive, 92
Ickes, Harold, 99
Ideas of Order (Stevens), 51
Idiot's Delight (Sherwood), 49
Idle Money, Idle Men (Chase), 22
Illinois Institute of Technology, 122
I'll Take My Stand (Twelve Southerners), 19
Index of American Design (*see* Works Progress Administration, Federal Arts Project)
Indian Americans, 200
In Dubious Battle (Steinbeck), 41
Industrial Workers of the World, 38
Informer, The, 91
Internationalism, 173, 178, 199
  (*See also* Interventionism)
International Society for General Semantics, 123
International Style, 62–64, 207
Interpretation of Christian Ethics, An (Niebuhr), 161
Interventionism, 176–77, 188, 194
  (*See also* Internationalism)
Iron, Blood, and Profits (Seldes), 165
Island God, The (Menotti), 210
Isolationism, 166–69, 172–73, 177–79, 188, 197
  (*See also* Pacifism)
Italy, 12, 32, 92, 95, 115, 167, 179, 186–88, 223, 225
It Can't Happen Here (Lewis), 35, 47

Jackson, Andrew, 135, 198
Jacobs, Lewis, 90
Jaffe, Sam, 48
James, Henry, 42, 55, 57, 203
James, Marquis, 135
James, William, 119, 181
Japan, 167, 179, 186–88, 192, 226–28
Japanese-Americans, 191–92, 200
Jarrell, Randall, 205
Jazz (*see* Music, jazz [swing])
Jeffers, Robinson, 25, 51
Jefferson, Thomas, 18, 66, 202
Jefferson Memorial, 66–67
"Jewishness" (*see* Religion, Jewish)
Jewish Theological Seminary, 155
Joan of Lorraine (Anderson), 204
John Brown's Body (Benét), 52
John D. Rockefeller (Nevins), 135
Johns Hopkins University, 136
Johnson, Allen, 133, 135

Johnson, Wendell, 123
Johnson Wax Company, Administration Building (Wright), 64
Jones, Howard Mumford, 177, 183–85, 220
Josephson, Matthew, 28, 31, 136
Journal of the History of Ideas, 137
Journalism, 85–86, 98–99, 212
  camera, 106–07
  magazine, 99, 101, 103–06, 212
  newspaper, 99–103, 212
  radio, 98, 212
  and Second World War, 212
Journal of Southern History, 136
Joyce, James, 27
Juarez, 92
Judaism (*see* Religion, Jewish)

Kaempffert, Waldemar, 112
Kahn, Albert, 206
Kallen, Horace M., 155, 220
Kaltenborn, H.G., 99
Kandel, Isaac L., 152, 218, 222
Kane, John, 74
Kantor, MacKinlay, 36
Kaplan, Mordecai, 155
Kazan, Elia, 48
Kazin, Alfred, 30, 38, 42, 44–45, 57, 106
Kellogg-Briand Pact, 170–71
Kempton, Murray, 31
Keppel, Frederick P., 68
Key Largo (Anderson), 49
Keynes, John Maynard, 13, 22, 127
  (*See also* Keynesianism)
Keynesianism, 14, 22, 127
Kidder Smith, G.E., 207
Kierkegaard, Soren, 160
Kilpatrick, William H., 143, 145
King Jasper (Robinson), 51
Kirchwey, Freda, 174
Korzybski, Alfred, 121
Koussevitsky, Serge, 80
Kroner, Richard, 160
Krupa, Gene, 83
Krutch, Joseph Wood, 48
Ku Klux Klan, Knights of the, 155, 173

Labor party, 225
LaFollette, Suzanne, 68
Land of the Free (MacLeish), 52, 106
Landon, Alfred M., 129
Language in Action (Hayakawa), 122
Languages, 222
  classical, 219
Larkin, Oliver, 76, 208
Lasswell, Harold D., 129, 165–66
Last Tycoon, The (Fitzgerald), 34
Late George Apley, The (Marquand), 35
Laughton, Charles, 97
Lavine, Harold, 176
Law (*see* Science, social)
Law and the Modern Mind (Frank), 124
Lawrence, David, 103, 105
Lawrence, Ernest O., 115
Lawson, John Howard, 48, 92
Lazarsfeld, Paul, 98
League of American Writers, 32
League of Nations, 159, 167, 170, 196, 199, 212
LeCourbusier, 62, 207
Lee, Irving, 123
Lee, Robert E., 135
Legal relativism, 123–25, 199
Legion of Decency, 88–89
LeRoy, Mervyn, 88, 92
Let Us Now Praise Famous Men (Agee and Evans), 106–07
Leuba, James H., 154
Levine, Jack, 70, 208
Lewis, Sinclair, 25, 35, 47, 49
Lewisohn, Ludwig, 55–56
Liberal education (*see* Education, general)
Liberal theology (*see* Theology, liberal)
Liberation of American Literature, The (Calverton), 54
Life, 105–06
Lilienthal, David, 16
Lindbergh, Charles, 101
Lincoln, Abraham, 49, 204
Lincoln, the War Years (Sandburg), 135
Lippmann, Walter, 20–22, 103, 109, 151, 195, 197–98
Litany for Dictatorships (Benét), 52
Literary criticism (*see* Literature, criticism)
Literary Digest, 103, 129
Literary Fallacy, The (DeVoto), 205–06
Literature, 25–58, 60, 133, 185, 201–06, 219

Literature—*cont.*
criticism, 31–32, 51, 53–58, 184, 205–06
fiction, 31–44, 201–03, 205–06
naturalism in, 26–27, 32, 34, 36, 39, 50, 184, 202
poetry, 50–53, 56, 205
radicalism in, 29–33, 37–41, 48–49, 51, 54–55, 205–06
and Second World War, 201, 203–05
theater, 45–51, 203–05
Little Caesar, 88
Little Foxes, The (Hellman), 49
Lodge, Henry Cabot, 212
Lomax, Allen, 79
Lomax, John, 79
Lombardo, Guy, 82
London, Jack, 26
Long, Huey, 12, 173
Long Day's Journey into Night (O'Neill), 50
Long Remember (Kantor), 36
Look, 106
Look Homeward Angel (Wolfe), 43
Lorentz, Pare, 91
Lorimer, George Horace, 104
Louis Pasteur, 92
Louisville *Courier-Journal,* 19
Lovejoy, Arthur O., 136–37
Lowell, Robert, 205
Lubitsch, Ernst, 91
Luce, Henry, 104–05, 187
Ludlow, Louis, 170
Ludlow referendum, 170
Lynd, Helen, 130
Lynd, Robert S., 130
Lytle, Andrew N., 19–20

McCarthy, Charlie, 95
McCarthy, Mary, 118
McCormick, Robert R., 102
McCullers, Carson, 203
Macdonald, Dwight, 194–95
MacDonald, William, 166
MacLeish, Archibald, 51–53, 97, 106, 173–74, 177, 181–85, 188, 192, 194–95, 205, 213
Magazines (*see* Journalism, magazine)
Magnificent Ambersons, The, 93
Mahan, Alfred Thayer, 196
Main Currents in American Thought (Parrington), 54
Malone, Dumas, 135
Manchuria, 167
Manhattan Engineer District, 214–15
Manhattan Transfer (Dos Passos), 37
Mann, Thomas, 175–76
Marching Song (Lawson), 48
Marin, John, 75
Maritain, Jacques, 119, 223
Marquand, John P., 35
Marsh, Reginald, 69–70, 207
Marx, Karl, 4, 55
Marxism, 4–5, 20, 29–30, 54–55, 57–58, 110, 126, 130, 136, 161–62, 184, 202
(*See also* Radicalism)
Massachusetts Institute of Technology, 110, 115
Mauldin, Bill, 193
Mead, George Herbert, 129
Mead, Margaret, 23, 132, 194, 216
Means, Gardiner C., 10, 127
Medicine (*see* Science, natural)
Mencken, H.L., 2, 34
Menotti, Gian-Carlo, 210
Merchants of Death (Englebrecht), 165
"Mercury Theatre of the Air," 97–98
Methodist Epicopal Church, 155
Methodist Protestant Church, 155
Metropolitan Museum of Art, 208
Metropolitan Opera, 76–77, 81, 96
Mexican-Americans, 200
Middletown (Lynds), 130
Middletown in Transition (Lynds), 130
Mies van der Rohe, Ludwig, 62
Milestone, Lewis, 211
Millay, Edna St. Vincent, 51–52
Miller, Glenn, 83
Miller, Henry, 203
Millikan, Robert K., 114–15
Millis, Walter, 164–66, 199
Mission to Moscow, 198
Mississippi Valley Historical Association, 218
Mitchell, Broadus, 126
Mitchell, Margaret, 36, 92
Modern Monthly, 55
Modern Times, 91
Monroe Doctrine, 197
Moon Is Down, The (Steinbeck), 201, 204
Moore, Douglas, 80–81

Moral Man and Immoral Society (Niebuhr), 160–61
More, Paul Elmer, 27, 55
Morgan, Lewis Henry, 132
Moscow trials, 32, 174, 198
Moses, Anna Mary Robertson, 74
Motion Picture Producers and Distributors Association, 89
Motion Picture Production Code, 89–90
Motion pictures (*see* Films)
Mourning Becomes Electra (O'Neill), 50
Mount Wilson Observatory, 115
Moving pictures (*see* Films)
Muller, Herbert J., 114
Müller, Hermann J., 116
Mumford, Lewis, 63, 72, 145, 177, 179–81, 184–85, 188
Munich conference, 98, 168, 187
Murals (*see* Works Progress Administration, Federal Arts Project)
Murrow, Edward R., 99
Museum of Modern Art, 63, 75
Museum of Non-Objective Painting, 75
Music, 60, 76–83, 208–11
  ballet, 210
  folk, 79–80
  jazz (swing), 80, 82–83, 96, 211
  musical comedy, 81, 210
  opera, 77, 81, 210
  radio, 77, 81–83
  and Second World War, 208
  symphonic, 77–81, 209–10
Musical comedy (*see* Music, musical comedy)
Mussolini, Benito, 20, 156–57, 167, 188, 191, 223
My Days of Anger (Farrell), 202
My Heart's in the Highlands (Saroyan), 49
Myrdal, Gunnar, 131

Nation, 33, 48, 61, 103, 117, 173–74
National Academy of Sciences, 110–11
National Art Gallery, 66, 208
National Association of Manufacturers, 17
National Board of Review, 88
National Broadcasting Company, 77, 94, 96–98, 213
National Cancer Institute, 110
National Council for the Social Studies, 218
National Defense Research Committee, 214
National Economic and Social Planning Association, 11–12
National Education Association, 141, 146
  Educational Policies Commission, 141, 146
National Planning Board, 13, 16, 111, 213
National Recovery Administration, 11, 126, 140
National Research Council, 110
National Resources Board (*see* National Planning Board)
National Resources Committee (*see* National Planning Board)
National Resources Planning Board (*see* National Planning Board)
National Youth Administration, 140–41
Native Son (Wright), 40, 204
Naturalism (*see* Literature, naturalism in; Philosophy, naturalism)
Nature and Destiny of Man, The (Niebuhr), 162, 224
Naziism, 33, 174–75, 186
  (*See also* Fascism)
Nazi-Soviet Pact, 33, 37, 55, 103, 174, 182, 198, 201
NBC Symphony, 77, 80, 86, 96
Negroes, 185, 200, 208
Neo-orthodox theology (*see* Theology, neo-orthodox)
Neo-Thomism (*see* Education, general; Philosophy, Thomism)
Neutra, Richard, 62, 65
Nevins, Allan, 135, 192
New Bauhaus, 175
New Criticism, 20, 55–56, 205
New Criticism, The (Ransom), 56
New Deal, 5, 10, 18, 20, 22, 40, 47, 72, 92, 101, 103–04, 111–12, 116, 126–27, 142, 156, 158, 163, 168–69, 171, 190, 194, 224–26
  and arts, 17, 41–45, 72–73, 79
  and education, 140–41
  and housing, 65–66, 72, 75
  and planning, 11–16
  and science, 109–11
New Deal, A (Chase), 7

New England: Indian Summer (Brooks), 57
New History (*see* History)
New Humanism, 27, 55
New Masses, 30–31, 38, 54, 103
New Republic, 4, 20, 56, 63, 103, 169, 173–74, 179–80, 201, 213
News broadcasting (*see* Journalism, radio)
Newspapers (*see* Journalism, newspaper)
Newsweek, 105
New Theatre League, 48
New York American, 70
New York Daily Graphic, 102
New York *Daily Mirror*, 102
New York *Daily News*, 102
New Yorker, 103
New York *Herald-Tribune*, 20, 199
New York Philharmonic, 77, 80, 96
New York Times, 56, 102, 112, 218
New York Times Book Review, 166
New York World, 20
New York World's Fair (1939), 75–76
Niebuhr, Reinhold, 159–63, 173–74, 180, 195, 224, 229
Nightmare at Noon (Benét), 52
Night Rider (Warren), 203
Nimitz, Chester W., 218
1919 (Dos Passos), 38
Nock, Albert Jay, 28
No Friendly Voice (Hutchins), 149
Norris, Frank, 26
North American Review, 103
North Star, 198
Northwest Passage (Roberts), 36
Norway, 177, 201
Note on Literary Criticism, A (Farrell), 55
Number One (Dos Passos), 202
Nye, Gerald P., 165
Nye committee, 164–65

Oboler, Arch, 97
Odegard, Peter, 129
Odets, Clifford, 48, 204
Odum, Howard, 15, 131
Office of Emergency Management, 207
Office of Price Administration, 212
Office of Scientific Research and Development, 214
Office of War Information, 199, 204, 212
Of Mice and Men (Steinbeck), 41
Of Time and the River (Wolfe), 43
O'Hara, John, 39, 202
Oklahoma! (Rodgers and Hammerstein), 210
Oliver Wiswell (Roberts), 36
O'Neill, Eugene, 25, 50, 204
One World (Willkie), 198
Only Yesterday (Allen), 1
Opera (*see* Music, opera)
Outlook, 103
Our Town (Wilder), 49, 204
Overture on an American Theme (Moore), 80

Pacifism, 169–73, 179, 205, 222
  (*See also* Isolationism)
Painting, 60, 67–76, 207–08
  abstractionism in, 69, 75, 208
  "American Scene," 69–72
  expressionism in, 69, 74–75, 208
  Fourteenth Street School, 69–70
  primitivism in, 73–74
  realism in, 68–69, 70–71, 208
  and Second World War, 207–08
  surrealism in, 69
Park, Robert E., 130
Parker, Charlie, 211
Parrington, Vernon L., 54
Partisan Review, 55–56, 58, 103, 163
Pauling, Linus, 116
Pearson, Drew, 103
Pearson, Norman H., 33
Pegler, Westbrook, 102
Peirce, Charles Sanders, 119
"People's Platform, The," 99
People, Yes, The (Sandburg), 52
Perry, Ralph Barton, 2, 177, 180–81
Peter Ibbetson (Taylor), 81
Petrified Forest, The (Sherwood), 49
Philosophy, 117–21, 133, 219, 223
  idealism, 119–20
  logical empiricism, 120–21
  naturalism, 119–20
  pragmatism, 118–19
  realism, 119–20
  Thomism, 119
Photography (*see* Journalism, camera)
Physics (*see* Science, natural)
Pippin, Horace, 74
Piston, Walter, 80
Pius XI, 156

Planning, national, 6–14, 21–22, 127, 225
regional, 14–17
urban, 64–65, 179
(*See also* Collectivism; Regionalism; Tennessee Valley Authority)
Planned Society, A (Soule), 7
Plough That Broke the Plains, The, 91
Poe, Edgar Allen, 42
Poetry (*see* Literature, poetry)
Poland, 33, 101, 166, 170, 172, 174, 182, 185
Political science (*see* Science, social)
Politicos, The (Josephson), 136
Politics: Who Gets What, When, and How (Lasswell), 129
Pollock, Jackson, 73, 75
Poor, Henry Varnum, 74
Pope, John Russell, 66–67
Popular Front, 20, 32–33, 37, 57, 103, 163, 173–74, 181, 203
Porgy and Bess (Gershwin), 81
Porter, Katherine Anne, 203
Potsdam conference, 226–27
Pound, Ezra, 51, 55
Pound, Roscoe, 123–25
Pragmatism, 11–12, 120–21, 153, 180
(*See also* Philosophy, pragmatism)
Preachers Present Arms (Abrams), 170–71
Prelude to War, 212
Presbyterian Church, 155
President's Advisory Committee on Education, 141
Press (*see* Journalism)
Princeton University, 98, 175, 223
Institute for Advanced Study, 175, 223
Principia Mathematica (Whitehead and Russell), 119
Pringle, Henry F., 135
Prodigal Parents, The (Lewis), 35
Progressive Education (*see* Education, progressive)
Progressive Education Association, 142, 144–46, 221
Prokofiev, Sergei, 209
Propaganda Techniques in the World War (Lasswell), 165
Protestantism (*see* Religion, Protestant)
Psychopathology and Politics (Lasswell), 129
Public Health Service, 110
Public housing, 61, 65–66
Public Speech (MacLeish), 52
Public Works Administration, 13, 65–66, 75, 140
Public Works of Art Project (*see* Treasury Deartment, Public Works of Art Project)
Puccini, Giacomo, 209
Pulitzer, Joseph, 102

Quadrigesimo Anno, 156
Quaker Graveyard in Nantucket, The (Lowell), 205
Quinn, Arthur Hobson, 50

Radicalism, 5, 23
in literature, 29–33, 37, 41, 48–49, 51, 54–55
in painting, 69–70, 74
(*See also* Marxism)
Radical Religion, 158, 162
Radio, 85–86, 93–99, 100–01, 107, 212–13
censorship and, 94–95, 212
and music, 96, 212–13
news broadcasting (*see* Journalism, radio)
and Second World War, 212
social effects of, 95
theater, 96–97, 213
Rain from Heaven (Behrman), 49
Ransom, John Crowe, 19, 56
Rauschning, Hermann, 176
RCA Victor Company, 77
Reader's Digest, 104, 225
Recent Social Trends, 131
Reconstruction Finance Corporation, 126
Reflections on the End of an Era (Niebuhr), 161
Refugee intellectuals, 175–76
Regionalism, 14–15
(*See also* Planning, regional; Tennessee Valley Authority; Agrarianism)
Regional planning (*see* Planning, regional; Regionalism)
Regional Planning Reports, 16
Religion, 139, 153–63, 222–24
Jewish, 155–56, 171, 223
Protestant, 154–63, 170–71, 222–23

Religion—*cont.*
Roman Catholic, 155–57, 171, 223–24
and Second World War, 222–24
(*See also* Theology)
Research Committee on Recent Social Trends, 23, 131
Research—a National Resource, 111
Reserve Officers Training Corps, Naval, 218
Resettlement Administration, 65
Revolt of the Beavers, The, 47
Rhapsody in Blue (Gershwin), 81
Richards, I.A., 55
Rich Land, Poor Land (Chase), 14
River, The, 91
Road to Serfdom, The (Hayek), 225
Road to War (Millis), 164, 166
Robber Barons, The (Josephson), 136
Roberts, Kenneth, 36
Robinson, Boardman, 70, 74
Robinson, Edward S., 124
Robinson, Edwin Arlington, 25, 51
Robus, Hugo, 75
Rockefeller Center, 61
Rockefeller Foundation, 98
Rocket to the Moon (Odets), 48
Rodeo (DeMille and Copland), 210
Rodgers, Richard, 210
Rollins College, 148
Roosevelt, Eleanor, 99
Roosevelt, Franklin D., 3–4, 7, 9–18, 21–22, 65, 72, 90, 98, 100, 110, 113, 124–25, 127–29, 157, 167–68, 170, 172–73, 177–78, 185–87, 190, 192, 194, 197, 199, 201, 204, 214–16 223–24
Roosevelt, Theodore, 135
Roper, Elmo, 129
Rorty, James, 93
Rosenfeld, Paul, 82
Ross, Edward A., 130
Rossen, Robert, 211
Rourke, Constance, 73
Royce, Josiah, 119
Rugg, Harold, 143
Russell, Bertrand, 119
Russia (*see* Soviet Union)
Rutherford, L.M., 114
Ruykeyser, Muriel, 51
Ryan, John A., 156

Sacco-Vanzetti case, 38
St. John's College, 151
Sandburg, Carl, 25, 51–52, 135
Santayana, George, 117, 119
Sarah Lawrence College, 148
Saroyan, William, 49, 97
Saturday Evening Post, 103–04
Saturday Review of Literature, 103, 228
Say, Is This the U.S.A. (Caldwell and Bourke-White), 106
Say That We Saw Spain Die (Millay), 52
Schlesinger, Arthur M., 136
Schlesinger, Arthur M., Jr., 11
Schneider, Herbert W., 159
Scholarship (*see* History; Philosophy; Science)
Schuman, Frederick L., 173
Science, 109–37, 147, 213–17
and Great Depression, 110–12, 214–15
natural, 109, 114–17, 128, 213–15, 222
and New Deal, 109–111
and Second World War, 213–17
social, 109, 121–33, 215–17
and technology, 111–13
Science, 112
Science Advisory Board, 110–11
Science—the Endless Frontier (Bush), 215
Science and Sanity (Korzybski), 121
Scott, Howard, 9–10
Scribner's, 103
Scripps-Howard chain, 101
Sculpture, 60, 67–69, 72, 75–76, 207–08
Second World War, 23, 76, 83, 105, 112, 137, 147, 162, 167–229
and arts, 201–11
attitudes toward, 168–201
and education, 217–22
and popular culture, 99, 211–13
and religion, 159, 222–24
and science and scholarship, 213–17
Seligman, E.R.A., 133
Selznick, David O., 92
Semantics (*see* Science, social)
Shahn, Ben, 70, 73
Sheeler, Charles, 69–70
Shoenberg, Arnold, 77
Second Rhapsody (Gershwin), 81

Seldes, George, 165
Seldes, Gilbert, 2, 85–87, 90
Sessions, Roger, 80
Shapiro, Karl, 205
Shaw, Artie, 83
Shaw, Irwin, 48, 171, 226
Sherwood, Robert E., 49, 204
Shostakovich, Dimitri, 209
Silver Shirts, 173
Sinclair, Upton, 34
Skinner, Dickson, 77
Skin of Our Teeth, The (Wilder), 204
Smith, Bernard, 54
Snow White, 92–93
Social Foundations of Education, The (Counts), 145
Social Frontier, 145
Social Gospel (*see* Religion, Protestant; Theology, liberal)
Socialist party, 30, 158, 162, 174
Sociological jurisprudence (*see* Legal relativism)
Sociology (*see* Science, social)
Social Science Research Council, 111, 133
Sockman, Ralph W., 158
Sokoloff, Nikolai, 79
Sokolsky, George E., 4, 11
Song of Russia, 198
Soule, George, 4–5, 7–8, 11, 168, 174
Southern Agrarians, 19–20, 55–56, 71–72
(*See also* Agrarianism; Regionalism)
Southern Historical Association, 136
Soviet Union, 6–7, 29, 33, 92, 118, 144, 162, 173–75, 197–98, 209, 225, 227
Soyer, Isaac, 69
Soyer, Moses, 69
Soyer, Raphael, 69
Spain (*see* Spanish Civil War)
Spanish Civil War, 12, 32, 39, 92, 155, 167, 173–74, 223
Spiller, Robert E., 56
Spykman, Nicholas J., 195–98
Stagecoach, 92
Stalin, Josef, 6–8, 30, 54, 174
Steffens, Lincoln, 6
Steinbeck, John, 40–41, 201, 204
Stevens, Wallace, 51, 56, 205
Still, William Grant, 80–81
Stouffer, Samuel, 193
Strauss, Richard, 209
Stravinsky, Igor, 77
String Quartet (Levine), 208
Strout, Cushing, 134–35
Studs Lonigan (Farrell), 40, 202
Sumner, William Graham, 3, 130
Symbols of Government, The (Arnold), 124
Symphony in G Minor (Still), 81

Tabloids (*see* Journalism, newspaper)
Tabloid Suite (Grofé), 81
Tansill, Charles C., 166
Tate, Allen, 19, 27, 56
Taylor, Deems, 81
Taylor, Frederick W., 9
Technical Alliance, 9
Technics and Civilization (Mumford), 63
Technocracy, 8–10, 113
Television, 97–98
Tender Is the Night (Fitzgerald), 34
Tennessee Valley Authority, 14–16, 19, 72, 110, 116
(*See also* Planning, regional; Regionalism)
That Which I Should Have Done I Did Not Do (Albright), 208
Theater (*see* Literature, theater; Radio, theater)
Theatre Guild, 48
Theatre Union, 48
Theology, 139, 158–63, 217
liberal, 158–59, 161, 224
neo-orthodox, 158–63, 217, 224
Roman Catholic, 223
(*See also* Religion)
There Are No Islands Any More (Millay), 52
There Shall Be No Night (Sherwood), 49
These Are Our Lives, 106
They Won't Forget, 92
Third Symphony (Harris), 80
Thomas, Lowell, 99
Thomas, Norman, 158
Thompson, Dorothy, 103
Thomson, Virgil, 80–81, 91
Thorp, Willard, 56
Tillich, Paul, 160, 162, 175, 203
Time, 104–05
Time of Your Life, The (Saroyan), 49
To a God Unknown (Steinbeck), 41
Tobacco Road (Caldwell), 40